PHILLIP HUGHES

PHILLIP HUGHES

THE OFFICIAL BIOGRAPHY

By Malcolm Knox & Peter Lalor

MACMILLAN
Pan Macmillan Australia

CONTENTS

From the Hughes Family

THE OPPORTUNITY TO SHARE Phillip's life with you in this book has brought great pleasure to our family.

In the pages to come we take you on the journey of our dearly beloved son and brother, from a child with big dreams to a young man who made those dreams come true.

We document how Phillip became an Australian Test, one-day and Twenty-20 cricketer, a cattle farmer, and a genuine, much-loved person. We hope that Phillip's dedication, class and humour shine through in these stories, and show how high he climbed and how hard he worked. We believe the risky, adventurous and positive strides he took to achieve his goals can be an inspiration to others.

Phillip was a unique individual and thrived at everything he turned his mind to. He had an infectious personality that left a mark wherever he went and he lived life to the fullest. As a family, we couldn't be more proud of our son and brother Phillip, and we will hold him in our hearts forever.

Before you read this book, it is essential for us to express heartfelt thanks to our family and friends for their unconditional love and endless support. We remain hugely grateful to the community of Macksville for giving Phillip a place to call home and for their devotion throughout his childhood and adult years. To the cricket community, who offered sustained encouragement through Phillip's playing career, and to the cattle industry, for the assistance they provided Phillip to help his passion and vision come to life, we extend our sincere appreciation.

Lastly, to everyone that has been interviewed for this book, we thank you all for the kind words and memories you have shared. To Phillip's manager James Henderson and the team at DSEG, we thank you for the constant support you've shown Phillip. And to the backbone of this biography, writers Peter Lalor and Malcolm Knox, and publisher Angus Fontaine and his team at Pan Macmillan, we thank you.

Phillip, we love you, we miss you, and we are forever proud of you.

GREGORY, VIRGINIA, JASON AND MEGAN HUGHES

Foreword by Michael Clarke

I FIRST MET PHILLIP HUGHES when he came down to Sydney from Macksville to watch a Western Suburbs club match. A schoolboy then, he was going to join our club when he moved to the city that summer, and he came to the post-match celebrations with Neil D'Costa, then my batting coach, and also Hughesy's. That Phillip would be playing at my club made him automatically a friend.

Never could I have guessed where that friendship would take us, but I was drawn to him immediately, and wanted to offer whatever advice I could in cricket and life.

It isn't hard to pinpoint why I, and every person Phillip met on his journey, would form strong bonds with him. Yes, he had a great sense of humour and, as everyone came to learn, he was a wonderfully loyal family man.

But it was also the way Phillip attacked life. Whether it was training, learning, working, partying or laughing, he would do it all with a genuine and infectious enthusiasm.

You could fill a book with stories about Phillip Hughes – and this is that book. It is a celebration of his life, and if there was one positive in the dark days when the cricket community gathered in Macksville in December 2014, it was that we could share some of these stories and take some time to be thankful to have known Phillip.

As a cricketer, he was the ultimate team man: a hard worker who loved training to get better. He played the game for the right reasons. He absolutely loved cricket and loved playing for Australia as much as anyone I have known. I believe he was good enough to go on and play 100 Test matches.

But more than anything, Phillip was my friend. We would always call or text each other, no matter where we were around the world, and help each other through tough times when required. When success came, we celebrated each other's as if it were our own.

Friendship was Phillip's great talent. Everywhere he went, he created new friends. That is a rare and special gift.

The Hugheses are amazing people, a salt-of-the-earth country family who loved that he played cricket for Australia but, above all, loved him for who he was.

Phillip's family have had their hearts broken – his death is more than just losing a son and brother. Their loss is always there.

We in the cricket world share their grief, and we owe them a debt for sharing their Phillip with us, a unique cricketer and a one-of-a-kind human being.

MICHAEL CLARKE

Introduction

THE PHILLIP HUGHES STORY is without a happy ending. In the way stories are told, it does not have a proper conclusion at all. It has a beginning, and the start of a middle, but the rest was taken away in the week before his twenty-sixth birthday. When Australia grieved for Phillip, a part of its sorrow was for the loss of possibility, as if the country had been absorbed in the first pages of a book, only to find that the rest had been ripped out.

There were many endings yet to be written. By the consensus of Phillip's peers in cricket, his story would have been one of precocious glory, severe trials and the hardening that came from disappointment and time in the wilderness, finally crowned by a comeback leading to 100 Test matches, 8000 runs for Australia, perhaps a World Cup. This was the story designed and expected by the leaders of Australian cricket, the selectors and the players, and would have followed a path trodden by Steve Waugh, Ricky Ponting, Michael Clarke, Justin Langer and a host of Australian greats.

Nothing is inevitable. Perhaps Phillip did not reach those heights, instead his career playing out in enduring triumph in first-class but not international cricket, like those of David Hookes or Darren Lehmann. Perhaps he retired early, left cricket behind, and followed his passion for cattle-farming.

Perhaps he did all of the above, and more.

Some story was waiting to be written. Instead, there is only a piece of a story, a story unfinished, with the ending we know but also the endings we can imagine.

One thing is certain. If Phillip had grown to his cricketing maturity and enjoyed the full arc of a career, his biography would be that of a cricketer, above all, as cricketers' stories are. Instead, because of the circumstances, this is a story about a boy and a man who remain forever young, and because his future as a cricketer was unfulfilled, his qualities as a human being come to the fore.

The impact of Phillip's death left a question hanging over Australia: what was it about Phillip Hughes that caused such sorrow? There were general themes of shock, the loss of innocence over our national game, which was known to be dangerous but not thought to be lethal, and the place sportsmen hold in our hearts.

But there was also something more, something unique to this young man. The grief over Phillip Hughes seemed somehow deeper than it would have been over any number of other public figures who had achieved more in their fields. There was some knowledge of him as a person, held inside the cricket community and the closer circle of his family and friends, that radiated outwards and was intuited by the wider world.

This book seeks to answer that question. Phillip Hughes might have become an archetype: a country boy, a child prodigy who flew high and fell before his time. But Phillip was also himself, a singular person; he remains the possession of those who knew him best, who still want to hold him close and refuse to have him taken away.

When looked at in the light of who he was, Phillip's story is not as incomplete as it might seem. His twenty-six years minus three days were rich and full of love and friendship and achievement. His is a story that highlights junior, school, country, club, 'pathways' and interstate cricket in this country. These levels are unique incubators for elite sportspeople, but they are also competitive arenas in their own right.

This was where Phillip was so often seen at his best, and where the stories began. Those who knew him best knew him through his games for New South Wales and South Australia, for his schools and his clubs and his underage teams, and in its way his career was a tribute to the calibre of those levels of Australian cricket. They deserve to be celebrated and not left in the shade, as they might have been in his story had Phillip Hughes gone on to play for Australia for another ten years.

The dominant voices in this story are those who were closest to Phillip, who will always feel his loss the most keenly. Many lay claim to a feeling that he was their intimate friend, which shows the type of person he was: a boy and a young man with the gift of collecting friendship. He had many, many friends.

Phillip's journey is done, belonging to him and nobody else, but in his own way, he has left much for us to remember and celebrate.

MALCOLM KNOX & PETER LALOR

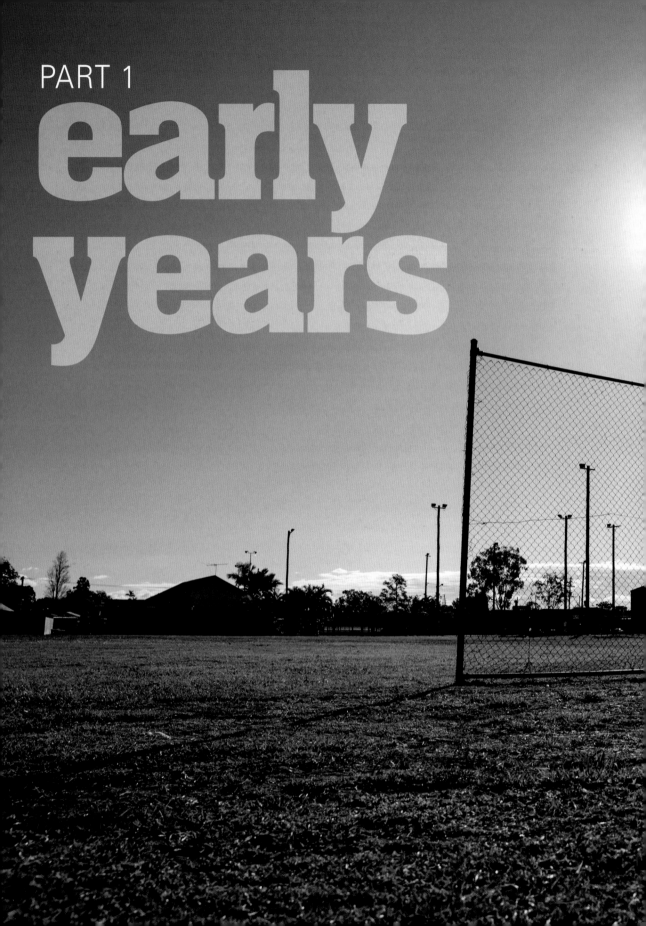

PART 1

early years

ONE

THE BOY FROM MACKSVILLE

There are only two pubs in Macksville. As the big rigs come down the Pacific Highway from the north, they drop gears and engage their brakes at the bend before the two-lane bridge across the Nambucca River. At night, the lights of the Star Hotel reflect off the water. The Star has the prime real estate, but a block back from the river the Nambucca Hotel – known as the 'pink pub' or 'Bonzer's' – was where the cricketers gathered. Year by year from the early 2000s, Bonzer's walls became papered with clippings of the banana farmer's son who was addicted to cricket.

STORIES ABOUT PHILLIP HUGHES? Pull up a stool. There are a thousand of them. He walked out to bat when he was barely stump-high, and that is where he stayed. He was making hundreds in junior cricket when a hundred was considered a good team total. He was in the middle when the innings started, and he was there as teammate after teammate came and went. Never satisfied, never in a rush to be anywhere else, he had found his place in the world.

They talk about Phillip sharing the C-grade player of the competition award with a 37-year-old opponent when he was twelve. There was the time he'd gone down to the big smoke and singlehandedly batted St Polding to victory in the state final. How does a kid score 159 not out

Just as he had been Macksville folklore, Phillip Hughes quickly became a figure of mystique and intrigue to the city kids with their coaches and flash gear. He seemed to make hundreds every weekend

in a 50-over match? No Australian batsman had achieved that in a one-day international.

There's plenty more where that came from. There's the time he hit a ball from the local oval into his grandfather's chook yard. All you could see was the feathers rising above the fence.

Nobody batted like Phillip. That big sweeping back lift, that uncanny ability to step back and cut the ball from the fourth stump line, from the off-stump, from the middle stump. Bowlers died the death of a thousand cuts. He developed the cut shot because when you are a kid and men are hurling the ball at you, it's the only way to get it off the square. He didn't have the strength to drive in those early days, so he gave the ball a tap on the head as it passed, letting all the frustrated bowler's effort take it to the boundary.

But Phillip was no one-trick pony. By the time he was a teenager, he would hurl himself into a cover drive or step boldly inside the line and pull.

Nobody in Macksville batted like him, nobody in the small towns around the valley, nobody in the bigger regional centres on the highway to Sydney or Brisbane, and nobody in those cities. Phillip Hughes had an insatiable appetite for runs and a quiet country patience that allowed him to weather storms in the middle and wait until the sun shone. Where else, after all, would you rather be?

4

It wasn't long before they knew how good he was. In every little town and farming community in the Nambucca Valley kids told their dads about the little left-hander, but their dads had seen him from the boundary already and were starting to talk to their mates. Men in the higher grades watched him walk out to the middle as a child and shook their heads in awe as he dug in.

Macksville is halfway between Brisbane and Sydney. Word spread across the narrow bridge and up the Pacific Highway to Urunga, Bellingen, Sawtell and Coffs Harbour, and south to Scotts Head, Crescent Head and Port Macquarie. Then word reached Sydney about this country kid who could bat and bat and bat.

Just as he had been Macksville folklore, Phillip Hughes quickly became a figure of mystique and intrigue to the city kids with their coaches and flash gear. He seemed to make hundreds every weekend. Nobody knew quite how he did it. Was it some kind of banana-country magic?

State Under-17 players, the best of their age, speculated that he didn't watch the bowler, but stared at the middle of the pitch and picked up the ball from there. Others said he'd developed his technique batting with an axe handle his dad used to harvest bananas. There's a story from an Under-17s trial when the best kids in the state were in the sheds talking about how many hundreds they'd got. One after another boasted that they had two, three, four; one kid had six. Phillip blushed a little when his turn came. He'd hit 50, maybe 60. He made hundreds for fun, someone once said.

Coaches of representative teams always insisted Phillip come to their trials, no matter how inconvenient or how much school he missed or how many runs he'd already made. It was as if they needed to see it again to believe it. There was the regional trial down in Sydney when the gun quick from Lismore ran in and did what good bowlers do: put the ball outside off-stump. And he watched as Phillip stepped back, his feet splayed wide until his eyes were almost at ball height, his bat raised that high you could see every stump . . .

First ball. Four.

Second ball. Four.

Third ball. Four.

Fourth ball. Four.

Fifth ball . . . you get the picture.

Each of the first five deliveries was pasted through or behind point. The scoreboard was spinning numbers like it was rolling its eyes. The opposition coach, in a state of panic, ran across to his counterpart.

'You have to get the kid off.'

'Why?'

'He's killing us.'

The Lismore bowler, the best in the region, had been earmarked to open in the carnival. Phillip was destroying his prospective teammate. The coach called him back to the sheds at the end of the first over. P Hughes 20 (retired).

Greg Hughes couldn't believe what he was seeing. He wasn't one of those fathers who hovered or meddled. Indeed, he sat away from the parents and selectors and kept his own counsel. But on this occasion he couldn't help himself. They'd driven 500 kilometres and had to drive 500 back, all for six balls?

It would be just another in a series of trips that would make Phillip and Greg as familiar with the highway in and out of Macksville as any of the truckers who hauled their loads in the night. This was their thing: driving and talking of cricket and cattle, and then driving some more and talking some more about the game they loved and the farm they would one day own. Phillip would bring a pillow to put his head down and dream about cricket and the farm. He and Greg became best mates, easy in each other's company.

'He gave his life to cricket,' Greg says. And cricket gave Phillip his life.

●

PHILLIP JOEL HUGHES WAS born at 4.50 pm on Wednesday, 30 November 1988, in Macksville District Hospital. Another baby, born two days earlier, lay in a bassinet in the maternity ward, and whenever he cried, Phillip would cry too. Phillip and Mitch Lonergan would be best mates for life.

The week Phillip and Mitch were born, Allan Border's Australians took on the West Indies in Perth in a Test match that saw Curtly Ambrose break Geoff Lawson's jaw and Merv Hughes take a hat-trick. Steve Waugh, who hit 91 in the first innings, would be the subject of a poster on Phillip's bedroom wall. It's still there, above the single bed at the back of the modest brick home in a room full of his rep shirts and mementos. The poster is titled 'The Final Campaign'.

Greg and Virginia Hughes are Macksville people. When they took Phillip home to join his elder brother Jason, they lived within a few hundred metres of two uncles and two sets of grandparents.

Virginia Ramunno's father Vince emigrated from the village of Pacentro in central Italy in the 1950s, having been sponsored to work on a banana plantation. The Nambucca Valley, fertile land irrigated by mountain rivers, had been populated by the Gumbaynggirr nation who fed on mullet and oysters from the water and Bangalow palms, lilly pilly and native grapes to supplement their hunting.

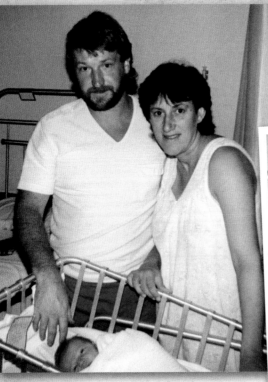

Left: Greg and Virginia were thrilled to welcome their second son, Phillip, into the world. He was a happy and placid baby from day one.

Below: Phillip loved bath time, especially when lots of bubbles were involved.

Above: Phillip as a toddler looking cool in sunglasses.

Right: From an early age, Phillip was always answering the family phone. This filtered through to his adult life where he called Greg and Virginia as often as he could.

Phillip could be like a farmer at the crease, with the sense that the centre wicket was his property, that he would stick it out here when things were tough and harvest when they got better

Old-growth cedar forests attracted the first Europeans in the late 1830s, but the real influx began in the 1860s when the colonial government broke up the large pastoral leases and allowed settlers to establish smaller holdings. The high rainfall and rich volcanic soils that had supported the indigenous people provided perfect conditions for farming. Two Scotsmen, Angus McKay and Hugh McNally, subdivided their leases to establish a township on the river: Macks' Ville. McNally built the two-storey Star Hotel in 1885 to take in passengers from the steamers that came up from the sea port of Nambucca Heads, 12 kilometres away. The railway arrived in 1919 and the road bridge in 1931, an event hailed at the time as the greatest day in Macksville's history, leading to the closure of the town's wharf.

When the cedar forests were spent, dairy farmers took to the lowlands and banana growers to the slopes. Bananas were a thriving industry for generations, supporting the Hugheses, the Ramunnos and many of their neighbours. The Banana Growers Federation and Co-op built offices in town and the banana displays at agricultural shows were keenly contested.

When he emigrated from Italy, Vince Ramunno had left behind his wife Angela with four young children, including twins born from triplets just before he set off. They followed him a few years later when he'd saved enough money to pay their passage by boat from Pacentro to another small country town on the other side of the globe. Their trip was not without incident. It was feared one of the boys had gone overboard, but he was found in the ship's shop looking at playing cards.

Virginia was born after husband and wife reunited. They lived in a big fibro house by the Nambucca River, where Angela still lives, famous for her pasta and other exotic dishes that were unheard of in a town where the only foreign food was the local Chinese. Phillip loved his nana's food, and his mum's baked dinners, and he loved that Chinese restaurant too – he told everyone that the food there was the best in Australia.

In the 1950s, the Ramunnos took to Macksville and the town took to them. Vince soon had his own banana plantation and the kids settled in as Australians, proving it with their love of cricket, rugby league and, in Virginia's case, basketball and squash.

The Hugheses had been hereabouts for longer. Greg's mother Edith was born in Kempsey, just down the highway, and his father Sidney was born in Maclean on the Clarence River 180 kilometres to the north before his family shifted to Bowraville, upriver from Macksville, when he was young. Sidney had a good job at the local abattoir and worked a banana plantation near Taylors Arm before moving into that business full-time.

Greg's childhood home was at the river end of East Street, the backyard divided by a creek where hundreds of ducks bred. They had chook pens that backed onto the Thistle Park cricket ground, and plenty of room for a barbecue and backyard cricket match, which became the family Christmas tradition.

Dreaming of becoming a cattle farmer, Greg went to Tocal Agricultural College near Newcastle for a couple of years but returned to banana-farming at home. It took a lot of money to get into cattle, but a man could rent a plantation and make a living from growing the tropical fruit. Thickset and calm, slow to anger but formidable when crossed, he played rugby league and a bit of cricket. Phillip's batting genes might not be here: Greg's highest score was about 70.

'Phillip always joked about that,' Greg says, adding that he didn't have time to train with the demands of running a property. There is talk in Macksville that Greg was a bit better than he admits.

'Phillip got it from me,' Virginia suggests with a grin.

Her solitary sporting trophy sits front and centre, surrounded by hundreds won by Phillip, Jason and their younger sister, Megan. Two tall bookshelves in the dining room

Vince took one look at the 9 lbs 4 oz boy and announced he was *boofono*, which, he said, meant 'big'. Phillip was dubbed 'Boof', sometimes 'Boofa'. The name caught on at home and in the streets of Macksville

are packed deep with gold figurines in various sporting poses, with more in the next room.

Virginia is a right-hander who played sport with her left, as would Phillip. He took his Italian stylings from her too, the dark eyes and the grin that sparkles with good-natured mischief. But Greg brought the understated focus and country calm, and Phillip could be like a farmer at the crease, with the sense that the centre wicket was his property, that he would stick it out here when things were tough and harvest when they got better.

Greg Hughes and Virginia Ramunno grew up not more than ten houses apart on East and River Streets, but hardly knew each other as kids. Their age difference, Virginia the elder by four years, meant they moved in different circles.

At 20, Virginia travelled to Europe and visited the medieval village her parents and siblings had come from. Pacentro, smaller even than Macksville, has an elevated castle, simple stone houses and shops around a small piazza.

Virginia had worked various jobs around town, and was working as a stewardess at the Macksville Ex-Services Club when she noticed Greg Hughes for the first time. That was around 1983, and in 1985 they married in St Patrick's Catholic Church. Virginia had gone to school here, Greg at the public, but they'd both funnelled into Macksville High to finish their secondary education.

They both loved and continue to love Macksville.

'It was a great place to grow up,' Virginia says.

'Magic,' Greg adds. 'Typical country childhood: rode your bikes, played till dark.'

'Very safe . . . just had to let Mum and Dad know where you were,' Virginia recalls.

'Come Saturday,' Greg chips in, 'you were down the river fishing until you got a bit older and there was a bit more to do. There wasn't a lot of cricket when I was growing up. We played a lot of football.'

'You were captain, Greg. And a cyclist.'

'I rode pushbikes. Track and road. Back in those days, when we rode track it was on dirt at the showgrounds, but we'd go away to carnivals at Tamworth, Taree . . . They had a tarred track.'

Jason was born in 1986, Phillip in 1988 and, after they caught their breath, Megan in 1995. They were already settled at their four-bedroom house in East Street when the boys were born.

Nobody could quite believe how big Phillip was. Virginia's father Vince took one look at the 9 lbs 4 oz boy and announced he was *boofono*, which, he said, meant 'big'. Phillip was dubbed 'Boof', sometimes 'Boofa'. The name caught on at home and in the streets of Macksville. It was that or Phillip. Never Phil, and God help you if Virginia heard you abbreviate it.

'He was just beautiful,' she says. 'He was so quiet right from the time he was born. You wouldn't know he existed. He was relaxed from the start; they really had to smack his bottom hard to get a reaction from him.'

'He had a bit of weight on him,' cousin Sharnie Barabas (nee Ramunno) confirms.

All the women agree that he was a beautiful boy, his eyes twinkling beneath a halo of fair curls.

'He was no trouble, loved his trucks,' Virginia continues. Finishing each other's sentences, Virginia and Greg share the account of his toddler years. 'Played in the little garden beneath the deck with his yellow Tonkas . . . Some stayed lined up on the veranda and others played in the dirt . . . They're in his room now . . . He would sit there and amuse himself . . . If the weather was bad, he would bring the clean ones inside and play with them . . .'

He had balance and coordination and was always doing tricks, racing a pedal car around the backyard before graduating to a skateboard. He played rugby league from age five and won his age group's swimming races.

The family loved the outdoors, often heading to the beaches at Scotts Head or Nambucca Heads on weekends. Virginia packed a picnic and the Hugheses would play ball games together on the sand between swims. Their tight unit was forged through physical recreation.

Above top: Phillip looked up to his brother, Jason, so much that he always wanted to wear what Jason wore.

Above: Phillip excited and ready for his daily visit to Macksville Park.

Below: A cheerful Phillip at age three.

Below bottom: From left to right, Mitch Lonergan, Phillip and Jason riding a horse out the back of East Street. The boys were inseparable and Mitch and Phillip would be best mates for life.

Above top: Virginia, Phillip, Greg and Jason on Phillip's fourth birthday. His impressive boat cake was made by the talented Aunty Kay Clews and the bowl of fresh bananas was picked by Greg that morning.

Above: Phillip posing for a photo with Virginia, his eyes twinkling beneath a halo of fair curls.

Left: Greg and Phillip, looking dapper, dressed up for a wedding.

Above left: Happy brothers Jason and Phillip getting ready for school at St Patrick's Primary.

Above: Phillip with a calf at the Macksville Show.

Left: Phillip and Jason won many medals and trophies with the Bowraville Tigers in junior rugby league.

Below: Phillip's passion for cattle started at a young age. At 11 years old he proudly participated in the Macksville cattle parade.

When Virginia took Phillip and Jason to the local swings at Macksville Park, she pushed them both, with little Megan watching from her stroller. 'The two boys were the best of mates from the start,' Virginia says. 'They adored Megan and both of them wanted to nurse her. I had to tell them to take turns.'

When Virginia was at work, Greg's mother Edith minded the kids. Edith was one of the first to remark on Phillip's physical skills. 'She threw balls to him, and commented from very early how well coordinated he was,' Virginia says. 'He was quick off the mark, too: she said she couldn't catch him.'

Cricket? Well, Phillip was a reluctant starter. At a young age, Jason had started to make representative teams, a good batsman but a star bowler in matches behind the Hughes's house at Thistle Park.

Then, Phillip's pride was challenged. Greg and Jason recall the moment.

'They tried to talk Phillip into going to play in the local side. His mates would, but not Phillip, he was not into cricket at all,' Greg says.

Jason takes up the story. 'It was Milo or Kanga cricket, I was ten, and we were in the back-yard that Saturday morning. He was seven or eight and we were a couple of players short. He didn't want to do it. He was, "Aww, like, is it a hard ball?" We'd just started playing backyard cricket and a few times I'd bowled the hard ball to him and he didn't like it because he was very young . . . I called him a pussy.

'In the end I just said come, and he came. We got in Dad's truck and he played and he killed it. He batted eight or nine and no-one could get him out. It was all my mates and he knew them and liked being around them. He liked it from then, I reckon. Even then you could see that cut shot. I noticed it then.'

Phillip would tell Megan that going to the ground that day was 'just another thing to do'. He was off the mark.

TWO **EAST STREET KIDS**

An Australian backyard is the cradle of invention, each with its own cricketing eccentricities. The backyard in East Street opened onto low-lying paddocks that would swamp up in heavy rain. A bowler had to start his run-up at the chook pens and turn a hard left to bowl to a batsman who was up against the back of the house by the barbecue.

JASON AND PHILLIP DEVELOPED a scoring system that made the most of the available architecture and impediments. A shot into the back fence was four. Over it and into the paddock, six and out: get it yourself and start bowling.

The garden bed where Phillip had played with his Tonka trucks was two, the side fence the same. At mid-wicket, the clothesline was 25 on the bounce but 50 on the full. Nick behind and 'auto wickie' took the catch, unless you edged it onto one of the narrow veranda poles; then the catch had been spilt and the boys would cry, 'Taylor's dropped him!'

Every game was a Test match and Mark Taylor was the slipper. He didn't drop many. The chook pens, which were at mid-on to a left-hander, were also four. The younger brother's cut shot was fed, but gained him only two runs, so he learned to work his drives toward the fence at mid-off where he could get four. You can still see the indentations at the point where he pasted ball after ball onto the off-side.

Some afternoons, Greg would let the chooks roam. A chook was 25 runs, an unfortunate bounty for one bird whose life ended when it got in the way. The luckier Hughes birds won prizes at the local agricultural shows, and the boys were given their own.

Above: Every element of the Hughes's backyard was a scoring opportunity. The fence was two runs, the shed was four, the Hills Hoist was 25 on the bounce and 50 on the full. Phillip's chickens, once worth 25 runs for a direct hit, still roam nervously.

Left: The Hughes family fence still wears the dings from Phillip's cut shot.

Competition was fierce between the brothers, the way it has been since Cain sent Abel in to bat, but the toss was a waste of time.

'He always batted first,' Jason says without rancour.

A bat was flung into the air and fell 'hills or flats'. If Phillip lost the first toss, he would call for best of three. If the next, it was best out of five.

'And if I won again,' Jason says, 'he would be like, "Mu-um! Mu-um!" and Mum would yell out, "Jason, Phillip's batting!"'

Jason would push off the chook shed, turn hard left and the game would begin. Behind Phillip, above slips to the left-hander, were windows. *Were*. He didn't mind lofting one over the cordon. While he usually got away with it in a game, in the backyard it resulted in shattered glass and exasperated parents. Virginia replaced that window a number of times and then gave up; the remaining glass was eaten away by cricket balls, shard by shard, until Megan, preparing for her eighteenth birthday party in the backyard, demanded that the window be fixed.

•

PHILLIP WAS FIVE WHEN he first made the papers. He was photographed with Greg, winner of Most Successful Exhibitor at the Nambucca River Show in 1993. A tough man to beat, Greg had previously won Best Commercial Bunch – Irrigated, Best Two Commercial Bunches, Heaviest Bunch of the Show (49.4 kg), Champion Bunch, Three Williams Hands and Heaviest Hand of Bananas.

'Greg, following in the footsteps of his father, has been growing bananas for 11 years,' the local paper reported. 'Greg leaves home for the plantation at 6 am every day and comes back at 4 pm. Part of his work includes cutting bananas once a week, every week.'

Following Jason, Phillip started at St Patrick's Primary School at five. Mitch Lonergan, whom he first encountered in the maternity ward, also made the journey across town and up the hill to St Patrick's, part of a rolling wave of boys obsessed with rugby league and cricket in East Street. Every few years, younger brothers joined the pack and were initiated into the ways of the bigger boys: the Lavertys, the Lonergans, the Ramunnos, the Martines, the Wards, the Hugheses and more who biked in from nearby. There was hardly a girl in sight, although cousin Sharnie rolled up her sleeves and joined in. They say she was tougher at football and more skilled at cricket than any of the boys.

The games advanced from one backyard to another and sometimes into the paddocks of the Donnelly Welsh Playing Fields. Each yard had its own cricket rules, but only the Hugheses' had lighting that allowed the game to roll on after sunset, only winding up when the last kid was summoned home for bath and bed.

If they weren't kicking or hitting a ball, they were riding around Macksville. Mitch Lonergan remembers going 'to town to get lollies . . . There were a couple of ways to go up to town. The first street, which was the quickest way, had magpies in two big trees. [Phillip] loved the thrill of the magpies chasing and swooping, but I was too scared and couldn't go that way, so I would go the longer way and had to meet him up town.'

The Hughes children's godparents, 'Uncle Winston and Aunty Kay' Clews, lived between Taylors Arm and the Tilly Willy Creek a couple of kilometres away. Winston had built a retaining wall by the river known as 'Winston's Wharf', a favourite fishing spot for the Hughes boys and their friends. There were rumours of a giant groper that lived beneath the bridge, one the kids dreamed of landing.

'He was competitive at that again,' Jason says. 'He would try and catch the biggest fish, but he wasn't really patient and after a few hours he would ring Mum to pick him up.'

To this day the groper remains unharmed, but the boys landed just enough smaller fish to keep coming back.

The kids from the area made Winston's Wharf their second home. Kay would bake cakes for birthdays, while Winston baited the hooks and freed the snags. Sometimes he took the kids out on his boat. Phillip would never forget the important people in his early life. Much later, he always visited the Clewses when he was back in town, or called them when he was away. When Winston got cancer, Phillip, by then a Test cricketer, dropped in with a signed cap and when Winston passed away, wore a black armband in the New Year's Ashes Test match at the Sydney Cricket Ground.

Left and right: Uncle Winston and Aunty Kay Clews' beautiful backyard led to a wharf on the river where Phillip and Jason spent many hours fishing.

Kay never cared for cricket, but became infatuated with Phillip's career. 'I would get so excited when he came on the news – I would jump up and down and kiss the telly,' she says.

Phillip gave her a coffee mug with his face and his shirt number, 64, on it when he returned from an Indian Premier League stint with the Mumbai Indians, another prized possession but no more prized than the memories Aunty Kay keeps of the chubby little boy with blond locks and cheeky smile.

Gatherings of family and friends usually took place at home. Aunty Kay's birthday cakes were the centrepiece of parties where the house was thrown open not only to the kids and their friends, but to the extended Hughes–Ramunno clans. 'We always had their birthday parties at home and they were lovely times,' Virginia says. Day-long Christmas barbecues took place in alternating years either at home or at Greg's parents' house. 'Phillip was happy with whatever presents he got, and he loved Christmas,' Virginia says. 'There was a lot of food, all the cousins and aunties and uncles were there, and before long there would be football and cricket set up, with everyone playing.'

Country life could never be too white-bread with the Ramunno connection. Virginia's mother Angela, or Nan's, riverside home is decorated in the mid-century Italian style, the front room bursting with ornate furniture, porcelain figurines and a wall covered in family photos, a slice of the old country in the heart of the new. Angela spoke both languages but favoured Italian around the family. The kids picked up enough words to understand her and insult each other.

'We have little words we would speak and continued for years to talk Italian to each other and we had Italian nicknames for each other,' Sharnie says. 'We probably don't really know what we mean.'

A traditional matriarch, Angela, or Nan, could be found mixing flour and eggs for fresh pasta and making Italian dishes every day in her 'pasta room' at the back of the house. The kids were encouraged to join in, and would get covered in flour and red sauce. Grandchildren on their way home from school gathered around the big table where dough was pressed and cut by hand or machine, and mixed with sauce made from Nan's home-grown tomatoes and herbs.

Sharnie, the daughter of Virginia's brother Geato Ramunno, who also lived on East Street, remembers getting in trouble for eating pasta raw. Nan was not a woman to meddle with, but Sharnie says Phillip had his way with women from a very early age.

'Boof got pretty much what he wanted from Nan – he was a smooth talker. Sometimes we would ask, "Nan, why are you making that type of pasta?" and you would see Boof laughing in the background. He was pretty cheeky that way.'

Jason recalls his younger brother loving Italian food. 'I wasn't a massive fan, but Phillip loved it. Loved it. There were days when he would go, "Oh Mum, could you get Nan to cook

me this or that?" and she'd just do it. Bolognese, pizza, pig's trotter . . . Phillip loved his Italian because the only other exotic restaurant was the Macksville Chinese. He moved to Sydney and he didn't know what was going on, didn't know you could go out for Indian or Thai. We didn't have those things.'

If Phillip got his way, it was because he had a charm that even an older brother couldn't deny.

'We did fight sometimes,' Jason says, 'but I reckon we have to be up there with the closest brothers going around. You just couldn't dislike him, you just couldn't. He had so much going on for him, and he just got what he wanted. When he was young, Mum gave him everything, but she was the same with all of us. She was good, Mum. There were a couple of times where we'd just have a day off school and Mum would take us to Coffs for new Nikes. If Phillip wanted them, he got them. Mum just said yes.'

Phillip adored his mother, and Virginia admits that he got his way too easily. He never had to ask; he just had a way of flashing that smile, twinkling that eye.

'Even when he'd left home,' she says, 'he would call if he needed something. If Greg answered, he'd say, "Dad, I don't need to speak to you, I want Mum on the phone". He would say Mum, Mummy or Vinny, and I knew straightaway what he wanted. All the kids were the same, they all came to me . . . He just had a tone of voice . . . He would never say, "Mum, I want money". He knew how to swindle, it was just a way he had. I'd say, "Okay, it'll go in today". But there was no mention of money. I could never say no to him.'

When he was ten, Phillip did a school assignment on the family. The work reveals a deep bond of love that is craftily manipulated for the task. Nan is in an 'advertisement' section that reads: 'Come one, come all, come and visit your elderly relatives. Pop in: Have a Cuppa: Have a chat: Have a hug but most of all come in and visit anytime. Family always welcome.'

PHILLIP'S BUSINESS CARD
SKILLS ARE:

Good Looking.
Good Cricketer
Good with Tools
Good At Jobs (Small or Large)
Good At fixing Anything
Good Boy
Good AllRounder
If You Are looking For
Another Member Please
Look at Bottom Two Corners
For Details.

② **KNOWLEDGE**

FAMILY

Families are good to have.

A family is important.

Mum is a nice person.

I think my family is the most important thing in the world.

Loving everyone in the family.

Yes what a family we have.

⑥

FOR SALE
JASON HUGHES. Good looking.
Excellent Cricketer.
Age: 12 years.

CHEAP BUY at PRICE
$6,200·00

Right: Fishing from the Macksville Bridge, Nino Ramunno remembers little Phillip almost going over the guard rail as he hooked a big jewfish. 'I ran over to help but Phillip stopped me in my tracks with an intense look of steely determination in his eyes. There was no way he wasn't going to land that monster all by himself. And he did.'

I predict when I am 30 my family will be as followed.

My Dad will be 58 years old. And probably still be a banana Grower, I Hope Dad will still be alive. I recond he will still have a beard, and I hope he will still play fantastic Cricket with me.

My Mum will be 62 years old, O boy, getting old; I hope mum will still be alive, I am sure mum will still be a terrific mum and friend to me.

My Brother Jason will be 32 years old, I guess he will be a Solicitor or doing Law, I hope he becomes a N.S.W. and Australian Cricketer because he is a Wonderful player, and I guess he might be married with children of his own, and I hope we will still be best mates.

Myself Phillip well I am going to be 30 years old. I do hope I become a famous Cricketer to play for N.S.W and also to be an Australian Cricketer. I don't know if I will be married and have children of my own. I do hope to own my own Cricket store and have my own Brand Name Cricket Labels example PHILLIP'S LABELS

My Sister Megan will be 24 years old. I guess she will be married. I don't know what she will do for work, probably medicine like my mum, dispense medicine etc.
At the end of the day my family will all be 20 years Older. O Boy!

Above left: Phillip won Champion Junior Boys Swimmer at St Patrick's. Swimming was a talent he picked up from his mum, Virginia. Phillip said: 'Mum tells me think positive and you will always do well.'

Right: Christmas Day is a big event in the Hughes household. Phillip was always the last one to go to sleep and the first one up. Greg, Megan, Phillip and Jason sit among the wrapping paper where Phillip had just unwrapped his beloved Tonka crane.

The words are arranged around a picture of Angela. Part of the task asked the students to imagine where they would be when they were 30. It's sweet and heartbreaking at the same time.

Virginia, who was working at a chemist's, drove him everywhere and passed on her talent for swimming. 'Mum tells me think positive and you will always do well.'

Dad is his cricket coach, Jason is a 'great mate' and bowls to him 'all the time, he has helped me to become a great open[ing] batsman in cricket'. Megan is too young and 'really hasn't helped me in anyway as yet . . . but I love her anyway'.

Megan was just two when Phillip did the assignment, but they would strike up a special relationship.

'He called me Mego or Sis,' Megan says. 'Everyone calls me Mego because of him. I don't know where that came from, I guess one day it just rolled off his tongue. Outside he was Phil, Hugh or Hughesy or something, but at home he was Bro or Boof, because when he walked through that front door from being away I wanted him to feel at home again.'

Like Jason, she says he was too lovable to argue with. 'You struggled to stay angry with him; he would always make you laugh and stop being angry. If he was irritating me, not making me angry, just playing with me, I would go, "You're annoying me, Bro", and the next minute he would do something funny and it was totally gone. I could not stay angry, he had the most beautiful heart.'

When the boys were young, Sharnie, already at high school, would look after them until Virginia got home.

Above: Phillip adored his younger sister, Megan, or 'Mego'. He used to hug and squeeze her until Virginia would tell him, 'Put her down!'

'We were together every day, basically playing football,' she says. 'Cricket started really creeping in when Phillip was around eleven or twelve, and it changed from backyard football to backyard cricket.'

The cover drive was born at home because it was worth double, but at the Ramunnos' the rules were different.

'That bloody cut shot,' Sharnie says. 'That's where he got it from. He would stand there the whole time. Cut shot, cut shot, cut shot, cut shot . . . until he got a hundred. And we were like, "Seriously, we can't get this bugger out". Sometimes we were glad when it was too dark to play because that was the only way to stop him.'

If it rained, Sharnie and the boys went inside and played 'classic catches', which involved kneeling on the carpet and pinging a cricket ball to an opponent also on their knees. Many a vase paid the price for not such a classic catch. China, windows, tin fences and chickens all paid the price for the cricket obsession that gripped the East Street kids.

'Cut shot, cut shot, cut shot, cut shot . . . until he got a hundred. And we were like, "Seriously, we can't get this bugger out". Sometimes we were glad when it was too dark to play because that was the only way to stop him'
– SHARNIE BARABAS

THREE

THE PERFECT PAIR

Knock.
Knock.
Knock.
Knock.
All day and into the night. Knock. Knock. Knock.

If you visited the Hughes house in East Street, your knock on the door would have been echoed from the backyard where Phillip and Jason were hitting cricket balls hung from strings. Over and over and over again.

WHERE JASON WAS KEEN, Phillip was obsessive. Nobody ever practised with such concentration. Ball under the eyes, elbow raised. Knock. Knock. Knock.

They figured out that if the ball in its sock hung by a simple string, it always followed the same arc. Too simple. So they knotted the string, causing the ball to swing left or right. Each boy had a ball a few paces apart, each at his own crease, moving in and out to play the ball at different points on the arc. Different balls were strung at different heights.

Through these sessions, Phillip developed his impeccable defensive technique. Everybody who saw him would be deceived by the flamboyance and audacity of the high back lift and the cut shot, and distracted from his defence. But young Phillip was rock solid. He was still, he waited for the ball, and he played it under his eyes.

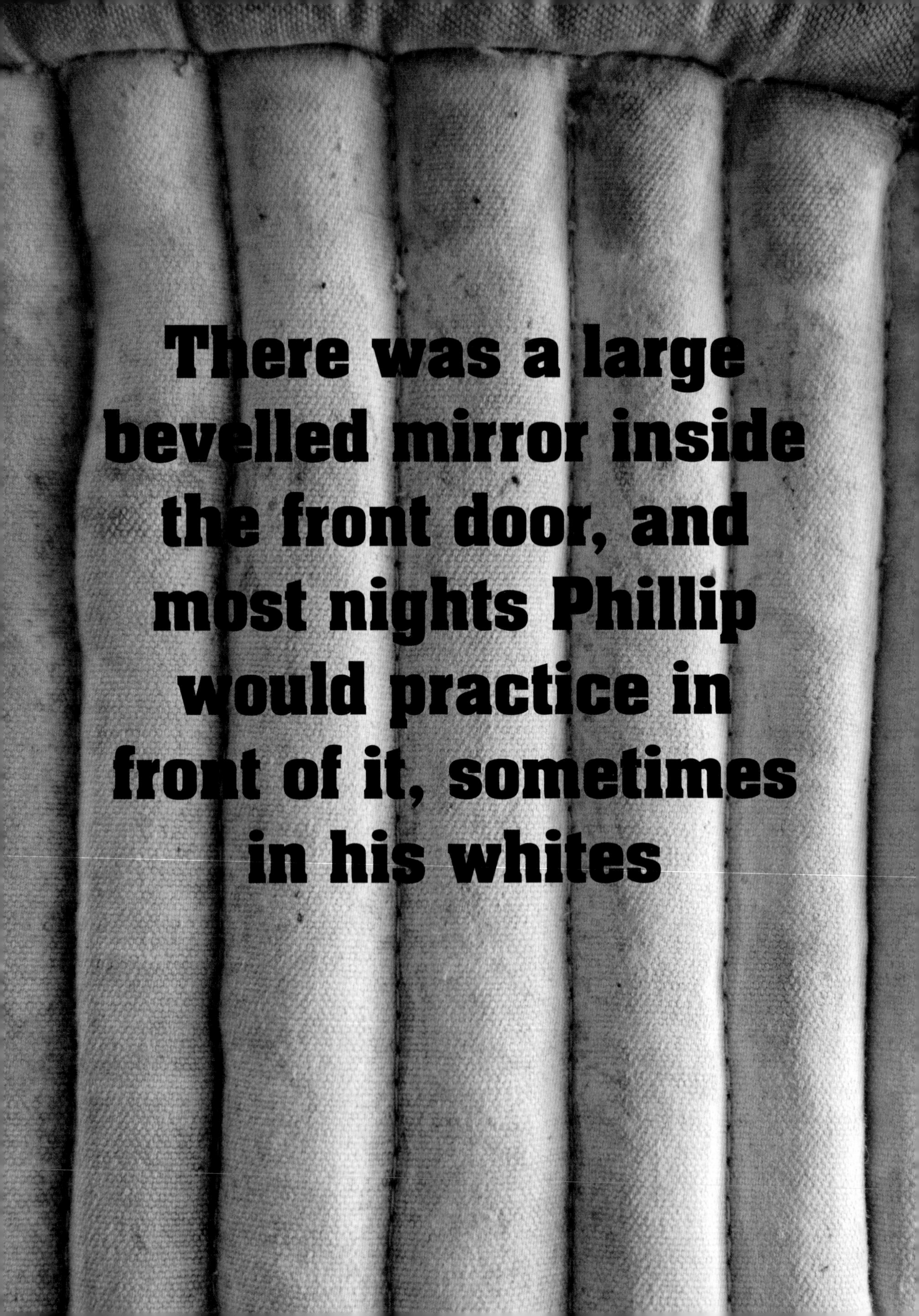

There was a large
bevelled mirror inside
the front door, and
most nights Phillip
would practice in
front of it, sometimes
in his whites

'You always have more time than you think,' he said. The best players always look like they have more time.

Phillip became as meticulous about practice as he had been about his Tonka trucks. In Year Three, Nathan Smith arrived at St Patrick's and became, with Mitch Lonergan, his closest friends. Two decades later, Smith remembers the sound when he arrived at the Hugheses'.

'You would knock on the door and ask if Boof was in, but you knew he was because you could hear the knock-knock-knock out the back.'

Greg gave the boy so many throwdowns locals worried his arm would fall off. When Smith visited, Phillip was happy to see him, but would not be distracted from his practice.

'Greg was always throwing him balls and he wouldn't stop. He would talk to you while he was doing it. If it wasn't throwdowns with Greg, he'd be hitting the ball in a sock on the back of the porch but still having a conversation with you. If you couldn't find him at home, he'd be around at Willis Street in the nets with Greg and Jason.'

Greg says the steady rhythm of Phillip hitting the ball in the sock would eventually be broken by a more emphatic knock as he played a decisive last shot, and then a clunk as the ball bounced onto the tin roof. A broom was always on hand to retrieve it for the next session.

Sessions didn't end when he came inside. There was a large bevelled mirror inside the front door, and most nights Phillip would practise in front of it, sometimes in his whites. Jason says mischievously that Phillip may even have slept in his gear. He is pretty sure he was sleeping with his bat.

Country life was fresh air, sport, sport, sport and then maybe a little bit more sport. After dark, if you stayed over at the Hugheses', you were co-opted into playing Test Match, the board game.

Phillip could focus on sport like few of his age, but at school he just got by. The reports from his early years are encouraging: his writing was neat, his attitude positive. Grade Four teacher Tony Kokegei noted that 'Phillip takes a lot of pride in the presentation of his work. He has worked very hard to improve in all subject areas. A very pleasing effort overall.' Grade Five teacher Stephanie Allan noted a rising restlessness: he 'tries hard to work well but can be

Right: Phillip and Jason in their rugby league gear ready to play for the Bowraville Tigers.

noisy at times when his enthusiasm gets the better of him. He is a polite, cooperative student'.

Virginia's and the family's love are obvious in the section devoted to parents' comments: 'Your improvement is noticed by Mum, Dad and brother Jason. Well done!'

In religion, Phillip had mastered some basic rules, writing that he'd learned to 'pray to God and pray for the sick people in hospital and don't hurt people by punching them or kicking them'.

Come the final year of primary, Phillip was increasingly focused on extracurricular activities. Asked to nominate something he had achieved in first term, he said he 'worked very well and played cricket for the school, and I did very well'. His goals were 'to be selected in the state side for cricket and do well in school work', in that order. His Grade Six teacher, Mrs Murphy, had taken a shine to the happy-go-lucky kid whose gifts were obvious: 'Phillip works well and strives to do his best . . . conscientious, enthusiastic and cooperative. He delights in his successes and has a pleasing attitude to school. If this persists he will continue to enjoy success in the future'.

The support Phillip felt from his family was crucial. It was, as he wrote in that earlier assignment, his mother who told him to believe in himself, and few fathers were as faithful to their children's sporting pursuits as Greg was with Jason, Phillip and Megan.

Phillip's cricket, however, became a religion that demanded much of the true believers.

Mitch Lonergan says that that the teachers had accepted early on that Phillip would succeed through sport and not academia. 'He realised he wasn't the smartest kid in the class, probably because he was so much in love with cricket and every other sport. He could be cheeky, but then he would grin and get away with it. Even when he was young, the teachers loved him and favoured him and I remember one saying, "When you make it big, don't forget your teacher". That was in Year Three or Four. They all knew Phillip was going to be something and were proud before he even made it. That's why he got away with everything.'

Joel Dallas lived along the river at Nambucca Heads but became good friends with Mitch, Nathan and Phillip. If they got into any trouble, he says, Phillip was generally an observer, and he had a gift for being 'loved by everyone's parents', who all found him respectful and polite. It was partly his nature, partly strategic. Virginia was not the last adult he could wind around his finger. Years later, Michael Clarke would say, 'My dad's friends became his friends. The minute he walked into a room, they became his mates.' Many others say the same. He became every dad's adopted son.

But everything else in life came second to cricket. Nathan Smith, who would go on to play league for the Canterbury–Bankstown Bulldogs and the Parramatta Eels, found that playing cricket against Phillip could become monotonous.

Above left: Phillip, ten, ecstatic with his trophy awarded for his hat-trick.

Above right: Ready to play for the Under-12s Macksville Ex-Services Club at age ten.

Left: Phillip in his cricket whites.

Above: Greg relaxing with Phillip, eight, Megan, two, and Jason, ten. Although he worked long days at the banana farm, Greg always had time to take the boys down to the Willis Street nets after school.

MID-COAST OBSERVER, Wednesday, March 31, 1999

Hughes joins state team

St Patrick's School cricketer Phillip Hughes (aged 10-years, pictured) has been ranked among the State's best Catholic Primary-age players.

The honour has placed him among his peers from public schools – winning a berth in the prestigious Primary Schools Sports Association (PSSA) State Titles in Tamworth from October 25-28.

Selected as a member of the Catholic (Polding) team, Phillip was ranked with the Catholic systems best cricketers in the northern half of the State. Phillip will now join one other Catholic squad MacKillop – (which covers the southern half of the State) at the Tamworth ...

GUARDIAN NEWS THURSDAY, FEBRUARY 11, 1999

Century helps in Urunga victory

A brilliant ...
out by Urunga
Moran ...
Coast ...
cil's ...
rep...
ea...

GUARDIAN NEWS THURSDAY, MARCH 25, 1999

GUARDIAN NEWS THURSDAY, OCTOBER 29, 1998

Locals shine in first junior inter-district cricket match

The first official under-12s inter-district cricket game of the 1998/99 season was played last weekend against last year's grand finalist Coffs Harbour on the Coffs home pitch.

PAUL WARD reports:

With five players from last year's premiership still eligible to play this season the foundation was set for a good season.

Nambucca/Bellingen lost the toss and was asked to bowl. The Coffs side was soon in trouble when opening bowler Matthew Ward (Macksville RSL) clean bowled the opening bats-man in his first over, leaving Coffs in the first over.

Further ...

Josh Law...

... the score was 1/6. This brought Josh Lawrence to join opener Phillip Hughes (Macksville RSL) and they produced some of the best under-12s batting I have seen, to record an 83-run partnership before Hughes was bowled for 40 leaving the score at 2/89.

Mathew Ward (Macksville RSL) joined Lawrence and they took the score to 146 runs before the rain fell and Ward was bowled by a skidder for 49.

Brendan...

Watch

PHILLIP RANK...

St Patrick's Primary cricketer Phillip Hughes (age 11 years) has been ranked among the state's best Catholic Primary-age players.

The honour has placed him among his peers from public schools - winning a berth in the prestigious Primary Schools Sports Association (PSSA) State Titles, held in Richmond from November 20-23.

Selected as a member of the Catholic (Polding) team, Phillip was ranked with the Catholic sys-tem's best cricketers in...

MID-COAST OBSERVER

GUARDIAN NEWS THURSDAY, DECEMBER 28, 2000

Captain Phillip

Macksville cricketer Phillip Hughes, 12, has been selected as cap-tain for the New South Wales State Cricket team.

Phillip, who is the only country boy to make the team, was recently in Newcastle with the state team for a three day competi-tion.

The state team played and won against Newcastle's Under-13 representative side – a side one year older than Phillip's team.

Phillip performed at a high standard. He gained 50 runs before retiring, and took 1/14 off 8 overs. He plays as an open batsman and change bowler.

Phillip, who is coached by his father Greg, will compete in the Australian titles from January 6 to 13 at Cobram/Barooga on the NSW/Victorian border.

Macksville's Phillip Hughes (left) – captain of the New South Wales Primary School's State Cricket team.

NEWS THURSDAY, OCTOBER 19, 2000

...' interdistrict win

Hastings batted and were dis-missed for 140. Nambucca Bellingen wicket takers included Jason Hughes (2/16), Reece Williams (1/11), Ben Maloney (1/26), Sean Takacs (1/14), Luke Pomroy (1/11), Danny Evans (1/7), Sean Cash (1/9) and Troy Grace (1/12).

Wicket keeper Ricky Welsh took two catches and a stumping.

Nambucca Bellingen under-12s: ... R Dawson 44, A Murrell ... S Fenson 2/3 ...

... under-16s ... to bat against ... district clash at ... Sunday (15th). ... Welsh and Harley ... a great start with 67 ... Schmidt (7) provid ... while Welsh was ... the other end ... included ...

Seaboard Valley Star • Wednesday, April 5, 2000

Dedicated young cricketer

Phillip Hughes

Phillip Hughes from St Patrick's School, has been ranked among ... Primary aged ...

his selection follows outstanding efforts as an opening batsman and change bowler.

Phillip plays Under 14's Saturday ...mings, C grade Saturday afternoon, in ...Coast Inter-district ...

MID-COAST OBSERVER, Wednesday, Dec...

SPORTS STAR
Phillip wins A...

St Patrick's School cricketer Phillip Hughes will play opening bats-man and change bowler in the Australian titles in ...uary after earning ...tion in the New Wales primary state cricket ...

...les will be held ...o/Barooga ...ry 6 next ...-year-old ...for the ...SL Cricket ...captain of ...

...ga were dismissed for 55 ...sville began their innings ...arley Schmidt and Jason ...s putting on 22. Michael ...hen joined Hughes and took ...score to 56. Hughes retired on ...

Ward continued on with his ...ings and was dismissed for 49 ...e was supported by Ricky Welsh (30), Evan Cotten (17) and Phillip Hughes (10).

Macksville were eventually dis-missed for 177 with Urunga's A ...Neil taking 4/14 and R Williams 3/ ...36.

Macksville RSL coach David ...Cotten was delighted with the win ...having taken the team through ...undefeated – including five out-right wins.

...House ...
...atrick's

'We all became bowlers because we never got to face a ball. You have no idea, we would just call it off after a while. It was just stupid – between him and Jason you couldn't get a bat, it was pointless. You'd think at some stage he might think he wanted to have a bowl or something, but he didn't. It was a pain in the arse. Both me and Mitch got plenty of practice bowling, that's why we never took up batting.'

He was so quiet about it, even Greg hardly noticed what was happening before his eyes

Phillip and Jason were the perfect pair. While Jason would go on to become an excellent batsman and boast the family's first double-century, he was primarily a bowler, which suited Phillip fine. The brothers would get the lawnmower out and cut the grass as low as they could. A hand-held concrete roller flattened the pitch. If that pitch became too worn and Greg began to complain about the bare patches, they would migrate to a new one. Often they had three on the go.

'Phillip and I played backyard cricket every day,' Jason says. 'I started taping the ball up and I used to nick him off all the time. No-one else could get him out, but I knew how to. There were times when he had five bats to my one. Ridiculous.'

Phillip couldn't figure out why he was having so much trouble. He didn't know that if Jason got home before him, he would 'get the hose out and water a patch on a good length. It would skid off and that really used to throw him. He had no idea.'

Jason's hold over Phillip didn't last, but he enjoyed it while it did. At twelve, Jason was the best of his age on the Banana Coast, and Greg was soon taking him for extra sessions. As the Hughes home backed onto the Donnelly Welsh Playing Fields, so they didn't even have to go out the front door. Across the road from the fields, Thistle Park would become home to the district's only turf wicket. Willis Street, where the nets were, was a block over on the way to town or school, but in the early days the run-ups were rough, so Greg and Jason would practise on the centre wicket. That's where Phillip became useful.

'When Jason was in Under-12s, he had been picked for the Polding PSSA [Primary Schools Sports Association] side,' Greg recalls. 'He was a very good bowler, very accurate, and I would be wicketkeeper but stand right back like a long stop. We stuck Phillip [with a bat] in front of the wickets and said, "Just block the balls". Jason was that accurate, Phillip had to block most balls. Hardly any got through to me. We only had three or four balls in those days. Most of them landed at Phillip's feet and he would tap them back.'

Too small to play shots, Phillip was developing his defensive technique. He was so quiet about it, even Greg hardly noticed what was happening before his eyes.

After a while, Jason realised his little brother was developing into a formidable opponent. 'I was opening bowler or first change for all the rep teams around. Phillip would just pad up and bat when he was ten or so. I would take it seriously and come off the long run-up, and after a while I couldn't get him out. I loved it, but he *really* loved it.'

●

IN SENIOR CRICKET THEY talk about a 'breakthrough year', a period when a young player rises suddenly through the levels. Phillip's breakthrough year began when he was facing Jason with the hard ball at Willis Street. In the spring, he would peel off a series of scores that would see his reputation sprout in the valley and spread far beyond. By the end of that season, the eleven-year-old from the bush would introduce himself down the highway in Sydney.

Short for his age, he looked like the little brother who'd tagged along and was given a game because somebody hadn't shown up. Except he usually walked out to open the batting and it didn't take many overs for sceptical opposition in the Under-12s, the Under-14s and the C-grade adults' competition to work out that Phillip Hughes was to be taken seriously.

'Your little bloke sure can hit a ball,' one coach reported to Greg, who at this stage was usually tied up with Jason's more serious cricket.

Greg didn't take too much notice. Jason was the talented son, and he couldn't expect another in the same family.

Phillip adored Jason and cricket was an entrée to the world of his older brother and his older mates, who had soon embraced him like family. At every game he was on the sidelines having throwdowns with Greg or whoever was available. Not content to be the tag-along little brother, when Greg took Jason to buy a bat, Phillip insisted he have one too. The Hughes family didn't have a lot of money, but what they had was spent on the kids and what Jason got, Phillip invariably wanted. When Jason graduated from primary school, he had to wear a dinner suit with bow tie and cummerbund. Phillip wanted the same, so he got the jacket, the tie and the cummerbund. But the tie and cummerbund weren't from the same set, and the budget didn't stretch to trousers.

One innings that season created a style that would endure onto the international stage a decade later. Early in the summer of 1998–99, trials were held for the Nambucca Bellingen inter-district team. The Hughes boys played junior club cricket on Saturday mornings for the Macksville Ex-Services Club, and in the afternoon the seniors played. Sundays were reserved for the representative teams.

Jason had Under-14 trials at the high school. Before he and Greg left, Phillip announced he would try out for the Under-12s at the Willis Street ground. Greg didn't take him seriously.

Above: Phillip (front, third from left) scored his first century as captain of the Under-12 Nambucca Bellingen district side at Bellingen Oval. The side were local inter-district champions and Phillip was lucky to share this championship with his friends Mitch Lonergan (back, second from left), Tom Schmidt (front, left) and Nathan Smith (front, third from right).

'It was all a bit tongue in cheek,' he recalls, but he wasn't going to stop him. Good luck to the little fella.

Warwick Lawrence from Urunga was the Under-12 Nambucca Bellingen coach. His son Josh was a very good cricketer who had played with and against Jason, but was young enough for another season in Under-12s. Greg knew the Lawrences and dropped Phillip at the nets on his way to Jason's trial.

When Greg got home, Phillip announced, 'I am playing next week in the rep side.'

'No, you're not.'

'Yes, I am.'

Greg rang Warwick Lawrence and said, 'What's this about Phillip? He says he made the rep side.'

'Only eight turned up, so I picked him,' Lawrence said. 'He'll be right.'

The rep games were at Kempsey, and luckily for Greg the Under-12s and Under-14s were on adjoining ovals. The father of the Hughes boys soon developed a habit of circulating between grounds. Greg still thought Phillip was too young, 'but I suppose we knew he had something because we had stuck him in front of Jason at practice and he could block them out . . . but Phillip was a baby. He was very short and solid'.

'He wasn't fat,' Virginia interjects. 'He was fit, but he was solid . . . he was beautiful.'

Warwick Lawrence batted little Phillip down the order and he played the only way he knew: blocking, turning over the strike and occasionally clipping the ball behind point with a late cut and other strokes that used the pace of the ball. Most nine-year-olds, especially those as short as Phillip, would find Under-12 representative bowlers intimidating, but his brother was opening the bowling in the Under-14s.

Josh Lawrence was batting when Phillip walked out for the first time. 'He came in at about number seven, striding out in those big bloody pads that were way too big for him – he looked too small to lift the bat. But I'd seen him at training having a hit when Jason was around and I said, "Mate, I don't need to say too much to you, do I?" He just shook his head.'

Memories vary, but Phillip scored somewhere between 17 and 21 that day and they could not get him out. The coach was impressed by what he saw.

'His defence was so good and anything short he would just flick behind square or off his hip, pull it even, but he didn't have the power in front of the wicket,' Warwick recalls. 'He was so very correct so early.'

After the game Warwick, who is both competitive and cunning, was at the pub with some mates. He told them he had found a nine-year-old good enough to open the batting in the Under-12s rep side.

'Down the order, he can hold up an end all day, but he won't get any runs because they pitch it up and he can't get it through the field,' he explained. 'If he opens, the difference is that if there is anything short with the new ball he can get runs behind point.'

Warwick had needed just one innings to decide that Phillip Hughes was an opener.

The North Coast Cricket Council stretches 230 kilometres from Iluka in the north to Eungai in the south. It comprises four associations: Lower Clarence, Clarence River, Coffs Harbour and Nambucca Bellingen. Inter-district games involve a fair bit of travel along the coastal highway. If you had two sons, you were torn.

Nambucca Bellingen's first round was against Coffs Harbour. Greg dropped Phillip at Sawtell on the way to Jason's game further up the road at Coffs. About 90 minutes later, his phone rang.

'That son of yours is a freak,' said Warwick Lawrence.

'What do you mean?'

'Well, I opened with him and he got 40.'

Phillip had batted with Josh Lawrence again. The pair had put on 83 runs against the previous year's premiers in a partnership that *Guardian News* cricket correspondent Paul Ward

reported 'produced some of the best Under-12s batting
I have seen'. Josh got 101 not out, showing Phillip just
how far you could go if you hung around.

After his tenth birthday, Phillip's team played Lower
Clarence at Rushforth Park in South Grafton. Greg
had taken Jason to Maclean, another hour up the road.

'Jason was trying out for the North Coast Under-14s
side, so I went with him.'

Meanwhile, Phillip opened the batting again. Josh
Lawrence came in at first drop and shared a big partnership with his mate's little brother.

'I remember that like it was yesterday,' Josh says. 'He
came off and he had the biggest grin on his face. He
was just as proud as punch.'

Phillip scored 64, his first half-century, a figure that
meant so much to him that when it came time to pick
a number for his one-day international shirt in 2012–
13, he chose 64. He wore 64 in the Indian Premier League, the Sheffield Shield, domestic
one-day and Big Bash League matches too. It is a number that will never be worn by an
Australian player again, having been retired from international service in the summer of
2014–15.

As the circle widened, more selectors were impressed. After his Nambucca Bellingen
performances, Phillip was selected in the North Coast Cricket Council team to play the Far
North Coast and the Northern Tablelands, and the then to tour Queensland. Phillip Hughes,
ten, was going places, literally. He top-scored with 59 (and took three for nine) at Ballina,
went to Beaudesert and Ipswich across the border, helping his team to more wins. In early
February they headed four hours inland, over the Dividing Range to Inverell. Phillip was
reluctant to travel without his dad, but was happy enough if he was with the Lawrences.

The Catholic primary schools had a well-structured state cricket competition and when
Phillip's new year started at St Patrick's, his performances in a trial at Wauchope won him
selection in a Catholic zone team for the diocesan trials in Lismore.

'This is a great achievement,' the local paper reported, 'as this extends from Laurieton to the

Queensland border. This is the start of a hat-trick for Phillip, as he has also been chosen to play for the North Coast Cricket Council team . . . Look out Mark Taylor'.

Phillip's appetite for cricket was insatiable. There was junior cricket for the Macksville Ex-Services Club on Saturday mornings, modified adult C-grade cricket in the afternoons, rep cricket on Sundays, and schools cricket during the week. Not only that, but he would bat for most, if not all, of the innings, and when his team was in the field, he would pull on the gloves and keep wicket before handing them over and having a bowl.

His rise through schools cricket, on top of his rep season, took him furthest afield. He made the diocesan team for the Polding area, which encompassed the north of New South Wales. The other diocese, MacKillop, took in Sydney, Canberra and further south. In the Polding trials, he caught the eye of Stan Gilchrist, a selector and a good judge of cricket flesh, having coached thousands of north coast kids, including his three sons. The youngest, Adam, was doing pretty well for Australia at the time.

'There were a lot of good cricketers,' Stan remembers, 'but Phillip was better than good.'

Despite two half-centuries for Polding, Phillip missed out on selection in the state primary

schools side. Greg, who took him to Tamworth for the carnival, which involved government and Catholic schools, says the selectors may have thought him too young.

Phillip didn't think, as a ten-year-old playing with Under-12s, that he was too young. On Saturday mornings he was playing in Jason's Under-14 team in Macksville before dashing to a C-grade competition made up of kids plus senior players who didn't want to clog up the

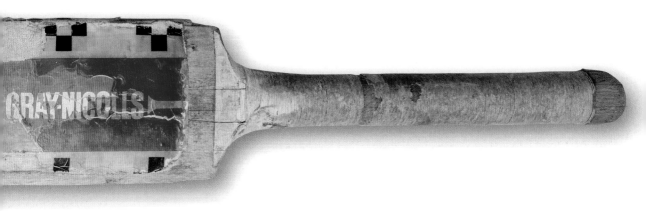

He would bat for most, if not all, of the innings, and when his team was in the field, he would pull on the gloves and keep wicket before handing them over and having a bowl

higher grades but wished to put something back into the game before they retired. Phillip was Macksville's youngest by a long shot. Coach David Cotten, who was approaching 50, drove a gaggle of youngsters to matches in his van. Another banana farmer, with a plantation on Whip Mountain, Cotten put in a long stretch as club secretary at Macksville.

'I used to sit up one end and let him bat,' Cotten says. 'He was too little to hit boundaries back then, but he used to stay there. The bowlers didn't take it easy on him, but they didn't target him. I used to open the batting and when Phillip came in I might score a run and let him face the rest of the over. After a while I didn't need to do that . . . My wife said, when he was 12, he would play for Australia. I thought so too a bit later. Not so much on his ability, but his attitude.'

The breakthrough season eventually had to end. After winning competitions with Macksville Under-14s and Nambucca Bellingen Under-12s, Phillip took a rest. During the year, he won Champion Junior Boys Swimmer at St Patrick's and played representative rugby league. But the next cricket season was never far from his mind.

FOUR

THE LITTLE CAPTAIN

The Ex-Services Club C-grade end-of-season report reckoned 'you must live in Alaska if you don't know about Phillip Hughes'. Against the mixed competition of adults and older boys, he won Player of the Year, as had Jason two years earlier.

IN THE SUMMER PHILLIP turned 11, he played in his own age group for the first time. He made it straight into the inter-district representative side for the Sunday competition, and his quiet cricket intelligence saw him chosen as captain despite, or perhaps because of, the fact he batted, bowled and kept wickets.

On 13 November 1999, he travelled north to Coffs Harbour for a rep match against Lower Clarence. It was an early start to get there before 10 am for the toss, which Nambucca Bellingen won. Phillip chose to bat. And bat he did.

Junior sides commonly made 100, maybe 150. The ball was hard, the grass was never short, the boundaries were long and scoring rates were low. When Phillip batted, however, his sides reached the 200 mark more often than not. His coaches, teammates, opponents and family say he had a feel for what was necessary. If wickets were falling, he would hang on and never get flustered; if the time was right, he would accelerate. Think Michael Bevan, who was steering teams to winning totals in one-day internationals, or Michael Hussey in years to come. This pre-teen boy was batting the same way.

Many of the later stories would come from his big scores made quickly, but Josh Lawrence marvelled at his patience.

'Phillip always valued his wicket. He could face out four or five maidens, just block, block, block. He'd say, "Mate, I am going to make these blokes bowl at me". He just had the mental capacity to go on.'

As a young cricketer, it was his ability to occupy the crease that stood out. His teammates could get frustrated at him digging in and not scoring, but he believed it was his job to be the backbone of an innings. The president of the North Coast Cricket Council, Ian Dinham, had a son, Braden, who played in representative sides with Phillip. Ian tells of a Combined High Schools trial game where Phillip hit a decent score, but faced 44 dot balls before getting off the mark.

'You just couldn't get him out,' he says. 'Phillip knew what he had to do to get his team a good total.'

Greg lost count toward the end, but he thinks Phillip scored 68 or 70 centuries before he left Macksville as a 17-year-old

In the 1999 game at Coffs, he watched four of his Nambucca Bellingen top order partners disappear. Most openers would be getting nervous by now. Tom Schmidt came to the crease and put on 69 with Phillip before getting out for 14. The little captain was scoring the bulk of the runs. The tail, like the top order, couldn't handle the Lower Clarence bowlers, and only Mitch Lonergan (17) showed any resolve.

Still, it was overs, not partners, that Phillip ran out of. He got into the 90s, but his chance of a century was ruined when two wickets fell in the 49th over. He ended up 95 not out. The fact that he'd only hit four boundaries shows how hard he had to work.

The following day, he opened the batting against Armidale and scored 77. As captain, he gave himself a bowl at first change and a return of three for 11 from four overs stopped anybody suggesting it shouldn't be so. In another match against Armidale, he scored 44 retired and then dismissed the top three batsmen on the way to figures of four for 10. Those who saw him bowl later are unanimous in poking fun at his run-up, action and speed, but in junior cricket he was canny, accurate and effective.

Tournaments and carnivals meant Phillip, Greg and Jason spent a lot of time out of town on the weekends, but Phillip managed to play in round one for the Macksville Under-14s, scoring 51 not out, and taking two for three. The annual report says that Phillip and Harley Schmidt (29) got 'Macksville off to a good start, although scoring at a slow rate'. Macksville beat Urunga by nine wickets, so it is hard to understand why the openers needed to be in any sort of a hurry.

The Hughes brothers were back in town for the semifinal against Nambucca and the grand final against Urunga, winning both. Phillip had been notching half-centuries all summer, including the 95 not out, and it seemed a matter of time before circumstances allowed him to climb the mountain to three figures.

In February, the Nambucca Bellingen rep side played their grand final against Grafton. Over the years, Greg would notice that his second son lifted for the big occasions. When the team needed runs in a final, it was usually Phillip who got them. Greg and Virginia were there to watch, another reliable indicator that this would be a big day.

He won the toss and, in humid conditions, batted. He watched partner after partner fall to the strong Grafton bowlers. His good mate Nathan Smith and Trent Matthews hung around for a while, but the six Nambucca Bellingen batsmen who were dismissed in the 45 overs he was in tallied 58 runs between them. It didn't bother Phillip; they were there long enough to enable him to score 103 runs. He had his maiden hundred. He took two wickets as Grafton fell for 101; he had outscored the opposition team all on his own.

Over the years, Phillip developed the habit of souveniring the game ball each time he made a century and noting the score and date along the seam. In his bedroom cupboard are two wicker baskets filled with balls. Sometimes he would get them out and line them up; he loved runs and he loved big runs. Greg lost count toward the end, but he thinks Phillip scored 68 or 70 centuries before he left Macksville as a 17-year-old.

Innings like his first century were not easily forgotten. Four years later, one of the officials from Urunga, Garry Matthews, wrote to Phillip to thank him for his contribution to inter-district cricket: 'As you are

Phillip's maiden century, 103 for Nambucca Bellingen. Having outscored the opposition on his own, he walked off to a standing ovation.

Phillip developed the habit of souveniring the game ball each time he made a century and noting the score and date along the seam

aware I am something of a fan of yours, your amazing talent and dedication on the field has impressed me over the years . . . I have a wonderful memory of your century in the Under-12s Inter District Final all those years ago indented in my head and I often reflect on that day with a wry smile. Usually those around me ask me what I am smiling about and I say, "I am just reflecting on a great memory".'

A week after making his first century, he again made it through all the school zone selection trials to play for Polding in the Catholic primary schools state competition. Selectors at trials never relied on his reputation, as he delivered on the day. Having had a taste, he became instantly addicted to scoring hundreds, and the following summer he would score five: two for Polding at the carnival, one for his state, one for the Macksville Colts and one for the Macksville Under-14s. If you were involved in junior cricket in New South Wales, you knew of Phillip Hughes.

●

POLDING HAD NEVER WON a Primary Schools Sports Association (PSSA) championship in any sport. The teams from the major centres took the PSSA very seriously, but Polding team manager Ken McNamara was more interested in the boys getting a chance to enjoy the competition. 'The carnival was all about boys enjoying playing cricket at a higher level . . . Winning was not a priority,' he says. To prove his commitment to participation, he ensured that all ten of his players (excluding the wicketkeeper) got a bowl in every match, whether they were good enough or not.

Phillip, however, had higher goals. Having scored well in the previous carnival, he quietly set his sights on the state primary schools' side. He wanted a NSW cap and he had three innings to earn it, unless the team defied history and made the final.

The diverse group of boys got together at ELS Hall Park at North Ryde in Sydney. When the rain stopped, they did training drills, which didn't reveal much. Almost every boy claimed to be an opening batsman, but Phillip got the job for the first match against Sydney East the following day.

Those who missed out on opening the innings breathed a sigh of relief when they saw the intimidating Shariful Islam mark out his run and deliver the first ball. The Bangladeshi-born all-rounder was the fastest bowler in the tournament. He and Phillip would meet many times in years to come, but this was the first time they had laid eyes on each other. It was a coming together of kindred spirits: talented, determined and quiet. Both had a job to do and on this day it involved beating the other.

Greg remembers, 'The first day was that wet, they bowled from [only] one end. We came up against this real fast guy, Shariful, with a long run-up. The kid was so quick the [Polding]

number three batsman said to the coach he would bat at ten. The kids weren't really into it.'

Shariful knocked over Phillip's opening partner and the first drop early in the innings on his way to figures of four for 22. The country kids couldn't handle his pace. Except one.

Phillip 'hit him everywhere', according to Greg. He scored runs at will as his new teammates were trundled out for next to nothing. Only three Polding batsmen made double figures, but when the innings was finished Phillip Hughes was still there on 108 not out, of a team total of 218.

Sydney East couldn't match Phillip's score and were all out for 97. Ken McNamara was so happy to have won a game that he announced, 'That'll do me.'

The manager was satisfied enough to go home with a win. Phillip, however, had other plans.

'I remember that game very well,' Shariful says. 'It was the first time I had seen him but I had heard a bit about him. He was the key wicket, we knew that, but I just couldn't get him out. He bombed me for six a couple of times. It was "wow". He was so talented. You could tell straightaway that he was the next big thing. From that day on I knew that this guy was going to be our next Don Bradman.'

After the game, the Hugheses met the Islams. The difference in backgrounds meant nothing. Shariful was born in Bangladesh and raised in Lakemba in Sydney's west. Both places are a world away from Macksville, but the boys had the game as common ground and a quiet resolve that bonded them in the years ahead.

Shariful remembers his first conversation with the batsman who was barely half his size.

'You were amazing out there.'

'You almost got me out a few times.'

'Yeah, but you were better.'

'I was trying to find out what he did better than the other batsmen and how he maintained that control,' Shariful admits now. 'He had a level of humbleness that he draws from his family. Then we spoke again during the presentations at selection and from there we stayed in touch through phone calls, because we both had the same goals and aspirations.'

Shariful's family grew to love Phillip.

'My mum cried when he got selected for Australia. She said, "This boy came to my house and ate my food". They were so pleased for him.'

Phillip only scored 30 next innings in the match against MacKillop, but it was easily the highest score of the innings. He took a great catch at first slip that had deflected off the keeper, and captured a wicket with his bowling. The country kids had won their second straight match.

The third and last game, against the imposing Sydney West side, would decide if they made the finals. Phillip's 23 was second-highest score in Polding's total of 101. While not a great score, good fielding and bowling (including two for 12 from the Macksville boy) got Polding over the line with ten runs to spare.

In the context of the matches and the age group, 30 and 23 were good scores, but Phillip was disappointed to have thrown away good starts, and also anxious about how they might have affected his chances of state selection. There was pressure, but Polding making the final meant he would get one more chance.

The excitement of the northern Catholic outfit making it this far was obvious in the cele-brations among kids, parents and coaches. The managers from other teams who were more experienced at this level couldn't help but be impressed with Phillip. Some suggested that Ken drop the idea of giving all ten kids a bowl for the final match against the Combined Independent Schools XI, but the Polding manager figured it had got them this far, so why not do it in the final?

The city sides would never do that, but they didn't have Phillip Hughes in their team. That the other managers offered advice suggests how everybody was hoping the boys from the bush might take down their private-school opponents, although they were a little taken aback when Ken told them, 'Thanks, but we will do it our way'.

The final was held at Waitara (later Mark Taylor) Oval in Sydney's leafy northern suburbs. The Hugheses got there well ahead of everyone else because, as Greg explains, 'Me not knowing the city and Phil not being the best navigator, we usually arrived early, just in case we got lost. Phillip would get lost riding his bike around town.'

They stayed with Greg's brother Ian, who lived in Sydney and came to the ground that morning. They were early enough to see the curator putting the finishing touches to the pitch. Phillip had played only a handful of games on turf wickets. It would be a few years yet before Macksville laid its own.

'What do you reckon, bat or bowl?' Greg asked.

'I'm not allowed to tell you,' the curator said.

Fair enough, they thought. Then the man gave them a bit of a grin and said, 'But I would love to bat on this myself.'

Father and son were struck by the beauty of a first-grade Sydney ground.

Greg says, 'White picket fence, mown grass, lots of turf wickets, Mark Taylor's name on the electronic scoreboard – we had never seen anything like it in our lives.'

Nor had city or country parents seen anything like what Phillip produced that day.

He won the toss and chose to bat. A flying start took the score to 110 before Nicholas Burrows was out for 27. The boy from the bush was already 64 and batting as if possessed.

Greg says, 'He absolutely smashed them, he was cutting the ball from the farthest pitch and they would be on their fourth run when the ball would hit the fence.'

The speed of this outfield was like nothing they had seen in the valley.

While Ken McNamara had been getting advice, so had opposition coach Steve Tomlinson, the director of boys' sports at the exclusive Barker College in Waitara. The night before the match, other managers had told him to be wary of Phillip Hughes.

After Nicholas was gone, Blake Creighton contributed 18 to a partnership of 93. When he was gone, Phillip just kept going. It was, Ken said later, 'an innings that was talked about all afternoon'.

Tomlinson says, 'We missed stumping him on 50 and thought, "How much is this going to cost?" . . . Phillip tore us to bits.'

In junior cricket, 60 or 70 was a great score. To reach a hundred was something else, but Phillip was not satisfied. Why stop when you are having fun? When the last ball of the 50 overs was bowled, he was 159 not out, in Polding's 214.

'The best I ever saw,' Tomlinson says.

Throughout, Greg was circling the ground. 'At first I think it was nerves and then as he started to build an innings I reckon it was excitement,' he says.

The hat-stand at East Street still bears the load of Phillip's many representative caps.

As Phillip pushed on, Greg stopped near a fig tree where the well-dressed parents of the private school kids had made their camp. He overheard one of them say, 'This is just not junior cricket.'

Which was a fair summation of what Phillip had done.

Ian Hughes knew his nephew was good, but that day he witnessed something extraordinary. He took a picture of the scoreboard.

'I didn't know a lot about junior sport, but I knew this was special. He was special.'

Abandoned by his restless brother, Ian got talking to an older man who was sitting watching the game.

'That was your nephew?' the stranger asked. 'That was the best batting I have ever seen by a young player.'

The highest ODI score by an Australian batsman was Adam Gilchrist's 154 against Sri Lanka at the MCG a year earlier. The highest ever percentage of a team's total in an ODI was Sir Viv Richards's 189 not out in a total of 272, or 69 per cent. Phillip had scored 74 per cent of his side's total, but that wasn't unusual, as he had been batting through innings with less competent batsmen in underage cricket. It was what he did.

'The biggest problem with junior cricket is batsmen never stay there,' Greg explains. 'Phillip knew there were no runs in the grandstand. Other kids who might be good bats would block three or four balls and then hit it in the air or get frustrated.'

Greg had watched a lot of junior cricket and believed that at this age a kid could only hit the ball 25 to 30 metres in the air, 'which was straight to the fieldsman'. Phillip knew to keep the ball on the ground, but had patience well beyond his years and a hunger for runs that knew no bounds.

'He always wanted more,' Greg says. 'And if he missed out, he wouldn't worry. "I'll get them tomorrow," he would say. Invariably, he did.'

Phillip's selection in the NSW team, announced after the final, was a formality. The Sydney South West coach and manager of the NSW PSSA team, Jason Ellsmore, remembered Phillip from his efforts the year before and during the day received a phone call telling him what was going on. Nobody could quite believe how big the Grade Six student had gone. Ellsmore says the selectors had already decided Phillip had done enough with his earlier hundred in

He'd set himself his goal and surpassed it. It was one proud boy who was presented with his first-ever NSW cap by former Test spinner Bob Holland that afternoon. Greg and Uncle Ian were pretty proud, too

the tournament, but they were more than pleased to see him go even bigger.

The shell-shocked private-school kids rallied to make 187. They might have got fewer if Ken McNamara hadn't stuck to his guns and given ten boys a bowl. Polding won the championship, its first in any sport. Phillip had scored 320 runs at an average of 160. His name was read out in the state team, but there was better news to come – he'd been appointed captain. He'd set himself his goal and surpassed it. It was one proud boy who was presented with his first-ever NSW cap by former Test spinner Bob Holland that afternoon. Greg and Uncle Ian were pretty proud, too.

Phillip was the first boy from Polding to be selected in the state side. Macksville was as pleased as the family, and his achievements were reported in papers. Everybody was claiming a piece of him. The Macksville Ex-Services Club devoted a full page to his achievements in its annual report, extraordinary for one so young.

He already had a bat sponsor. Earlier that summer, Andrew Maggs, a cricketer from down the river at Nambucca Heads, had brought his C-grade side down to play in Scotts Head, an

Left: After leading them to the state championship, Phillip made history as the first Polding boy to be selected for NSW.

isolated seaside hamlet off the highway south of Macksville. A long drive along the Scotts Head Road delivers you to the postage-stamp ground between the caravan park and the bowling green, right by the sea.

'I was fortunate enough to have a few talented kids in my side and they were older than Greg's kids,' Andrew recalls. 'But you could see straightaway that Jason and Phillip were outstanding young cricketers.'

Andrew and his wife had bought a franchise for Callen Cricket, an equipment range owned by former Test player Ian Callen. Andrew had been told that if he saw somebody with genuine potential, he ought to do something for them. After the game at Scotts Head, he said to Greg Hughes, 'Mate, I have never seen a kid bat like that, he is really something special. I think he will play for Australia one day.'

'It was the way he did it,' Andrew says. 'They had lost a lot of their top batsmen. This little kid came out and we had good bowlers on. All of a sudden he plays this late cut for four. I was like, "Great shot!" I was in slip, clapping every shot he played: a couple of cover drives, the cut shots . . . he just had it. I had seen a lot of kids play cricket up and down the coast, I had seen a lot of good cricketers, but I had never seen anyone like Phillip.'

Maggsy had a special Callen bat at home and said he would do the Hugheses a deal. If they bought the matching equipment, he would give them the bat.

The company gained plenty of local exposure, as Phillip was rarely photographed without that bat in the next few years.

Phillip was always grateful for the support he received. A few years later when a cricket-loving boss gave Nino Ramunno time off to pick up his cousin at Sydney airport and the flexibility to drop him at tournaments, Phillip, without any prompting, autographed a bat and gave it to Nino's boss in gratitude.

One of the people Phillip sought out after the PSSA final at Waitara Oval was Andrew Maggs, exclaiming, 'Maggsy! It was the bat! Every time I hit something in the middle it went to the fence.'

Maggs tried to let him know it wasn't just the bat.

Two months later, Phillip got to wear his blue NSW cap when he led the team onto the field for the first match of the School Sports Australian Primary Cricket Exchange in Cobram

Callen Cricket gained plenty of local exposure, as Phillip was rarely photographed without that bat in the next few years. Phillip was always grateful for the support he received

Barooga, near the NSW–Victorian border. Greg, Phillip, Jason and Uncle Ian made the trip and set themselves up in the local motel. It was more than a 1000-kilometre drive from East Street, but Phillip made sure his family had not made the trip in vain.

It was dry and hot and the flies were terrible, but the cricket was good. NSW played a combined side in the first match at Strathmerton Cricket Ground, a dot on the Murray Valley Highway. Phillip opened the batting.

Under competition rules, coaches and managers couldn't talk to the kids between the first ball and the drinks break. The opposition captain decided for the first session that he didn't need a third man. Big mistake – Phillip was like a kid in a lolly shop.

'It was not real smart. He just kept cutting them to the boundary,' Jason Ellsmore remembers. 'By the break he was about 60 runs and 40 had gone through that area of the ground. He smashed them, and when I say smashed them, he absolutely blazed away.'

A third man was eventually put in, but when he went wide Phillip hit the ball fine of him, and when he moved finer, Phillip hit it wider. He was toying with them.

Phillip was retired on 115 so the other kids could have a hit. The combined side was all out for 95. He'd beaten a team single-handedly. Again.

It was the first time the other states had seen Phillip Hughes in full flight, but they wouldn't forget him. Phillip left the tournament with the highest aggregate and the highest average (55).

Ellsmore discovered something that teammates would comment on for years to come. 'When he got out, he didn't throw his bat or carry on. He was disappointed, but it was that disappointment when you are having fun and the fun stops. He was a quiet boy with a big grin and wide eyes and he had a reasonable sense of humour too. He had an absolute love of the game.'

The tournaments allowed like-minded kids to catch up, and there were gatherings around the motel pool. One night, at a barbecue by the Murray, the boys swam as the men turned the snags and drank a few beers.

Ian remembers that from the moment they had arrived there was a buzz around his nephew. 'Everyone seemed to know Phillip or had heard of him.'

When he batted, people stopped to watch the kid who made their sons look pedestrian.

You didn't forget Phillip Hughes. Some years later, Ian ran into a man who remembered his son coming home from a game of cricket and telling him he'd just played against the best cricketer he had ever seen, a little kid from Macksville.

The NSW PSSA team manager Damian Toohey had been watching Phillip for a few seasons. 'We used to talk about playing "in the V" until you are comfortable but the cut shot was something he sweated on with the new ball. He could hit any ball outside off-stump for four through point or behind gully . . . People talk about him being unorthodox, but he put himself in a position

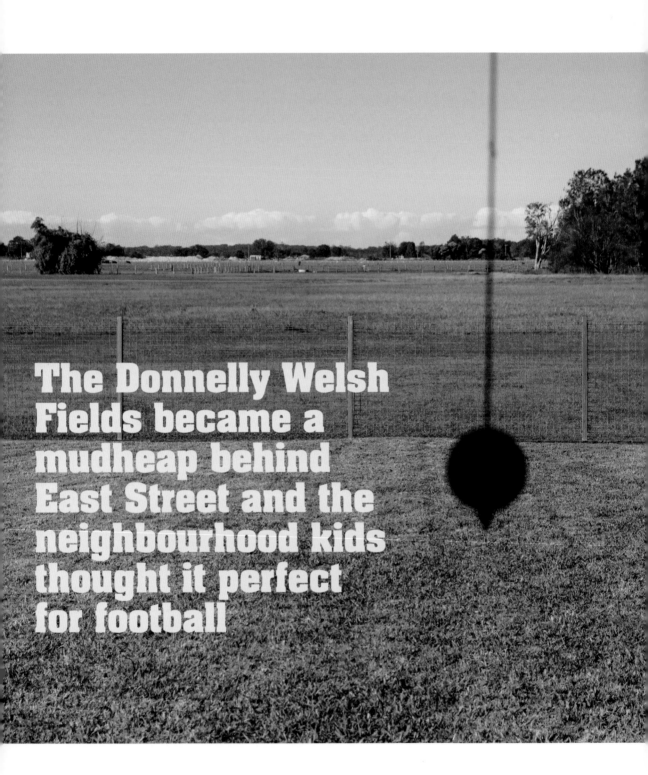

The Donnelly Welsh
Fields became a
mudheap behind
East Street and the
neighbourhood kids
thought it perfect
for football

to hit balls more often than not. He could wipe a team quickly without going out there to belt them. He did it by putting away the bad balls.'

On turf wickets, it was Phillip's cricketing brain, as much as his hunger for runs, that left a mark on Toohey. 'The beauty of carnival cricket is that the wickets vary considerably. You could go to a four-day carnival and play on four different wickets. Phillip could adjust to any wicket and took his time to get used to the wicket before playing shots. When he got to Barooga and the wicket was flat, it was playing into his hands and he could bat for four days. At carnivals he could bat for as long as the team needed him to bat. He always had a good understanding of the game situation.'

On day three of the carnival, NSW had to play at Strathmerton again and Jason Ellsmore noticed something strange. 'All these farmers had rolled in and were waiting for the toss. They had heard about Phillip and downed tools on the farm for the day to come in and watch this 12-year-old bat. We lost the toss and bowled, so they went home, but they came back at lunch in their utes wearing shorts and boots and stuff. Phillip to some degree failed. He got 20-odd runs, and with that they all left. I am sitting there thinking, "This is like the stories my old man used to tell me about Bradman".'

●

It may seem Phillip Hughes had a single obsession, but elite junior cricketers were yet to be monopolised through the winter. As a rugby league player, Phillip was elusive and fearless, though he displayed a physical aggression that was at odds with his calm at the batting crease.

His dad, his uncles and Jason were all good players and Phillip had, according to some judges, great ability at league. He represented Polding while at primary school, played representative football at high school and was a star player for the Bowraville Tigers, the same club that produced rugby league great Greg Inglis, who lived 200 metres from the Hugheses in Wall Street.

Nathan Smith, who would be good enough to play in the NRL, says, 'As much as everyone will say he was dedicated to cricket, which he was, he was just as dedicated to anything he was doing at the time. When we were playing footy in the backyard, he was 100 per cent dedicated to it.'

The Donnelly Welsh Fields became a mudheap behind East Street and the neighbourhood kids thought it perfect for football. Mitch Lonergan remembers playing in knee-deep water and coming home in clothes stinking like a swamp to a disgusted mum. Mitch and his father Morrie remember one game Phillip played for Bowraville in particular.

'In the Under-13s or 14s we beat a side by about 100-plus to nil and Phil scored 66 points himself,' Mitch says. 'He was freakish. I was pretty sure it was against Orara Valley at Bowraville. He scored five or six tries and kicked every goal.'

Morrie, another parent who adored Phillip, coached him at the Tigers and was as impressed by his football skills as by his manner. He first had Phillip with Greg Inglis in the Under-7s, and watched him and Mitch play for years. One year Phillip won best and fairest despite missing half the season with injury.

'He played five-eighth, halfback, second row – he would play anywhere. To be honest, he tore this side apart with his ferocity,' Morrie remembers. 'He was only a little fellow but he was that hard . . . he was a very tough boy. Nothing worried him. He was fearless even though he was half their size.'

Teammate Joel Dallas says, 'Whenever he played sport another side of him came out. You used to see this aggression – he just loved the competition. He was a fast runner, he was tough, he was a little ball of muscle, he just went for it pretty much. There was no holding back. I reckon he could have played professional league if he wanted to.'

Phillip was keen to go as far as he could, but was often playing cricket when the winter sport season started and finished, and he would miss the football trials. But he couldn't let go of the code. When he was in his late teens and on the verge of touring India with the Australian Under-19 side, he showed up to football training and announced he wanted to play a season with his mates in the Macksville Under-18s.

'He played and did his ankle and we all looked at each other and knew that was the end of that,' Morrie recalls. Phillip had broken his ankle and that was indeed the end of his football career, but he always harboured the desire to go back and have another crack. When, after establishing himself as a cricketer, Phillip made plans to retire to Greg's farm with his own cattle, he had clear plans for weekends, according to Mitch Lonergan.

'He always said, "You'll be living back at home when you're 36, I'll be living on the farm, and, us and Jason, we'll play reserve-grade footy for Macksville". That's all he wanted to do.'

Morrie Lonergan believes Phillip was good enough but wonders if his height would have held him back. 'Being a rugby league man through and through, I would tell you he had the capacity, the skill, the toughness and the determination, but knowing the way these NRL people pick sides, I don't think he would have made it. Not because he wasn't good enough, but back then they were looking for six-foot-two halfbacks.'

FIVE

DOING IT FOR THE KIDS

Macksville is a small but intense sporting community that cares for its kids and is often happy to put their sporting priorities above all else. The trips to Sydney, Cobram, Newcastle, Coffs Harbour and the like were demanding on Greg, particularly as Jason was still pursuing his cricketing dreams too. Fortunately, the banana plantation was not high maintenance so Greg could often leave someone else in charge. Virginia would sell raffle tickets at the Ex-Services Club to raise money for teams, and eventually the cricket club invested in a Bola bowling machine. Some in Macksville joked that the machine was purchased to save Greg's arm.

'FINANCES WERE OFTEN STRETCHED at home but Greg and Virginia put the kids first. Dad busted his arse on the bananas,' Jason remembers. 'You could see it in Mum and Dad's eyes sometimes that we were struggling. You don't make much money when you are a banana grower, but we never missed out on anything. Phillip put in a lot of work and without a lot of help, really, from anyone outside the family.

'Dad's real consistent. If he says, "When you get home I'll have the ball machine on the back of the truck", he's going to be ready to go. That was good for us that he was on the ball. With the job he had, he could knock off at 3.30 pm and start at six in the morning.'

The Bola lived in the Hugheses' shed during winter, and helped Phillip practise his batting year-round. Greg would drive it to the nets

Left: Standing nine-foot tall and spitting balls at fearsome speed, the skittish Bola bowling machine honed Phillip's fighter-pilot reflexes as a batsman.

on the back of the truck and set up its legs and connect it to the car battery while Phillip got ready.

The bowling machine practice sessions became an institution in Macksville. 'If Dad's truck was at the nets, people would stop by to have a look at Phillip,' Jason says.

Cousin Nino had moved to Sydney and remembers that he would turn off one street early on his way home 'just to say hi to Greg and the boys – they were always there at the Willis Street nets'. All of Phillip's mates knew where to find him.

Greg says he didn't know a lot about batting technique. 'All I really knew was about getting your front foot down the wicket, keeping the bat and pad together, that sort of thing.'

There are two broad types of cricketers. One is coached correctly but is often a little mechanical. The other, rarer beast is homespun, intuitive and often far better than his cookie-cutter peers. The downside is that if you don't look technically perfect you have to make more runs, for every failure is evidence of a 'flaw'.

The upside, as bowlers discovered, is that an unconventional player is hard to dismiss in conventional ways. Without planning, Greg had developed the second type. Phillip raised his bat higher than the textbook prescribed, brought it down in a sweeping outside-in curve rather than mechanically down the line of the ball, and opened his front leg to the on-side while slashing to the off. None of these idiosyncrasies was 'correct', but good judges would see through the surface eccentricities to the heart of batsmanship.

Warren Smith is a batting coach from Wagga Wagga who first encountered Phillip in NSW country and underage sides. Warren is legendary in the southern half of NSW for his creative coaching techniques and was credited with nurturing Michael Slater through the junior ranks. One day as an adult, Phillip, feeling gloomy about criticism of his technique, sat down with Smith.

'Don't worry, mate, you have got a special gift,' Smith said. 'The three worst bats I ever saw were Sir Donald Bradman, Allan Border and you.'

Confused, Phillip said, 'What do you mean?'

'You know how David Gower looks elegant and Greg Chappell looks elegant?' Smith said. 'Well, you don't. You aren't pretty to look at, but you have two beautiful things.'

'What's that?'

'You have very good eyes and quick hands.'

Looking back, Smith says, 'When Phillip hit the ball, it was right under his eyes. Look at Bradman. When he went at the ball he looked like he was all over the place, but when he hit it he was still. Border was one of the toughest and best I have ever seen. He was hard. If Bradman played today they would never hold him. They have covered the pitches and brought the boundaries in and he would be away. You look at Border, Bradman and Hughes, and they had a special approach.'

Phillip's unorthodox approach and uncanny ability had some very good bowlers throwing up their arms in despair. In 2009, Andre Nel had retired from international cricket but found himself bowling for Surrey against Phillip, who was batting for Middlesex. The South African Test paceman gave up all hope of getting him out and even bowled a beamer in frustration. Phillip made 195 and Nel declared that Phillip, then 20, was the most difficult batsman to bowl to in world cricket.

Phillip developed his own style through years of practice in Macksville, but he complemented it with another great advantage that was also intuitive but, unlike his aesthetics, straight from central casting.

Greg and Phillip believed that 'there are no runs in the grandstand', but it took a special patience to hang in there and keep batting as Phillip did. That innate temperament, between the ears and in the gut, inherited more than learnt from Greg, was Phillip's key edge over bowlers and his batting rivals.

Shariful Islam remembers an intimidating calm confidence. 'I can only talk about this now because I have learnt the game a lot better than back then, but at that age he had this maturity to dominate all bowlers. He was already ten years ahead of his time. That's what really amazed me.'

Matthew Day, who would become Phillip's flatmate and close friend when he moved to Sydney, first saw him bat in a Polding–MacKillop primary schools match. What he remembers best is not the technique so much as the mental application.

There are two broad types of cricketers. One is coached correctly but is often a little mechanical. The other, rarer beast is homespun, intuitive and often far better than his cookie-cutter peers. Without planning, Greg had developed the second type

'He ebbed and flowed with his innings. He could take an hour and a half to make ten runs, then score 20 or 30 in a few minutes, then go back to slow. He was always a boundary hitter, so when he was grafting it was a lot of dots and then a lot of boundaries. He knew how to wait.'

It was Phillip's patient defence that had him picked as an opener when he was barely stump-high, and Greg insists that he was seen as an orthodox batsman until commentators became distracted by the way he played on the off-side. Sam Robson, the England opener, played in representative underage sides with Phillip and remembers he was 'solid and orthodox . . . As Phil got older, he would be remembered as being unorthodox. Less was made of that when he was young. He played pulls and hook shots off the faster bowlers. Compared to him, the rest of us were run of the mill. We were ducking or getting out of the way of short balls, but he was hitting them for four.'

Matt Day thought the same. 'Early on, he was never the most orthodox but he never stood out as being unorthodox either.'

Stan Gilchrist had Phillip and Jason up to a camp in Lismore when the younger brother was around 12.

'Boy, oh boy, he was an incredible talent,' Stan says. 'Absolutely awesome. He just shone. Jason was good, but Phillip was something else. Not a great technique, but I had seen Allan Border as a young kid and he wasn't textbook and technically wasn't great, but his grit and determination and timing and absolute focus . . . A lot of the kids would come to those camps and have a good time. They would do the cricket things and then muck around. Phillip was just focused. He'd ask for extra minutes on the bowling machine . . . I never asked Adam [Gilchrist] to practise. He always asked me to come down and feed the machine. Phillip would have been exactly the same.'

A father willing to give that time and support was critical. 'Greg and Virginia gave the boys whatever they required to get where they needed to go and that needs to be applauded as well' – STAN GILCHRIST

Having a father willing to give that time and support was critical. Part of the reason Steve Smith developed into a Test cricketer was a similar relationship with his dad Peter, who was at home every night after school to take him to the nets or for throwdowns in the yard, and who was there at every turn. Michael Clarke, the Waugh twins, the Chappell brothers – it is almost an essential ingredient for greatness. Adam Gilchrist had the same fortune.

'I've always said that the commitment is not only that of the player, but also that of his support team,' Stan Gilchrist says. 'Greg and Virginia gave the boys whatever they required to get where they needed to go and that needs to be applauded as well.'

Nobody has done the maths, but it wouldn't be surprising to discover that Greg Hughes drove 1000 kilometres for every century his son made.

●

PHILLIP HAD SET HIS mind on playing for Australia very early, and at carnivals he and Shariful Islam spent hours discussing exactly how they were going to do it. The Sydney all-rounder would develop into a handy cricketer, but admits that Phillip, who was always a class above him but might not have realised it yet, became something of a mentor for him.

'He always had so much to give to everyone, even at that age. He genuinely cared. When we were batting he would say, "Watch this guy, bro, he is trying to do this or that". I never had much advice for him.'

Jason eventually found himself in a similar situation. 'I used to worry a bit about my technique and what people thought of me, but Phillip just backed himself. He didn't care what anyone thought about him, he just backed his own ability and he used to tell me to do the same.'

When the boys moved to Sydney, the tables would turn; Phillip would become his elder brother's guide and advisor, encouraging

Left: Phillip always took pride in his appearance. Before a match he followed a careful routine of laying out his equipment and rubbing the marks off his bat. Virginia always made sure he took the field in freshly washed whites.

him to come to the Western Suburbs club and make a life. Like Shariful, Jason would be good but not great, yet in Phillip's eyes that did not matter – nor did it stop him caring.

Cricket, for Phillip, had always been embedded in his family life. As he improved, the Hughes home in Macksville developed a cricket rhythm, with rituals and processes that comforted the young batsman, and eventually, by having Jason move in with him in Sydney, he would try to reproduce that comfort.

Megan remembers fondly the evenings before Phillip would set off to a tournament. 'I remember every time, the day before the game, the night before and not too late, he would come home from whatever he was doing, have a shower and then take up the entire lounge room with his gear. It was like he wanted us to be part of it. I remember he would lay out the gloves, the pads, towels, the inners, the grips, the water bottles to be frozen, everything he needed. That was the routine. Every Friday night Mum would cook, and we would chill and talk about the game and the weekend and how he felt. I think that took the stress off his shoulders, knowing we were around, or that we were going [to watch him] no matter what. That was his routine. Mum and Dad, I feel, have built this family in this home on love and trust and we just bounce off each other. Phillip loved that and every week we would do that. I think Phillip loved us around on the night before his games.'

The rituals of preparation calmed the boy. They bordered on obsessive, but he found something soothing in paying attention to the process of packing for a game or a tournament. He would take the bats to the back veranda and, with a rag, set about taking the marks off the bats he would use the following day. Other days he would just arrange the century balls he had collected on the carpet.

'The mirror got a good workout,' Jason observes.

It wasn't only for batting practice either; Phillip was renowned for the attention he paid to his clothes and hair.

'He would say, "Come on Vinny, let's get a double shot",' his mum recalls. 'Next thing I know, he was changing out of his tracksuit pants because he couldn't go down the street in anything but his best clothes.'

Virginia was kept on her toes. He had to have clean whites for every game and everything ironed. If he played two games on Saturday, he had to have two sets of whites. He would never

> **Cricket, for Phillip, had always been embedded in his family life. As he improved, the Hughes home in Macksville developed a cricket rhythm, with rituals and processes that comforted the young batsman**

take to the field in dirty clothes or to the streets in a crumpled shirt. Macksville is a town of farmers, flannel and muddy utes, but Phillip was particular.

'He always had to be neat,' Greg says. 'If you saw us in the mud with the cows he was fine, but if you saw him out in public he was immaculate. When he went away, the first thing he had to learn was to iron and wash his clothes. He would never put on a creased shirt. Before then he didn't know what an iron was or where the washing machine was. Virginia did it all for him. If we went up to the pub on a Friday afternoon, I could go as I was, but he would iron his clothes and make sure his hair was right. If he had time out, he would buy new clothes. He always liked nice clothes. If we were going out at five, he would have the iron out at ten to.'

The other ritual was the car rides. Father and son spent a lot of time on the road together, and Phillip grew particular about this too.

'He wanted me to go all the time,' Greg says. 'You might think that was silly, but it was *all the time*.'

In the car Phillip would talk about his ambitions in cricket. Over the years, he started to talk to his dad about his dream of buying a cattle stud when he made it. The plan was for father and son to run the farm, with the others involved.

Greg and Phillip were as much best friends as father and son. The relationship was remarked upon by almost everyone who encountered them in the cricket world

Greg developed his own rituals, too. He disliked anything that smacked of cricket politics. Greg watched alone on the other side of the ground. Being away from the scorers, Greg would sometimes tally Phillip's runs with stones or twigs by his folding chair and check it during breaks.

'He never liked me talking about their performances,' Greg says. 'Jason was the same – you would turn up at a rep game and parents would say how their son got a 100 or five wickets last week . . . Phillip didn't like that, he didn't like us boasting and he never boasted either. If he had made the state side, he'd walk up the street with his mates and get on their bikes and he would never mention it.'

Greg, who admits he has a bit of a temper, says Phillip taught him to be calm. They learned to deal with upsets by giving them distance. They'd talk in the car or at home. If Phillip kept calm about these things, so could Greg.

Nino Ramunno observes that Greg and Phillip were as much best friends as father and son. The relationship was remarked upon by almost everyone who encountered them in the cricket world.

The Hughes and Ramunno families had spread to the cities, offering alternatives to being billeted or paid accommodation. In Sydney were cousins Nino and Sharnie as well as Greg's brother Ian to stay with. Sharnie had an apartment and a flatmate.

'Greg and Phillip would stay with us,' she says, 'and we would sit there and watch him play cricket. He slept on my couch, the poor bugger, but he didn't whinge once.'

Ian and Helen Hughes had a house in Lidcombe in Sydney's west. At least there the boy got a bed – one of his younger cousins was moved in with Ian and Helen so that Phillip could have a good night's sleep. The family remembers Greg and Phillip arriving tired after the long drive from Macksville, but the first order of business for Phillip was to get out a bat and have throwdowns in the backyard. They also had a ball on a sock on their veranda, and when the men grew bored or wanted a drink, the boy would do what he did at home. Helen says that after a game Phillip would come home and go straight outside and hit it into the summer night. The neighbours still talk about coming home from work and hearing that knock-knock-knock-knock deep into the night.

SIX

GAMES AGAINST MEN

There's a bloke in the town of Dorrigo who tells people he got Phillip Hughes out once. Takes a sip of his beer and admits he was 32 years old at the time and Phillip was 12. He takes another sip and adds that the kid had already scored a hundred. He says it is his only Test wicket. There are a few in the area with the same boast, but not many, because Phillip didn't make a habit of getting out.

PHILLIP HUGHES STARTED TURNING out for the Macksville A-grade team when he was 12. The sight of the boy wandering out to the wicket initially caused some looks and words between opponents and spectators. He may have been small, but sledging only doubled Phillip's determination. The Year Seven student went on to score 38 runs, then completed two stumpings and two catches behind the wicket.

These games against men were important. He was a kid who wanted to take on the world, and he would start by taking on the men's world of his home district.

'I was very young and they were grown men from 20 to 35 and even 40, and on the synthetic wickets back home and the cement wickets, when they came in with the new ball, and they were grown men and I was only a young guy, they wouldn't hold back and I think that gave me a lot of confidence moving down to the city,' Phillip said nearly a decade later in an interview with cricket writer Mike Coward recorded for the Bradman Museum. 'They'd give it to the young guys and I think that was something I used to thrive on and that just gave me that confidence.'

He might have batted like a veteran, but away from the game he was still a cheeky kid who rode his pushbike about town with his mates, went fishing, got swooped by magpies and whispered about the forbidden wonders of girls

Cousin Nino Ramunno says Phillip was growing into a young man ready to engage with life in all its roughness. 'The worst thing you could ever do to Phillip was sledge him. He would just become quiet and more focused.'

After making centuries from one end of the state to the other in the previous season, his reputation was widespread. Phillip had only just started high school, and he was still a child. He might have batted like a veteran, but away from the game he was still a cheeky kid who rode his pushbike about town with his mates, went fishing, got swooped by magpies and whispered about the forbidden wonders of girls. At the exchange in Cobram Barooga, he had been called on, as NSW captain, to address the teams at the end of the tournament. Centre-stage was not his thing, but he handled it almost as easily as he'd handled the bowling.

On his return to Macksville that January, he was called on to brush up on his public speaking again. Phillip was awarded the Junior Sportsperson of the Year Award at the Australia

Day ceremonies in the Ex-Services Club. Andrew Stoner, the local member, wrote to the young cricketer, telling him he could invite friends and family and would be expected to say a few words. Phillip rose to get his certificate after the Macksville Bowlers Ladies Number 3 team (team of the year), and acquitted himself with quiet confidence.

Phillip started secondary school at Macksville High, directly opposite St Patrick's Primary School, two years behind Jason. By day Phillip shared his classroom with boys, but on the weekends he was rubbing shoulders with men. Even though he cracked a foot larking around at school early in the summer and missed some cricket, Phillip was soon back in the swing of things.

He handled A-grade cricket on Saturday afternoons in the valley. After two half-centuries, the youngest player in the entire competition top-scored with 36 in the first innings of the grand final and followed it up with a determined 23 in the second, but he couldn't get the men over the line.

Picked in the Nambucca Bellingen Under-14 rep team that summer, he travelled to the Gloucester Carnival and notched scores of 40, 73, 70, 65 and 49 against teams from Manning, Penrith, Armidale, Gloucester and Sydney. He didn't play in the Under-14 inter-district grand final but made a controversial appearance in Jason's Under-16 team that February.

Phillip was originally not picked, as he had played in the lower age group all season. Before the match, he went camping on a Bellingen property with a mate. Greg thinks Phillip might have had an eye on the farmer's daughter. The Under-16s were a good team, with many of the players representing at a higher level, but on the Saturday before the final one of them got sick and withdrew from the game. Warwick Lawrence, who had asked Phillip to open in the Under-12s two years before, was coaching the side.

'Where's Phillip?' he asked Greg. 'I want him to play tomorrow.'

Greg explained he was away camping, but Warwick wasn't put off. They came up with a plan that Greg would ring the farmer, who would take Phillip next morning to the side of the highway, where coach Lawrence could pick him up. The family got his cricket gear together, and all arrived at the ground to take on Coffs Harbour in the final.

The Coffs people were furious when they saw the short kid warming up with the Under-16s. They knew exactly who he was and complained bitterly. The rules were that you couldn't drop down and play for a team you hadn't been in that season. There was, however, nothing to stop you moving *up*.

Their misgivings proved well founded. Phillip opened the batting and made 104 as Nambucca Bellingen racked up an imposing 297. Josh Lawrence got 66 and Jason, who was captain and had been itching to get a hit, blasted a quickfire 32 in the final overs.

'He absolutely whacked them that day,' Jason says. 'I remember he brought up his 100 with a shot through the gully. I was spewing for the first 30 overs because all I wanted to do was get in there and have a hit, but he wasn't going anywhere.'

An overwhelmed Coffs could manage only 135.

The following month, the Under-14s made a trip south to Kempsey to play the local team at the Verge Street Oval for the Kempsey Observer Shield. Phillip scored 120 not out, 20 more than Kempsey managed in reply.

Too old now for the Under-12 state team, he had nowhere to go at the highest level in junior cricket. The states had introduced an Under-15 carnival the year before, but there was no room in the calendar for the schools to sort out the best players in 2001–02. They invited boys eligible for the next season to try out at the Sydney Cricket Ground. Somehow the coaches chose 25 out of hundreds of hopefuls and sent them to Northbridge for a trial match the next day.

One of the fathers at the Northbridge trial remembers seeing a small boy walk into the indoor centre with a cricket bag twice his size and thinking he would not have a hope – and then watching in amazement as bowler after bowler failed to penetrate his defence. Phillip batted well, but was not picked among the state's best players up to two years older than him.

●

SCHOOL CRICKET OFFERED A chance to play with Jason under the coaching of Barry Lockyer, who had come to Macksville High the year before. Barry played cricket locally and knew the younger brother was as good as the elder. The three became good friends, and if Greg couldn't drive the boys to a carnival, Barry did it. They called him 'Baz' but tried to do the right thing and refer to him as 'Mr Lockyer' at school.

'I tell my son I have a Test wicket,' Barry says. 'I managed to bowl Phillip in the nets once. It was the only time it happened.'

Macksville High played in the Combined High Schools competition, which linked with the Alan Davidson Shield against teams from Sydney. With Phillip and Jason, Macksville became a force. Barry Lockyer remembers the day they had to play Mullumbimby in a final at Thompson Oval, Brunswick Heads. Mullumbimby, having only made 149 thanks to some good bowling by Jason, decided the best way to get out the young opener and win the game was to attack him verbally and physically.

'They absolutely gave it to him that day,' Barry recalls. 'These blokes could bowl pretty quick, he was only a little fella and there

'Phil was in Year 9, batting against Year 11 and 12 bowlers. Our team was sledging him, bowling at his body, but he was so determined, he just never wanted to get out' – SIMON KEEN

were some big mouths out there. I thought, "This will be interesting". Phillip only got 34 not out, but he carried us that day: he put his head down, turned the strike over and basically got us home. Jason got about 30 runs. Phillip and Jason were calm fellows. Nothing rattled them.'

Simon Keen, who would go on to play for NSW and the Sydney Sixers, was at Westfield Sports High School, a selective school that specialised in sport. He remembers encountering the Hughes brothers around this period. 'They played us in the Davidson Shield, it was a semi or a final [in Dubbo]. Phil was in Year 9, batting against Year 11 and 12 bowlers. Our team was sledging him, bowling at his body, but he was so determined, he just never wanted to get out. He was not satisfied with just making some runs. You could see how other guys felt they had accomplished something when they got 60 or 70, but not him.'

Phillip and his brother had driven to Dubbo with Barry Lockyer; others had gone with the principal or parents who could make the eight-hour drive. To keep the costs down, they stayed at a hostel. They lost to Westfield but finished third in the state, an incredible achievement for such a tiny school.

After the semifinal, the umpire asked Barry how many kids attended Macksville High.

'Oh, about 700, but it's co-ed, so it's really 350.'

'How many play cricket?'

'You are looking at them.'

Macksville High never held a try-out; the 11 or 12 kids Lockyer told to come to training got a game. Thanks to the efforts of Phillip, Jason and a few of their mates, they had beaten schools with specialist coaches and far greater resources.

Over the years, Jason and Phillip put together some big partnerships. In January 2003, they played for Macksville A-grade against Bowraville at the Thistle Park ground behind their grandparents' house. It was a grand day for the family. Phillip, who was 14, scored his first A-grade century and Jason made 113. They put on 213, which the *Guardian News* said

The Government of New South Wales

Presented to

Phillip Hughes

in Recognition of Your Selection to Represent New South Wales

2003 Australian Schools Cricket Championships

Premier

of the State of New South Wales in the Commonwealth of Australia

Sydney,   25 March   **20** 03   *Member of Parliament*

'would have to go down as the highest by brothers in local A-grade cricket'. The paper also hazarded a guess that Phillip was the youngest player to get a century at that level.

Jason recalls that they didn't really say too much when batting.

'He was quiet. I would sometimes say something to him about not getting out or not playing a certain shot and he would nod, but he was a cheeky little bugger and he would go and play it anyway and get a four.'

Years later, after Phillip had made his debut for Australia in South Africa, cricket writer Mike Coward asked him if he was scared to face the new ball as a boy playing against men.

'No, not overly sometimes, you can be if there's real quick bowler and there is a hard ball, a new ball. But that's something I've always loved, I see it as a challenge. Go out there and show myself as early as I could, so that's why I liked it.'

Jason finished the summer with 705 A-grade runs at 117.6 (highest aggregate and second-highest average), while Phillip finished with 422 runs at 70.3.

Phillip was bouncing up and down the age groups. On Sundays, in Under-14 representative cricket, he took Nambucca Bellingen to an inter-district final win with an unbeaten century to

'There were Chinese whispers; all the kids talked about this kid from the country' – SIMON KEEN

Phillip shaking hands with future Sheffield Shield player Michael Hill at the Under-15s All-Schools Championship at Adelaide Oval No. 2.

cap a season of 408 runs – his Australian Test number – at an average of 139. Through his performances for Macksville High against boys up to 18 years old, he made the NSW All Schools 15 Years cricket team to compete in the Australian Schools Championship in Bathurst.

Simon Keen said that by now everyone had heard of the prodigy from Macksville. 'He had an aura. Coming from the country, people spoke about him. There were Chinese whispers; all the kids talked about this kid from the country.'

Phillip survived for an hour, after which the sun had dried the pitch. When things settled down, he got going and was eventually retired. The harder it was, the more determined he became.

Phillip had a reasonable tournament in Bathurst, but nothing outstanding. His scores of 30, 26, 62 and 33 could not be considered a failure, but others shone more brightly, including Shannon Hurn, who made 111 for South Australia against NSW. Hurn eventually quit cricket for a chance to play in the Australian Football League, going on to captain the West Coast Eagles.

Simon Keen recalls batting with Phillip when a spectator fell victim to his cut shot. 'My mum and dad and Phil's dad were in a tent in line with his cut shot. The ball just flew off his bat. My mum didn't have time to move, and it hit her. She had to get taken away. Phil was really apologetic, he was so worried that she was going to be okay. It got her in the face and cut her eyebrow.'

Phillip had set the bar so high that what looked like an ordinary performance was in fact above average. His 30 opening the batting with Chris Ridley in the first match helped set a NSW first-wicket record (101) and he also set a fifth-wicket partnership record (55) with Manjot Singh, who would become a good friend and a club and state teammate. The selectors were impressed enough to include him in their Australian Under-15 side. While it existed in name only, it was his first 'national' representation.

The following summer started with the usual chaos of carnivals – the Under-17 Northern Country Carnival on the Central Coast, the Bradman Cup on the South Coast – and meanwhile Phillip was fitting in Macksville A-grade games, breaking a record with a 221-run partnership with Jason against Bowraville, who must have been heartily sick of the both of them. Two days later, Phillip made 108 against Wauchope High School, who replied with 98.

It might have been tempting to remain a big wheel on the coast – he averaged 189 that 2003–04 season for Nambucca Bellingen – but Phillip now had a clear goal to play cricket for Australia. When he'd plotted it with Shariful Islam, he wasn't joking. Nobody on the north coast had any doubt, and Sydney got the message through the state Under-12s and Under-15s.

It was time to take things up another notch.

SEVEN

MANY WAYS TO GET TO 100

'Some people are put on this earth to play cricket for Australia. Ricky Ponting, Michael Clarke and Steve Smith are, and Phil Hughes was another of those.'

FORMER AUSTRALIAN HEAD COACH Tim Nielsen makes this simple observation to describe his first impression from 2009, when Phillip entered the Australian Test team. The extraordinary thing is that even as a boy, Phillip knew it too.

All young Australian cricketers dream of the same thing. Macksville's premier batsman set his goal early and privately, but was happy to share it with a chosen few. 'It's something I've always planned for. You want to get in there and get the job done very quickly,' he admitted later.

Few doubted he would get there, but even fewer knew just how hard he worked. Every night of the week, summer and winter, he was at the Willis Street nets with his dad. With every trial match, every tournament, every hundred, every time he walked to the crease, he had to prove himself again.

This all-consuming ambition left little time for school. At Macksville High, a class teacher reported to Barry Lockyer that Phillip had told them not to harass him about an overdue assignment because it was cricket season. Lockyer, who doubled as cricket coach, was pretty sure the boy had his priorities right.

Phillip wanted to leave school early, but his parents were keen for him to stay and finish his Higher School Certificate, as Jason had.

His Aunt Helen remembers having a quiet talk to him at a family function about keeping his options open.

'He said, "I am going to play for Australia. Cricket is my life". He was that determined.'

Any hope she had of convincing him to have a Plan B evaporated when she heard that quiet announcement.

'School wasn't for me,' Phillip told Megan for one of her school assignments. 'I didn't really want a normal job.'

He and Shariful Islam spent a lot of time on the phone talking about their goals. 'He had made up his mind at the age of 12 he was going to play for Australia,' Shariful says. 'When I look back, I see he made a choice at that age and was able to execute that perfectly.'

He did press on at school – because of cricket. Greg convinced him that there were good options through the school system to play representative cricket, and he accepted that. For the time being.

'Once he got past Year Eight he was hardly there,' Greg admits. 'I think one year he did 15 trips between here and Newcastle, Wollongong and Bathurst in the summer period, and that starts to eat into your schoolwork. I think it was around Year Nine where out of seven weeks he was at school seven days, and the rest was cricket.'

The people who administered cricket had little sympathy. 'They would do things like have state trials in Sydney the Monday *after* September school holidays finished,' Greg says, 'so that means Tuesday is also gone for the drive home, and they had Wednesday off for senior kids. It amazed me: a fortnight of holidays and they would do that.'

Phillip's school report at the end of Year 11 confirms he had one interest only. 'We are expecting a better effort from Phillip in 2006, despite his many sporting interests,' class teacher Mr Bogema suggested. 'He needs to improve his performance in Standard English, Industrial Technology and Senior Science. While we expect him to captain Australia some day, there is a remote possibility he may need to make a living like ordinary folk! Let's work on all sides of the future.'

Greg concedes that a lot of parents wouldn't have let their children miss as much school as Phillip, but he and Virginia could see his focus and his talent. 'And, I have to admit, it was bloody enjoyable,' Greg says. 'For all the driving we did to all those carnivals, I can tell you that at least eight times out of ten I drove away with a hidden smile because he had done so well.'

Keeping track of Phillip's centuries would have been hard work if he wasn't doing it himself; he racked up his twenty-fourth by Year Ten at school. And school did fulfil Greg's promise of

Leading his teammates onto the field as captain of the Under-15s NSW XI.

throwing up cricketing opportunities. Phillip was top run scorer and Player of the Carnival at the Combined High Schools Championships on the central coast where he notched up 134 against the Western Area team, averaged 66 and was duly selected in the CHS First XI.

CHS cricket coordinator Damian Toohey says Phillip especially loved taking on teams from the cities. 'Phillip loved playing at these carnivals and giving it to the city kids. He always played in a competitive fashion and was very respectful to everyone. Unfortunately at this time a lot of the people involved use to call the North Coast the Phil Hughes XI, which certainly was none of Phillip's doing, but sections didn't like that.'

In March 2004, as a 15-year-old, he impressed everybody at the NSW Schoolboys Lord's Taverners Championships, scoring a century in a partnership with captain Usman Khawaja for the CHS Firsts.

'I was playing first grade at the time,' Khawaja says. 'I was thinking, who is this little guy? He was hitting them to all parts.'

England opener Sam Robson ran into Phillip around this period. 'I remember it clearly because of how much better he was than anybody else at that age. The guys in Sydney always fancied ourselves over the country boys. Playing grade was looked on as pretty impressive, playing with the men. All of a sudden Phil turned up and I was staggered. He played every single shot and was miles ahead, and he was from this little town that we'd never heard of.'

Usman, Ben Way and Ben Jonas were selected with Phillip for the NSW Schoolboys team, and he received the Steve Rixon Perpetual Trophy as Player of the Year. Because of his age, he was able to play again the following year and picked up the same award, this time shared with future first-class all-rounder Will Sheridan. (Phillip let Sheridan have the handsome trophy for a year.) The only other players to win it twice were Adam Gilchrist and NSW Sheffield Shield player Corey Richards.

OVER SCORE	POOL	MATCH BETWEEN		NEW SOUTH WALES	AND	NORTHERN TERRITORY
	PLAYED AT PARK 25, ADELAIDE			TOSS WON BY NEW SOUTH WALES		1st INNINGS OF NEW SOUTH WAL

TIME In/Out		BATSMAN	SCORE	BALLS FACED	MINS
9.30	1	P. HUGHES	224 5 4 44 4 4 1 23 3 2 4 1 3 14 3 214 4 12 24 1 4322 1 422 2 244 4 1144 2 114221 4221	156	199
9.50 10.30	2	N. TAYLOR	2 1 21 3 3 W	49	60
10.51 10.52	3	J. DYBALL	1 11	13	21
10.53 12.66	4	S. ISLAM	2 1 2 2 1 3 2 3 34 1 214 4 12 2 3 1162	70	105
12.57	5	C. DASH	1	4	10

Being younger than the other boys, Phillip returned for another shot at the Under-15s national tournament as captain of a NSW team that included his mate Shariful Islam. That year the carnival was held in Adelaide, a future happy hunting ground. He gave the locals a taste of what was to come with a record score for the competition: 166 not out against the Northern Territory.

Phillip's love of batting was infectious. In that game, NSW lost two early wickets before Phillip was joined by Shariful, who recalls, 'His hand–eye coordination was amazing. After one cut I said, "Man, what was that?" and he just said, "Yeah, well if he keeps bowling there I'm going to keep doing the same thing". No batsman in that comp was able to play the shots that he did. I never saw a batsman in any of the other states who could bat even close to Phil. Bowlers were doing what they were trained to do and he was putting away their good balls . . . It was absolutely frustrating for the bowlers.'

The pair pinned their ears back, and Phillip's scoring toward the end of the innings makes stunning reading: 4 2 2 2 1 1 2 4 4 4 4 1 1 4 4 2 1 1 4 2 2 1 2 4 2 2 1.

In his last 28 deliveries, he hit nine boundaries, made 64 runs, and failed to score off only one ball: the last.

Teammate Daniel Burns, who was watching that innings, remembers Phil getting down on one knee and scooping the bowlers onto the leg side.

'It was like a switch getting flicked,' Burns says.

He knew, however, that a Hughes innings could go through many phases. 'He always batted at his own pace, he wasn't rushed and didn't panic and if you played against him and he got to 30 you knew you were going to pay. Sometimes it was a slow and painful death. He just knew so many ways to get to 100.'

Shariful and Phillip set a third-wicket partnership record of 175 before Shariful was dismissed for 62. Phillip's 166 alone accounted for the Northern Territory, but it would also have been enough to win 11 of the matches in a week when wickets were damp and difficult. Phillip was equal top score (35) for NSW in the semifinal against Victoria, and his 33 in the final play-offs was the second-highest for the Blues.

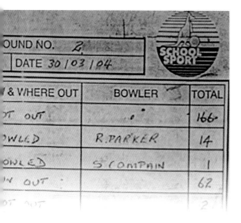

& WHERE OUT	BOWLER	TOTAL
T OUT		166
OWLED	R. PARKER	14
OWLED	S COMPAIN	1
N OUT		62
OT OUT		2

ROUND NO. 2
DATE 30 / 03 / 04
SCHOOL SPORT

Phillip's scoring toward the end of the innings makes stunning reading

'The batting,' the team report stated, 'was disappointing, with only two batsmen performing consistently well. On and off the field all players behaved creditably at all times and the team spirit and cohesion was exceptional. Phillip Hughes performed his duties well as captain.'

Phillip's reputation had become, says Victorian wicketkeeper Brett Forsyth, a distraction. 'For the first two days of the carnival, we were playing on a ground next to where New South Wales was playing and we could see him batting and had wondered who the little bloke was . . . I remember him scoring over 150 in one game. We were just amazed that someone at that stage wasn't scoring 40 or 50 or 60, but was batting all day and making big scores. That was the first we'd heard of him and then we played against him in the semifinal. I am pretty sure we had him caught out behind early but he wasn't given out and we were getting into him. We had our plans in place, but he just kept cutting. I think he got 30 or 40 that day, even bowled a few seamers at the back of their innings. I am pretty sure he got me out that day.'

Brady Jones, the Tasmanian wicketkeeper, says: 'There were rumours flying around about the kid from New South Wales who had scored so many hundreds and you just thought he was going to be this huge kid who was bigger than everyone and would belt everyone around, but he wasn't. We thought he would be a man child . . . He was small, but he just did it.'

Mitchell Harvey bowled brilliantly in Adelaide. A left-arm quick from Dorrigo on the northern tablelands 75 kilometres north of Macksville, Harvey had played against Phillip for years.

'I never got him out,' Harvey says. 'Growing up, he was the best batsman I ever saw. I played a lot of cricket at a high level and he was the outstanding player. He could just produce when he had to. There were kids from other states with big reputations, but he made them look secondary.'

Simon Keen, who would be Phillip's state captain at Under-17 and Under-19 level, says Phillip's feats were the talk of junior cricket. Another batsman told him of a time 'Phil was slog-sweeping sixes all day . . . he was slog-sweeping for fun. All the other kids were making up theories about how he did it, like, he didn't watch the bowlers, he just watched the middle of the wicket, that was his secret. There was a story that he learnt to bat by using an axe on his banana farm. He was already this bigger-than-life character.'

There was a prize at the end of the carnival that meant more to Phillip than any trophy. He was picked to play for an Australian Under-15 selection in a tournament against Indian and Malaysian teams in Delhi later that year. Cricket was luring the Macksville boy further afield.

EIGHT

COLOUR AND MOVEMENT

There are no beggars, monkeys, dancing bears, dusty pitches or squat toilets where Phillip Hughes comes from. In 2004, Macksville boasted a population of 2500. Where Phillip was going, that many people could squeeze into one city block.

INDIA IS AN ASSAULT on the western senses. Its streets swarm with people day and night, its air is as polluted as any on the planet, and it is a place of eternal noise, movement, colour and aroma. It shocked adult cricketers from the big Australian cities. How confronting was it for a 15-year-old country kid like Phillip Hughes?

The boys of the Australian 15 Years School Sports Association tour gathered in Sydney for a couple of days' training before flying to India. They were put up at a Randwick hotel close to a fast-food outlet where one youngster from Macksville proved to be quite a hit with the local girls.

On 25 September the boys left those familiar things behind and flew to Delhi. To say they were ill prepared is an understatement.

'It's real hot here, smelly and dirty,' Phillip informed his family in a postcard.

'The food was not so good,' he wrote in another letter.

Indian restaurants were scarce on the NSW north coast, and curries can be confronting for the uninitiated. His roommate on the tour, Daniel Burns, remembers the pair of them running for the toilet in the airport and being confronted for the first time in their lives with holes in the floor. No seats, no toilet paper, nothing they could recognise.

Nonetheless, Phillip kept his mind open because it was cricket and a taste of what life on tour must be like.

'Phillip and I just looked at each other, shrugged and laughed,' Burns says. 'He was like that for the rest of the tour. Other kids got homesick and let things get to them, but he just enjoyed it. Everything he saw he took in his stride.'

Keeping Phillip in cricket was a costly exercise. The trip was expensive, but the North Coast Cricket Council chipped in $500. Every time he made a new representative team, Greg and Virginia paid for the shirts, caps and jackets, petrol for the car ride and accommodation if the tournament wasn't in Sydney where they had relatives. Then there were the expenses of being on the road.

The team's coach, Damian Toohey, remembers raised eyebrows when Phillip was not named captain for the tour. 'The national secretary had told us the selection committee had decided on Michael Hill and Kurt Pascoe. I don't think this was well received in the Hughes house at this time, as Phillip had captained the NSW team. The most impressive part was his attitude in respecting the other boys. I think he had captained most teams he'd been in but he was relaxed being one of the boys. He led them shopping, and meeting other people, and creating stories. He had some mischief in him, but always respected what he was doing. He was funny in our pool recovery sessions, and he ordered lots of chips from room service, apparently.'

The kids found themselves on buses for hours in the morning trying to get to the ground and would arrive drained shortly before play. The same trip home would take a quarter of the time.

'It was a tough trip,' Burns says. 'A lot of us were sick and the organisation wasn't great, but Phillip just enjoyed himself.'

Daniel, Phillip and Mitch Harvey roomed together, the Macksville boy hammering room service and staring out the window in wonder at the mysteries of India. Other boys were confronted with the mysteries of two beds in a room for three people.

When asked about the tour a decade later, teammate Brett Forsyth's memory is that Phillip *was* captain. 'The thing that stood out was his leadership. I was pretty sure he was joint captain with

Left bottom: Bowling as much as batting won Phillip 'Player of the Tour' on his first Australian rep tour, a 2004 odyssey through India.

Right: Phillip in front of the Taj Mahal. He enjoyed the sights, not so much the food.

Michael Hill . . . Those two were the most credentialled but I remember that Phil stood out in everything he did. Even if he wasn't captain he was a leader, and any challenge, he took on. The personality didn't change. He was always having a laugh, he just loved it, he was always happy to be there and I suppose that's the thing I remember: a country boy with a mullet who just loved cricket and loved being there. The touring stuff didn't bother him, he just loved being around the boys. A positive person. He was very driven, even at a young age. Most of us hoped we would do it but he knew he would. He believed in himself.'

On arrival, still tired after their flight, the boys were taken to Agra to see the Taj Mahal. Piled on a bus first thing in the morning, they were told it would take four hours to get there. It took eight. The vehicle pulled up at a questionable-looking north Indian roadhouse for lunch, but as they got off the bus the Malaysian team coach told his Australian counterpart not to let anybody eat the food. The bus wouldn't stop again and made the return journey without once pulling up for food, despite pleas from one and all. They only returned to their hotel at 2 am.

There was a bizarre itinerary for the tour, which was organised by the Commonwealth Youth Sports Development Council. It involved a lecture and a play by local students about AIDS awareness, seminars on Commonwealth values and gender equity, plus factory visits and a reception with representatives from the Australian High Commission.

One by one, the young cricketers fell ill. It wasn't until later that they realised the drinks they were given during games had been mixed with tap water. The boys would only eat naan bread for lunch, and, later in the tour, some of the fathers who made the trip would get food from a nearby pizza chain. Mitchell Harvey lost 14 kilograms on the tour; he reckons Phillip might have lost the same.

Like many first visitors to the subcontinent, it was the poverty the 15-year-olds found genuinely confronting. When one boy gave money to a beggar, he was given a stern warning by the liaison officer, who told the kids that beggars were professionals, and giving money only encouraged them. It was a moral dilemma none had faced before.

A colourful religious festival that passed the hotel enchanted the visitors, but when a man confronted them with a dancing bear on a chain one of the boys threw money at the handler and yelled at him, 'I want you to dance, mate! Not your bear, YOU!'

Phillip wrote a postcard home during a trial game: 'We had our first game today. I'm 44no. I was smashing them. The Taj Mahal was sick. I miss use so much I think I'm getting home sick, can't wait to see you. Love you so much. Love Boof. PS keep ringing me.'

The boys struggled with cricket conditions so different from anything they had seen. It rained every night and the wickets were a challenge. The Indian spinners preyed on the batsmen while the Australian fast bowlers struggled in the humidity. Nobody was healthy. In the second game against Malaysia, Phillip saw the quicks struggling, grabbed the ball and took six for 24 from ten overs. He made 41 of the team's 120 runs and took three catches, but the tourists were still beaten. It was his best performance of the tour.

Michael Hill remembers that Phillip 'bowled these dreadful medium pacers – they barely got down the other end, and he took six wickets in one of the games and I think that was his best figures ever. I was captain and I bowled him the rest of the tour after that'.

Mitch Harvey describes Phillip's bowling action as 'horrible': 'He was looking at his feet when he let the ball go – it was almost like he bowled off the wrong foot.'

Daniel Burns says Phillip's bowling was 'a farce, it was really hilarious'. He has no memory of him bowling in the nets, but he recalls the almost wrong-footed action and the way he angled the ball in: 'It barely bounced above ankle height, it was travelling so slow.'

As amusing as Phillip's bowling was for his teammates, Toohey remembers him bowling Virat Kohli, already a star, for a duck.

Brett Forsyth was impressed with Phillip's batting. 'He just adapted so quickly to the conditions. Where for a lot of us it took us a long time on the spinning tracks, he would get out there and start sweeping from ball one and just took the game on.'

Phillip wrote a postcard home during a trial game: *'We had our first game today. I'm 44no. I was smashing them. The Taj Mahal was sick. I miss use so much I think I'm getting home sick, can't wait to see you. Love you so much. Love Boof. PS keep ringing me'*

Damien Toohey saw that it was a result of hard work behind the scenes. 'Against the new ball he was great. The interesting thing was our kids against spin, because the [Indian] kids bowl flatter and into the wickets. There was a lad who was about six foot who bowled around the wicket and into Phil's pad, full and at good pace. Our kids grew up waiting for the ball to be tossed up and would come down the wicket, and he had to work out how he was going to bat against that. At that stage he wasn't a good sweeper of the ball and he went away and practised and practised before we played them again. That was the sort of kid he was, you could see him sitting there thinking, "What am I going to do?"'

Toohey says Phillip seemed to be casing India for when he would return with more senior sides. He was moved to have an unusual heart-to-heart with the boy.

'I do remember sitting Phillip down at our mid-tour review and saying to him, "You need to focus on becoming a first-class cricketer. You are that good". [Team manager] Neil Findlay said to me at the time, "I've never heard you say that to a kid before". I said, "He needed to hear that from us". At the time I wasn't sure if he was that focused off the field. It was his first trip without Greg, and I reckon he was cutting loose a bit.'

Phillip would always seek out the better players on the other side and try to engage them in conversation, hungry to learn more. Kohli says he remembers Phillip from that tour and later visits with Under-19s and an Australia A side. He, too, fell for the Hughes charm.

'He was pretty excited to be where he was, playing for Australia, you could see that,' Kohli says. 'He was happy to be on the pitch and interacting with people that he liked. I never found him hostile. He was calm and quiet and friendly. He seemed happy to be doing what he was doing. You could see he loved batting.'

Phillip's attitude to cricket and life made a profound impression on Brett Forsyth. 'Once your cricket is finished, you let go of it all and move on, but some people you hang on to and he was one for me . . . he had this country thing, he was content, he wasn't needy, he was firm how he went about things, but he had this infectious personality. I was a massive fan of him as a person and a player even when I was playing against him. It was also his mental application, the way he went about it. He didn't worry about failure from what I could see; he just didn't see cricket that way. He went out there and played the game and was positive, and that set him apart. He was inspiring, his personality. I wanted to be like him, I wanted to walk about without that fear and not worry if I was good enough or anything else. He didn't have that fear of failure, which is a big thing in cricket. Everyone was comfortable with their talent, but the personality is what gets the player to the next rung.'

Burns was equally impressed with his roommate's attitude and ability. 'We saw Steve Smith and Usman Khawaja and David Warner when they were young, and he was head and shoulders above them in terms of junior cricket. He was the perfect teammate too. When I think about it, I realise there was never a time when you felt he wanted to be somewhere else or to be doing something else. He just wanted to be there. He was funny, relaxed, focused, and he never got cheeky with coaches. In the rooms after a game, he would be the first with a joke or a laugh and it didn't matter if he'd made a duck or a hundred, he was always the same.'

By the last game in India, however, Phillip was exhausted and was excused from playing. He took to the dressing room and slept the whole day. Toohey says it was a hard choice. He thought they could win but he had to prioritise the boys' health.

Phillip finished the series with 8 wickets at 13.25 and 135 runs at 33.75. His feats with the ball earned him the Bowler of the Series award. The Player of the Series was

Kohli. Phillip's peers voted him best player in the Australian squad. He was the complete all-rounder at this level. The squad needed a back-up keeper, so when he wasn't taking wickets he would relieve Brett Forsyth behind the stumps.

'Phil was sharing the gloves, leading the team when he needed to, and bowling. Whatever challenge he had, he just did it,' Forsyth remembers. 'He didn't look like your traditional keeper, he probably had short sleeves on. It was bizarre. I saw him on TV when he took the gloves when Matthew Wade bowled in the Test in Tasmania [against Sri Lanka 2012–13] and the grin he had was exactly the same as the one I remember from India. It was Phillip having a laugh and saying, "How good is this?"'

On his return, Phillip wrote a letter of thanks to the North Coast Cricket Council, signed off, 'Yours in Cricket. PHILLIP HUGHES 15'. He told them it was 'good to be home to a baked meal' and apologised for the delay in writing, 'but I had an arm in plaster for three weeks due to a broken bone in my right hand'.

There was a story behind that.

The young cricketer had recently become a boxing fan and worshipped Anthony Mundine, a former rugby league star who had given up football to follow in his father's footsteps as a boxer. The former world champion was a controversial figure, but, as Greg says, 'Phillip didn't know anything about politics'. He took to carrying a small picture of Mundine in his cricket kit and was intrigued by his hero's craft.

After India, Phillip and Greg were training every night of the week at the Willis Street nets.

'He had this country thing, he was content, he wasn't needy, he was firm how he went about things' – BRETT FORSYTH

Greg patiently set up the bowling machine while the boy got ready, and then he would feed in ball after ball after ball. They had more than 100 balls ready to go before reloading. Hardly a word was said. Occasionally Phillip wanted the balls aimed in a certain spot, but even that could be done with a gesture.

The nets weren't in great shape. The wire developed holes and fell away in places. Later somebody would suggest that the club ask Phillip to fix them.

'Why?' they were asked.

'Well, he wore them out.'

It was a fair point. The crooked structures still stand today and somebody has patched them up, but nobody is there on a winter afternoon, especially now that newer nets have been installed at the nearby Donnelly Welsh Playing Fields.

When Phillip was finished, he and Greg would pack up and drive to a local house where there was a gym and a punching bag.

'Feel me muscles, Mum,' he would announce with a grin.

A batsman, like a boxer, needs quick hands and feet. It was a truth coaches Warren Smith and later Justin Langer preached, and one the Macksville boy knew before he met either of them. He was, fortunately, blessed with both. That high back lift convinced bowlers in the split second after they released the ball that they were a chance, but in a blink the gate was closed, and the bat was colliding with the ball at the last possible moment, right under his eyes.

Sparring became a favourite activity and it was during a session with Jason, who was as strong and quick as Phillip, that a bone in the hand broke. Right on the eve of the cricket season.

After India, Phillip and Greg were training every night of the week at the Willis Street nets. Greg patiently set up the bowling machine while the boy got ready, and then he would feed in ball after ball after ball

Jason can remember an incident in which he might have given Phillip a broken nose during a similar workout.

Needing to get to Bowral for cricket trials, Phillip had the plaster removed two days before he had to bat. The family was told that he would need a doctor's certificate clearing him. That was arranged and faxed off. The night before leaving, Greg gave him some throwdowns in the backyard. Phillip's arm was weak and sore, but he didn't let on.

'We didn't realise how much strength he'd lost,' Greg recalls.

In a first practice match in Bowral, Phillip was run out for not many, which might have been a good thing, as he had to play against a City side the following day in a match called the Brett Lee Cup.

Matthew Day had first seen Phillip in the PSSA tournament when he scored 159 not out at Waitara Oval. As an opening bowler for City, Day had been hearing things about the country kid for years and they had occasionally crossed paths. The Country–City match in Day's last year of Under-17s was Phillip's first competitive game back from his broken hand.

Day recalls: 'Our coach said, "Let's test him out early". I took the first over and the first three balls were bouncers. He went, four, six, four. He had fourteen after three! All pull shots. He was renowned for his cutting, but in junior cricket it was pulls, pulls, pulls. Everyone joked that the six had hit Bradman's house. Phil said, "I think I've woken the old fellow up!"'

The Don, who had died three years earlier, would have been delighted to be disturbed from his eternal rest by an unorthodox country boy who was challenging the game with the weight of his talent and magnitude of his scores.

'He slapped these guys,' Greg remembers. He scored 120, but was in pain through the whole innings, and the coaches said he wasn't allowed to field. City won, and Phillip was sent home and told not to play cricket for a month.

The 120 proved more than enough to ensure he was selected for NSW in the Under-17 National Championships. Again he was getting in early: he was young enough to qualify again 12 months later.

The layoff kept Phillip out of cricket up to Christmas, which gave him time to finish his school year and collect an award. He had decided to stay on at school beyond Year Ten, but the North Coast School Sports Association already awarded him a Sporting Blue, usually reserved for those in their last year. He received a certificate listing his achievements that concluded: 'Phillip has set himself very high goals and seems destined to achieve them. Taking into account the size of his hometown, its isolation from first class sporting venues and limited competitive opportunities against boys of similar ability, one cannot underestimate the enormity of Phillip's achievements compared with other boys from metropolitan centres across Australia. Congratulations on a well deserved "Blue" in the sport of Cricket.'

In January 2005, Phillip went to Tasmania for the Under-17 tournament. Greg would follow after attending to some business at home. Phillip missed out in the first matches against Victoria at New Town Oval and Queensland at R. Ferguson Park, but then Greg arrived for the third match against Western Australia at King George V Park in Glenorchy. The 16-year-old put on a show for his dad, scoring 114 – the exact winning margin for the Blues.

'Everyone joked that the six had hit Bradman's house. Phil said, "I think I've woken the old fellow up!"'

It was only a taste of what was to follow. The following day Phillip hit 160. NSW coach David Patterson sang Phillip's praises to the *Coffs Coast Advocate*: 'His cutting and cover driving was exceptional as were the shots he played off his pads. The best part about both his centuries was the way he hung in there as an opener when we were in trouble at 4–55 and 3–42. He really held the innings together.'

Phillip was named in the Under-17 Merit Team, made up of the best players in the tournament, but he was not considered for the Australian squad for the Under-19 World Cup.

His incredible form continued through that 2004–05 season. Having opted to play for Sawtell in the larger Coffs Harbour District Cricket competition, he found himself playing against Nambucca Bellingen in the Under-16s inter-district grand final. There were mutterings in the Macksville and Bellingen pubs about this new turn of events, but rules were rules, and Phillip was Phillip: he scored 129 not out to win the match.

At the 2005 NSW Schoolboys Championships in Barooga, batting for North Coast, he made 120 not out against Riverina and 107 against Sydney East (who had another up-and-coming young batsman by the name of Steve Smith, who responded with 60). South Coast defeated North Coast in round three and Phillip was out on his favourite number, 64.

When that was done Phillip pulled on the pads to bat for Sawtell against Coffs Harbour in the Coffs Harbour and District Cricket grand final alongside Jason. The match preview in the local paper claimed his nickname was 'Superstar'. While that was not true, it may as well have been. Phillip's efforts in that game are best recounted by *Coffs Harbour Advocate* journalist and Coffs Harbour cricket captain Brad Greenshields, who wrote about them four years later when Phillip was picked for Australia, under the headline 'The Day I Knew Phil Hughes was Special'.

'His reputation had preceded him. Nevertheless, being the captain of the opposition team I was quietly confident that the pressure of a first-grade grand final would be enough to unnerve someone of such tender years . . . Oh how wrong I was.'

Greenshields, like so many before and after, believed the best way to get the 16-year-old out was to keep off his pads and bowl an off-stump line to dry up his scoring opportunities.

To that end he put in a slip, two gullies, third man, backward point, short cover and mid-off. The game was at Richardson Park, with beautiful views of the mountain ranges and an ocean breeze that takes the edge off the heat.

'I don't know why I even bothered,' Greenshields wrote. 'Hughes possesses a cut shot that could get through a gap in a budget surplus.'

Phillip didn't show off; he just built up a steady half-century.

'When Hughes rocked onto the back foot he looked like he had all the time in the world. His defence showed no sign of weakness and he hardly said a word, no matter how much my team tried to verbal him'.

Sawtell won the grand final and while Greenshields was disappointed to lose, at least he had a story to tell.

Hundreds were filling up the baskets in the back bedroom of the East Street home. Matt Day remembers, 'The teams that got him in the first few overs, they got really pumped. When he got to 20, they'd get very deflated, because he was away, and he made hundreds for fun.'

Sam Robson was sitting with Phillip at a state Under-17 trial game in Canberra. 'The guys were in the dressing room talking about how many hundreds they'd made. Someone would say two, or three, and someone would say six. Phil said he had made 50 or 60, an astronomical number.'

Despite all the centuries, things got confused the next summer and Phillip suffered a setback that, like many first rebuffs, left a deep scar. He was going so well, Cricket NSW told him that

When the NSW Under-19 team was read out, two words were missing: Phillip Hughes. Phillip was told he would be in the Under-17s instead

he should captain its Under-17s but also try out for the Under-19s, so he skipped trials for the first and went to the second, in Manly after the September school holidays. In the second trial in Blacktown he scored two Under-19 half-centuries, dominating alongside fellow left-hander Usman Khawaja. It should have been enough, but the Under-19s decided to have another trial the next day.

Phillip took a deep breath. 'Now I have to prove myself again,' he said to Greg. And he did, with another half-century.

When the NSW Under-19 team was read out, two words were missing: Phillip Hughes. The selectors had opted for Steve Cazzulino as an opener, even though Phillip had performed better in the trials. Cazzulino was picked on the strength of his runs for NSW Under-19s the

'Most of the times I bowled against him he had the wood on me, like he did on everyone, but that one day I was going all right. Then he did *that* to me' – MICHAEL TOWNSEND

previous season. Phillip was told he would be in the Under-17s instead. Cricket NSW had indicated that Phillip might play in both age groups, as all-rounder Moisés Henriques had done the previous season, but they changed their mind after talk that it was too much cricket for one boy.

Greg and Phillip were stunned. He was, after all, a batsman. Nobody had ever suggested Phillip Hughes would be better for less time at the crease.

Greg was perplexed. He had made two 1000-kilometre round trips for the trials, taking time off work that stretched his limited resources.

'It was a very upsetting day,' Greg admits. 'Freddy [David Freedman, the Under-19 coach] was nearly in tears when he told him, "We are not picking you, we can only pick you in the Under-17s". Phillip said nothing. I said, "Why is he at the Under-19 trials when you were never going to pick him?"'

But the Hugheses were not a family for ugly scenes. Part of the reason Phillip wanted his dad to never sit with other parents was that he disliked parental influence. The other players were also surprised. Matt Day recalls that Phillip 'did incredibly well in those trial games at Blacktown and they didn't pick him, which was a sore point for Phil and the family. They're a country family who never had heaps of money. They'd come to a trial and he'd done really well. For them it was a big expense and no result'.

Usman Khawaja was also surprised. 'It threw a spanner in the works, him making runs, because Steve Cazzulino had made a lot the year before and they had him and me down as openers. The coach pulled Phil aside and said he wouldn't be picked. It was a hard thing for the coach to do.'

Cazzulino admits 'it raised some eyebrows . . . That was the last time I got picked ahead of Hughesy'.

Performing at an Under-17s trial in Newcastle for Northern NSW, Phillip blasted the ball around the park for two days running. Another century in the bag. They were going to rest him for the third day and let some others have a bat, but it was rained out. Then it was off to play for North Coast in the Colts, where he got another century.

Freedman points out they had some fantastic batsmen in the team that year, but 'I am happy to admit we got it wrong'. The Cricket NSW talent coordinator says Hughes, along with Moisés Henriques and Josh Hazlewood, were the best young cricketers he ever saw.

'The thing about Phillip was he wasn't aesthetically pleasing but it never compromised the way he played. He had an insatiable appetite for runs. We'd heard about him at the North Coast Zone academy and knew he was good by the mountain of runs he scored.'

NSW won the Under-17 carnival in January 2006. Phillip hit 259 runs, including three half-centuries, and was selected in the merit team. The Under-19 carnival was a chance of being chosen for an authentic Australian team. That was another reason why his non-selection hurt.

School cricket was a light workout these days, and in the spring of 2005 Phillip duly hit three centuries for Macksville High and would have got a fourth if he hadn't been run out for 91. His last innings for his school was 115 not out – in a total of 134! He played cricket in the local competition again and was part of the Ex-Services Club A-grade side that beat the Nambucca Hotel team in the grand final at Thistle Park.

Michael Townsend, a fast bowler for the pub team, was bowling well that day. Phillip nicked one through slip and later in the over was ruffled by a short ball. Some say it hit the badge of his helmet, while the bowler says it skimmed past.

'It's funny, I never intentionally tried to bowl bouncers to anybody and I think that's what surprised him,' Townsend says. 'Most of the times I bowled against him he had the wood on me, like he did on everyone, but that one day I was going all right. Then he did *that* to me.'

At Thistle Park, it was always a bit of a thing to aim the ball at the chook sheds over the on-side boundary. 'I am a tail-end slogger like most fast bowlers, but I could never get it. It was cow corner for right-handers,' Townsend says. 'It was even more annoying that he cover-drove me into them. A few blokes got it in over the years. It is a fair hit, they were all right-handers, though. I've never seen it hit square that way he did it.'

The feathers went flying and the din from the chooks could be heard across Macksville.

The mild-mannered quick was so impressed, he congratulated the batsman. 'I never got him out,' Townsend admits. 'My brother did. My brother was living in Sydney and they brought a team up from Strathfield to play and I was in Phil's team; we had a selected team from the local comp. My brother was the fast bowler and he got him. He was pretty proud of that. He photocopied the scorebook and everything. He must have known things were coming.'

Like many opponents who had taken a beating from him, Townsend got on well with Phillip off the field. 'My parents owned the Retravision store in town, and every now and then I would go and help the Hugheses with the computer at their place. Whenever he came home, he would come by the shop and ask you how you were going. He was a nice kid. He would approach you for a chat. You didn't have to chase him down to say hello.'

Phillip scored 777 runs in A-grade that season; Jason proved difficult to remove and averaged 312.

'He went berserk,' Greg says. He swung the bat like he had nothing to lose. Six of his last 12 scoring shots went for six

'They reminded me of a Steve Waugh–Mark Waugh type of thing,' Townsend remembers. 'Jason was a bit more flamboyant with his shots, a bit more like Mark Waugh, whereas Phil had his head down a bit more and concentrated on things.'

There was one last sour note that season. The trials for the NSW Combined High Schools side were held early in the summer, but the Hugheses found themselves trying out for the state Under-19 team in Sydney the day before and would have had to drive overnight to Lismore to make the game.

'I needed to work at some stage and nobody else was going that way, so we couldn't do it,' Greg says.

Phillip just couldn't get there.

The North Coast region ruled that as Phillip had not made the trials he was ineligible to play for CHS, despite the fact he had played the previous three years and been player of the carnival in the last two. It was patently ridiculous.

'They were following their guidelines and there wasn't much that could be done,' Damian Toohey says. 'I remember saying to Virginia, "Phillip has bigger fish to fry in cricket, and he will be doing great things". I have no doubt if he had attended the carnival he would have batted for four days!'

The local scene had clearly grown too small, but Phillip had one last sign-off for Macksville Ex-Services Club, *his* club, in a game at Willis Street against Urunga. Phillip had accepted $100 to go to Port Macquarie and do the presentations for the junior cricket club the same afternoon. The Macksville team batted first, and Phillip got to his half-century when it became obvious that it was time to go.

'He went berserk,' Greg says. He swung the bat like he had nothing to lose. Six of his last 12 scoring shots went for six. The scoresheet shows the sequence: 4 2 4 2 6 1 2 6 6 4 4 1 6 1 1 6 6 6 1.

Sorry Urunga, there was somewhere he had to be.

big
time

NINE

SUMMER IN THE CITY

Rain was falling on Mona Park, a tree-ringed oval in Sydney's western suburbs, when Neil D'Costa arrived to watch an Under-17 representative match in the 2005–06 summer. Or rather, D'Costa was there to watch a player. He had his doubts that play would start in the weather, but he was prepared to take the chance.

D'COSTA, AN EBULLIENT, FAST-TALKING former grade batsman, was club coach at Western Suburbs, one of several Sydney clubs who actively scoured country and junior cricket for new cricketers. Wests, the club of Bob Simpson, Alan Davidson, Greg Matthews and Warren Bardsley, battled with the St George club over bragging rights of having produced the most Australian Test cricketers out of any club in the country. St George, as well as Manly, were also chasing Phillip Hughes, but no club had a coach as persuasive as D'Costa.

He remembers the day well. 'It was horrible and wet, but I'd told him I would go. The wicket was diabolical, but this little kid was hosing them out. He was small, but he was solid. He looked like a rugby league halfback. He was a muscly little fellow, and as a batsman he was so smart. He'd hit the ball and say "Two", and it was always two. He competed – he played like a seven-year-old in the backyard against the kids from the street all the time. He had a sense of the game as a contest. He just wanted to get runs and win games.'

D'Costa came with some advantages over other club coaches. He was already well known as the mentor to Michael Clarke, who had burst

onto the scene the previous year with a century on his Test debut in Bangalore and another in his first home Test in Brisbane. Clarke had subsequently struggled in the 2005 Ashes series and been dropped, but for young aspirants in Australia there was no more glamorous young cricketer than Clarke. He played for Wests.

D'Costa had other links to Phillip. He coached Shariful Islam, who had talked about the kid from Macksville since primary school days. 'When Shariful came back from the PSSA championship,' D'Costa remembers, 'I said, "How did you go?" He said, "Pretty good, but you should see my best friend Phillip Hughes play." I said, "How good can he be? Can he be better than you?" He said, "Oh, he's much better than me." This guy was peeling off hundred after hundred, so that got me wondering.'

By 2005, Shariful was Phillip's number-one advocate at Wests. They were regularly talking by phone, and D'Costa introduced himself by jumping onto the calls.

Shariful remembers: 'I always had it in my mind that Phil needed to be in Sydney. Phil needed to play grade cricket. I said to Dave O'Neil [a barrister and then Wests' club president], "I have this person called Phil Hughes, he is amazing, have a look at his stats." I explained to him the story from Under-12s to Under-15s. Neil didn't know a lot about him. At a game one day, we sat down and I said, "We should recruit Phil." They were asking me why, and I said, "This guy is going to be the next Don Bradman!" Neil did his research and looked at his stats and was very impressed. Then Dave said, "We need to do what we can to bring him to the club".'

Shariful was straight on the phone to Phillip. 'Look, mate, you have got to come to Sydney, you have to play grade. I know that you are young, but you have to play here.

Shariful also played the Clarke card, suggesting that the rising star of Australian cricket could be a valuable friend and mentor at Wests. 'Because Phil and I had that bond, he did trust what I said. He knew that I always had his best interests at heart. I said, "There are a couple of ways you can look at it. You are in a comfort zone playing for country teams and doing well, but I think you need to test yourself if you want to play for Australia. The guys in Sydney are more experienced and you will be playing against players who have been playing grade cricket for a long time."'

Briefed by Shariful, D'Costa watched Phillip bat at Mona Park in the rain then invited him and Greg to a first-grade match between Wests and Randwick–Petersham at Petersham Oval in January 2006. D'Costa also brought Moisés Henriques, the 18-year-old captain of the Australian Under-19 team and Phillip's future NSW and Australian teammate. While Phillip

and Moisés chatted, Neil spoke with Greg and organised lunch at the Pine Inn, a pub on Parramatta Road in Concord.

As they took a table, D'Costa, always direct and provocative, asked Phillip how ambitious he was.

Phillip looked him in the eye and said, 'Play as high as I can.'

D'Costa, who loved a game of any kind, recognised that he and Phillip were in a kind of light-hearted shoot-out.

'How high?' D'Costa fired back.

'Play for Australia.'

'Where do you want to play?'

'Replace Matty Hayden.'

Greg laughed. Phillip and D'Costa did not. Hayden, in 2005–06, was a giant of Australian cricket, with 79 Test matches and nearly 7000 runs to his name. He was 34, but after a difficult 2005 Ashes campaign had returned to form against the West Indies and South Africa at home that summer, scoring four centuries and averaging 73.

D'Costa replied, 'If that's your goal, then come to me. If that's *not* your goal, we can finish lunch and go our separate ways.'

He was prepared to take Phillip Hughes as seriously as the boy was taking himself.

'I knew what he could do,' D'Costa says now, 'but the question was, could he get comfortable in Sydney, could he stay out of trouble?'

Outside the pub, Phillip got in the car and told Greg he wanted to go to Wests.

'Neil was very good, very switched on,' Greg remembers. 'NSW weren't offering rookie contracts yet, but Neil said to Phillip, "You're not ready for first-class yet but we'll make you ready".'

Another of D'Costa's strengths was how quickly he could organise contacts to make logistical arrangements. Although Phillip could take or leave his last year of school, the adults felt it was important for him to do his HSC. D'Costa sprang into action, calling Dr Ian Paterson, headmaster of Homebush Boys High and a keen cricket parent, to get Phillip enrolled. Shariful was already attending the school, so Phillip would have a friend close by. Acquainted with the developer of a new housing complex at Breakfast Point on the Parramatta River near

Above: Phillip (on one knee without his cap on) with his NSW Under-17 teammates in Tasmania.

Concord, D'Costa also organised for Phillip to move into a unit with Matt Day and another Joey's old boy, Matt Costello. Within the month, Phillip's move was under way.

'I wanted to get to the city as soon as I could,' Phillip would tell journalist Mike Coward in 2009. 'I knew if I wanted to be a professional cricketer and play at the top level, I knew I had to move to Sydney and I thought to myself the sooner the better to get down to the big smoke.'

D'Costa, whose cheeky nature was a good match for Phillip's, was ecstatic. He got to work practising with Phillip but could not resist a crack at his rival Andrew Fraser, the leading light at the Manly Cricket Club, who had also been seeking to sign Phillip.

One day when he was with Phillip, D'Costa phoned Fraser and asked, 'Who's that kid from Macksville?'

'Phillip Hughes,' Fraser said. 'He's coming to us, he's going to be great!'

'Yeah. I was just talking with someone about him. I'll put him on.'

D'Costa handed Phillip the phone.

'G'day.'

'Who's that?' Fraser said.

Left: With teammate and future Australian captain Steve Smith, opening for NSW Under-17s at Bankstown Oval.

Right: Phillip (front) taking the field for a NSW Under-17 one-dayer at Mona Park, Auburn.

'Phillip Hughes.'

D'Costa grabbed the phone and chuckled, 'You're not so confident now, Frase, are ya!'

As it had been in junior cricket, stories built up around Phillip Hughes as soon as he moved to Sydney. David O'Neil took a phone call from St George's cricket manager John Jobson.

'Congratulations,' Jobson said.

'For what?'

'You've got Phil Hughes. He's the best young batsman we've seen. We were interested, but I knew it was over when a big limousine came to pick him up that D'Costa had organised.'

O'Neil's brother, Chris, another Western Suburbs cricketer, had died in 1998, and a scholarship was set up in his name to help country cricketers move to Sydney. Some of these funds were put aside to assist Phillip.

'Like all clubs, we have our strengths and weaknesses,' David O'Neil says, 'but we were very good at bringing new players into the fold.'

D'Costa rarely brought young cricketers to meet O'Neil at his chambers, but he made an exception with Phillip. D'Costa sat him down in front of the lawyer–president and said, 'This is the bloke to come and see if you get into trouble. Not that you will get into any.'

Full days of attending school with cricket practice before and after kept trouble at arm's length. Dr Paterson picked Phillip up from home and took him to meet D'Costa at the nets.

'He was really proud of his first week, that he attended every class,' Matt Day says. 'His uniform was immaculate. He loved ironing. That was the one household task he did do. His shirt and pants looked great.'

Phillip never compromised on looking dapper. The next year, he attended the Cricket Australia Centre of Excellence on a residency program in Brisbane. His fellow student Michael Hill recalls, 'We were 18 or 19 years old and away from home and single. Every Friday and Saturday night, we would be waiting for Hughesy ironing his shirt. He would change his shirt three or four times, change his hair three or four times, he always wanted to look good. We never left on time.'

Hughes's care for his appearance had a reason: he liked girls who liked boys who looked good. He liked girls a lot. But during his first week going to school in Sydney, he was puzzled and disappointed about one thing. He phoned his cousin Nino and said, 'It's good, but there's no girls here.'

Nino laughed. 'Did the name Homebush Boys not give it away?'

D'Costa says that this was another reason he had wanted Phillip to go to that school, 'to keep him away from the girls, which worked, for a little while anyway'.

Sometimes D'Costa picked him up after school and dropped in on Dr Paterson to ask how Phillip was going.

'He's not exactly a good student, Neil.'

'He doesn't have to be a good student. Is he turning up?'

Dr Paterson nodded. The quality of Phillip's schoolwork was in inverse proportion to the quality of his cricket, but his charm instantly won over everyone, from the headmaster down.

After Phillip's schooling was sorted, it remained for Wests to have him registered and graded so that other clubs would give up any hope of luring him away. The last game of the 2005–06 season was against St George, and rather than have him travel to the first-grade away game, Wests decided to play him in second grade at Pratten Park, their home ground, where a welcome barbecue would be put on after the match.

D'Costa picked Phillip up from Breakfast Point, and gave him a hit on the Pratten Park wicket before having breakfast. The last over of the one-day fixture is something of a Wests legend. St George batted first and scored 250. Phillip opened, and at the beginning of the fiftieth over he was 135 not out and the scores were tied. The bowler was Steve Green, a future first-grade regular. His first five balls to Phillip were dot balls. Some witnesses say Phillip did it on purpose, to build the tension, while others say he smashed each ball straight to a fieldsman. Either way, it came down to the final ball of the day, which Phillip hoisted over the mid-wicket fence into what might one day be called the Phillip Hughes Nets.

'That's how he rolled,' D'Costa laughs.

Through the winter, D'Costa worked with Phillip on aspects of his technique at the Activate Cricket Centre at Breakfast Point, later co-owned by another Wests player, Ash Squire.

'He was the first player to hit in the nets once they were finished,' Squire recalls. 'I had to

kick him out because the glue on the carpet was still setting . . . Net 5 was always his – he didn't want anyone else to use it. I had to tell him I had to run a business!'

Concentrating on Phillip's technique, D'Costa 'didn't buy into the

Left: Phillip 'The Charmer' (middle) with his school friends at Homebush Boys High.

116

The quality of Phillip's schoolwork was in inverse proportion to the quality of his cricket, but his charm instantly won over everyone

idea that it was unorthodox. It was a different package, but everything was in the right place at the critical moment. Experience was what he needed, not technique.'

D'Costa didn't want to mess with Phillip's instinctive appetite for runs.

'What I brought was working on his angles. He played too much through and behind point. We had to straighten up his defence and get him working on his on- and off-drive and cover-drive. He had a three-finger pinch grip with his bottom hand. His left pinkie didn't touch the handle. It was on the side, like playing a flute. We turned that bottom hand down into more of a tennis grip. Otherwise he couldn't hit a full ball through the leg-side.'

There were also weak spots in his back-foot game. 'When he played off the back foot to a hip-high ball, he was hopping back and his weight ended on his front foot,' D'Costa says. 'We helped him step and slide. Mark Taylor and Mark Waugh played that shot the best. Watch the ball in, watch it out. Get his head still. Turn his elbow over.'

This was a project of D'Costa's for years to come: a mixture of not getting in the way of Phillip's strengths but working hard with him on his weaknesses. D'Costa also took him frequently to Michael Clarke's unit at Breakfast Point to talk about cricket and how to train.

'The fact that he was playing at my club made him automatically my friend,' Clarke says.

Clarke had broken back into the Australian team for the tour to South Africa and Bangladesh early in 2006, and created a deep impression on Phillip with his fanatical dedication to his preparation, which was now aimed at the 2006–07 Ashes series.

He didn't need to try too hard, as Phillip already idolised him. 'I didn't know that he would take a picture of me to the hairdresser in Coffs Harbour and ask for the same haircut,' Clarke laughs. 'As it happened, I also knew the hairdresser and that's how I found out. Hughesy would love telling me that story all the time, and I was saying, "No, don't tell anyone!"'

Left: The first of many English summers, this time with a NSW youth team in June 2007.

118

'Off the field, he was almost timid. But when he walked out there ... There was something about him' – DANIEL SMITH

In June and July, Hughes went to England with a New South Wales youth team for nearly four weeks. His group included previous underage teammates, including Day, future Test fast bowler Jackson Bird, Steve Smith and Sam Robson.

'It was a great few weeks and a lot of us remained friends,' Robson says. 'When you go away with someone, you know them for the rest of your life, you'll always have those memories.'

Day remembers Phillip's conversations with other players. 'It was mainly cricket and girls for Phil. Everyone liked him. When we talked cricket, it wasn't about past players or the game as a whole, it was about what we did today, what we were going to do tomorrow. Sam Robson was the complete opposite: he knew every stat.'

During his HSC year, Hughes was in the unit with Day and Costello one night. He came out of his bedroom and said, 'I've got to write an English HSC essay tomorrow on a book I haven't read. What am I going to do?'

Costello got him to locate the book in his school bag. The three of them read the blurb on the back cover before Day and Costello jotted some ideas for the essay.

'I've never seen anyone study like that in my life,' says Day.

The three young men were accepted into the little community around their home – the IGA supermarket, the Breakfast Point Country Club and the Palace Hotel, the pub across Tennyson Road into which Phillip was warmly welcomed.

'The publican looked after us, the locals all knew us and kept an eye out for us. It was a good community to be part of,' Day says. 'With the unit, it was a brand new development so to have three young guys moving in was a bit of a concern. But Neil told them we were serious about sport and the unit would be fine. We paid the rent upfront and it was all fine.'

With the 2006–07 cricket season approaching, Phillip managed to get through his HSC exams and prepare for his first-grade debut for Wests against Manly at Manly Oval. It was in the lead-up to this game that he met Daniel Smith, the Wests first-grader, NSW state player and punishing right-handed batsman who, though seven years older, would become an influential and beloved member of his inner circle.

'We became friends pretty much straightaway,' Smith says. I had been around for a while, and took it upon myself to make new guys feel welcome. Matty Day was a friend too. We hung out and trained together, and it went from there.'

In that first game at Manly, Smith watched Phillip closely. 'He was pretty nervous and hadn't come out of his shell. Off the field, he was almost timid. But when he walked out there, you could tell he believed. He made about 70 and we felt we had a good one. There was something about him. We didn't know how far he'd go. We just felt we had a good one for the club, and if he went beyond that, anything more was a bonus.'

Through the club season, however, Phillip struggled to adapt to the intensity of adult cricket in the city. His heart was still in Macksville: Ash Squire remembers that when Phillip's Western Suburbs mates took him out to a nightclub, The Ranch, in Epping, on his eighteenth birthday, 'the first thing he wanted to do was step outside and phone his dad'.

The homesickness took time to fade, and made for a tough first season at Wests.

'He was quiet but keen to learn as much as he could about the game. He picked your brain and did that with a lot of guys,' Daniel Smith says.

Above: Back home in Macksville with Dad and Mum, cutting the cake for his 18th birthday.

Opening with Steve Phillips, who was Michael Clarke's best friend and a mate of Phillip as soon as he met him, he averaged in the thirties but did not feast on adult bowling as he had in the past. The standard was considerably higher, as Shariful had promised. Later, Phillip would say that this period of adjustment was one of the hardest of his career.

Under-age cricket offered some relent. In midsummer, he went to Adelaide to play in the Australian Under-19 Championships, where his captain was Simon Keen and his teammates included Day, Robson and Steve Smith. Stepping down to teenage bowlers, he scored 324 runs at 54, came third in the overall averages and fourth in the aggregates against players up to two years his senior, and helped NSW to a first-place finish.

A highlight of his tournament was at the Pembroke School ground in Kensington against Western Australia, whose opening bowler was the towering future Australian paceman Nathan Coulter-Nile.

Above: Picking the gap with a trademark punching cover-drive at Mona Park.

'Before I even saw him in the Under-19s, my father's mate had watched him in Queensland. He said Phillip Hughes was going to play for a long time for Australia,' Coulter-Nile says. 'He was definitely a class above the rest of the Under-19s.'

Phillip opened the batting, lost his partner David Murphy for 40 and then Steve Smith for a duck, but set about a huge partnership with Keen, who came in just before lunch. As they walked off the field for the break, Phillip said to his partner, 'I just want to get back out there. Why do we have to stop?'

Keen says, 'Other guys would have been satisfied with however many he'd scored, but Phil would never let the bowlers off.'

As Phillip proceeded to score 167 off 208 balls, adding 195 with Keen, the bowlers were tormented, among them Coulter-Nile.

'Bowling to him showed me how hard it was to bowl to guys without any weaknesses. He cut the ball off the off stump, right where you wanted to bowl. He was the hardest batsman to bowl to, because he'd be 20 not out before you were forced to change your line to leg stump, and by then he was away.'

The innings set up NSW for their win in the tournament, and embedded Phillip in the minds of players in other teams, including future top-level teammates Matthew Wade, James Pattinson, Kane Richardson, James Faulkner, Nathan Lyon and Mitchell Marsh.

Robson was in awe of that 167. 'I remember that game clearly. It was a massive score, but for him it had become the norm. Anyone there, if you asked them who were the best players, they would have said Phil for sure. His ability to make big hundreds at that age set him apart. He was certainly confident in his ability and you could tell that deep down he had the confidence I imagine that champion players have. He was very quiet though, not up himself, very much one of the boys.'

Back in Sydney, however, things were not flowing. After the encouraging first game at Manly, he had scored few half-centuries and not one hundred. D'Costa would drop in on games to watch him, and leave thinking only of new facets to work on. Through the week, he was drilling Phillip with practice and fitness work in the gym at Wests Leagues Club at Ashfield. Phillip was working hard but not producing results.

D'Costa sometimes resorted to shock tactics. 'I'd never yell at Phil in front of anyone else, but I went over to his place and made a big show of saying, "What are you doing? Do you want to play for Australia? If you don't want to, you can go to Macksville and stop wasting my time!"'

Towards the end of the season – D'Costa reckons it was the game after that grilling – something clicked. Wests were facing Bankstown in a two-day semi-final away from home. Bankstown's attack included future NSW representatives Aaron Bird, Scott Thompson and Keen. On the first day, Hughes scored 140 and Wests were three for 300.

'That was the moment he changed,' Day says. 'He felt he belonged and could dominate first grade.'

Keen remembers the day vividly. 'Neil D'Costa had told him not to play the pull shot. He grafted his way to 100 without much flair. At 100, he loosened up with the most unbelievable shots of all time. I was saying, "Where do I bowl? Can the captain please take me off?" Generally, we just hoped we could be bowling to him on a day when he'd decided to graft. He'd make a hundred either way, but a good day for us was when he wanted to work on something in his game and get his hundred slowly.'

●

THE CONNECTIVE TISSUE OF cricket is the tales players tell about each other, and Phillip Hughes, while quiet, was already the focus of yarn-spinning on the Sydney scene. Because of how rapidly his career accelerated, he would not play a great deal of first-grade cricket in Sydney, but Hughes stories began spawning.

One story involved a club game the day after the Under-19 Championships in 2006–07. After a night out celebrating, Hughes and Day caught a 6 am flight from Adelaide to Sydney, where they were expected to play a first-grade game the same day against Campbelltown at Raby Oval, on the city's south-west fringe. Day's parents drove the weary boys to the ground, where they discovered a fast green wicket, a fierce Campbelltown attack, and a lost toss. Phillip was permitted to bat down the order, but it didn't matter: Wests were soon five for 40 and Hughes and Day were the next men in.

'We batted so badly they couldn't get us out,' Day says. 'We were nicking to slips and they'd drop us. They realised how badly we were travelling. Their opening bowler Mitchell Claydon was running in, flapping his wings at us like a bird, but we just couldn't get out. We laughed and laughed the whole time. In an hour and a half, Hughesy might have got 30, and I might have got three or four. They got stuck into us and still couldn't get us out.'

Daniel Smith tells another story about Phillip's lucky streak in club matches. 'We were playing at North Sydney on a very ordinary wicket, chasing 170. I said to him, "I'm not going to last if I bat properly out here. I'm going to swing from the hip." He did the same and we ended up putting on 140 in 12 or 13 overs. We both got out for 70 and were sitting on the sidelines feeling pretty happy with ourselves. We ended up scraping through seven or eight down, so maybe we didn't quite take ownership of it.'

Things didn't always go their way. Sydney University were a top-performing club with rising and established players such as Greg Mail and Ed Cowan, and also the redoubtable

Matthews said, 'The guy I feel sorry for is your dad. All you've cost me is eight runs, but you've cost him a hundred bucks in petrol money to get down here!'

Greg Matthews. Now at veteran age, the one-time Wests legend dismantled grade teams for the students with his unique mix of guile and chatter. Phillip didn't care about names but Matthews had a fair bit to say about the young boy's reputation as the next big thing. Phillip responded by hitting him for two fours off his first two balls. Then Matthews got him out.

Matthews walked alongside him all the way off. In a loud voice, knowing that Greg had driven down from Macksville and was watching from the fence, Matthews said, 'I don't mind, but the guy I feel sorry for is your dad. All you've cost me is eight runs, but you've cost him a hundred bucks in petrol money to get down here!'

Fruity verbal exchanges have always been part of Sydney first-grade cricket, and Phillip was often on the receiving end. Usually, though, his adversaries were not crowing over success like Matthews, but ranting in exasperation. It wasn't limited to his batting.

Day tells a story of Phillip's moment of glory as a bowler for Wests. 'He was a horrible bowler, but in that Under-15s tour to India he'd got bowler of the tournament, and he clung on to that as his bowling achievement. One day at Wests I was captain and he was nagging and nagging me all day for a bowl, and I kept saying, "You're kidding yourself, you can't bowl". We'd spent all day in the field and got a few wickets at the end. The opposition was nine wickets down and he said, "Come on, give us the last over, you've got to give me a bowl now". So I did, and his first ball got hit for four. His second nearly bounced twice but the bloke missed it and it bowled him. The batsman's language, swearing at Phil all the way off the field, made it even funnier.'

When it came to sledging, Phillip was a non-participant. On a NSW Under-17 trip to Hobart, at the light-hearted end-of-match fines meetings, nobody could think of anything to fine him for. In the end, they invented the 'Church Mouse' fine for him, and he had to pay $2 for not saying a word all day.

Many would attribute his silence on the field to his kind nature, but others think that Hughes simply accepted that he was no good at sledging, which often requires a quick verbal wit. At the end of his first season at Wests, he represented the Australian Under-19 team in five matches against Pakistan Under-19s in Brisbane and Caloundra. His captain was Keen, and his teammates included Day, Coulter-Nile, Robson and Hill. The Pakistan captain was future Test opener Ahmed Shehzad, and an enthusiastic talker. He gave a serve to most Australian players, whether he was batting or in the field. In one of the games, Pakistan lost three early

wickets. Shehzad was at the other end, and Phillip finally lost patience. Having held his silence, he walked up to Shehzad and said, 'It's all on your shoulders now, come on, let's see how good you are!'

Shehzad gave the small boy a contemptuous glare and said, 'Lucky I have big shoulders.'

Unable to think of a comeback, Phillip retreated. He'd proved to himself why he didn't sledge. His approach was, "I don't need to say anything because I'll do it with the bat". And he did.'

That Australia–Pakistan tournament was another watershed, showing how far ahead of his contemporaries Phillip was. The bowlers included whippy left-armers Mohammad Amir and Junaid Khan, both soon destined for the Pakistani Test team, bracingly fast and possibly not quite under 19. Opening the innings, Phillip scored two centuries and two fifties,

Right: Opening the innings for NSW v Victoria in the Under-17s final at Bankstown Oval.

Above: Phillip at training with the captain of the NSW Under-17s, Manjot Singh.

averaging 96.75 and guiding Australia to their 3–2 win. No other batsman on either side scored a hundred.

'Amir was the same size he is now and really fast,' says Robson, 'but it was no problem for Phil. Batting with him, he was really determined but also laidback and calm. He was clearly the best player on either side.'

Keen, who was rooming with Phillip, remembers that 'playing days were always his happiest. He'd wake up with a big smile on his face, he couldn't wait to play. I'd say, "Another hundred today, braz?" He had his cheeky grin. "Yeah, braz." His attitude was, "I'm not going to boast about it, but that's what I'm going to do".'

That winter, his first out of school, he settled in at Breakfast Point and frequented the Palace Hotel with his close mates including Daniel Smith, Day and builder Lloyd Andrews, who knew him through Neil D'Costa and became a friend he would see or speak to on a daily basis. Occasionally Jason, who had followed Phillip to Western Suburbs but was living with an aunt on the North Shore, would join them and spend the night sleeping on the floor of Phillip's unit. Sometimes the boys would arrive at the Palace to find Steve Smith waiting on the doorstep, a long way from his home in Menai, saying he would like a steak and a punt but, being underage, he wasn't allowed in anywhere else.

The boys got up to boys' tricks. Annoyed by a 'No Parking' sign outside the Breakfast Creek development that had no obvious reason, Phillip and his mates swung on the sign until the cement block came out, put it in their car and swapped it for a two-hour parking sign nearby, which they had also ripped out of the pavement. The space near their home remained a two-hour zone for years. Phillip had a keen eye for fun but, being so quiet, was the least likely to get caught.

Money was always tight. The NSW rookie contract that he was offered during 2007 netted $11,000, which he supplemented with a job at Wests Leagues Club at Ashfield.

University was never an option – when his HSC results arrived, he joked to his flatmates, 'If you add all my marks up, I get nearly 100!' – but he had set himself on the course of professional cricket, which meant, at this speculative age, relative financial hardship.

His total after-tax income that year was $192 a week. Virginia would send him envelopes of banknotes from Macksville. It was a bread and water lifestyle. Typically, whenever a care package from Virginia arrived, he would shout his mates dinner, in return for the many times they bought for him.

Phillip remained extremely quiet and polite among strangers. Wests Leagues Club gave him a job behind the bar, but he was too timid. He was moved down to the cellar, managing deliveries, which he enjoyed, fitting in shifts around his training and playing commitments.

He was away a lot that winter, with a stint at the Centre of Excellence in Brisbane (the Australian Cricket Academy had moved from Adelaide and been renamed in 2004),

He established close bonds with fellow cricketers he regarded as 'genuine people'. 'He didn't like people he thought were fake.' He made no discrimination based on anyone's background, but took them as he found them. This won him friends who might have seemed unlikely at first

bracketed by a tournament against emerging players' teams from India, South Africa and New Zealand in July and a two-week tour to Chennai, India, in August. He scored consistently rather than heavily until the last match in Chennai, where he made 107 against a Tamil Nadu adult team and added 170 for the first wicket with one of his new friends, Ed Cowan.

Hughes's longest-standing mates say that he kept a dividing line between them and the friends he picked up through cricket. He played so much, he came into the lives of hundreds of cricketers through the years, and not all could be his best mate.

D'Costa says, 'In a lot of those junior teams, he didn't talk much, and the rest of the time he was batting. No-one knew Bradman because he was always batting. Before he was eighteen, Phil would go to the game, score runs, and go home to bed. His teammates loved him because he was winning games for them and then being so modest he wasn't walking around telling everyone how good he was.'

But he also had a powerful gift for making friends, and as Day says, he established close bonds with fellow cricketers he regarded as 'genuine people'. 'He didn't like people he thought were fake.'

He made no discrimination based on anyone's background, but took them as he found them. This won him friends who might have seemed unlikely at first. Matthew Wade, the

Victorian wicketkeeper, had antagonised the NSW players during under-age championships, and Day says he was always 'butting heads' with Wade. But at the Centre of Excellence, Wade and Hughes became friends for life.

'We hit it off straightaway,' Wade remembers. 'We had similar builds, so we were put in drills together. He said he flogged me. When we had to go for a run, he was the first to get his shirt off. He was pretty happy with his rig! We also worked on wicketkeeping together, but I never got the vibe that he wanted to do it at the next level. Everyone knew he was going to be an outstanding batter, and that was what he was focused on.'

As he rose in the cricket world, Phillip attracted sponsors. The Callen Cricket sponsorship had been superseded by Sommers, Kookaburra and Adidas, and Wade laughs at the memory of going into Phillip's room later in their careers. 'It was all lined up: pairs of shoes, pairs of cricket spikes, more bats than you could poke a stick at. And it had to be just the way he wanted it. He was really fussy about his gear. When you went near it, he'd say: "Don't touch that!" I saw that as an invitation and used to take the mickey out of him by moving his gear around or touching his bats. He hated it!' His roommates while at the Centre of Excellence were West Australian wicketkeeper Luke Ronchi and Victorian batsman Aaron Finch. 'I'd heard about this 18-year-old superstar,' Finch says, 'but being Victorian, I was sceptical. When I arrived at the apartment we were living in, he'd taken the biggest room and had hung all his things in the wardrobe. He had this massive beaming smile and said, "G'day, I'm Phil, I got here an hour before you, so I've taken the big room". He had so much charm you had to let him get away with it. From that moment, we got on like a house on fire.'

Another example of his gift for friendship was Ed Cowan. By background and personality, Cowan might as well have come from a different planet. An old boy of the privileged Cranbrook School in Sydney's east and a protégé of the

'He had this massive beaming smile and said, "G'day, I'm Phil, I got here an hour before you, so I've taken the big room". He had so much charm you had to let him get away with it'
– AARON FINCH

'His hours and hours of practice gave him a fearless personal belief. Playing against him, you felt that … I thought I was half a chance with his slog sweep. History shows I wasn't!' – BEAU CASSON

English cricketer, writer and broadcaster Peter Roebuck, Cowan was a polished, educated, literate individual seven years Hughes's senior. But they recognised something of each other's quiet determination and history of being underestimated, small left-handed openers who were anything but replicas of Matthew Hayden. Their friendship would grow strong near the end of Phillip's life, but when they first met at the Academy, they clicked via their work ethic.

Cowan 'found him very quiet but comfortable. He wasn't cocky, just comfortable with how he batted. I fed endless balls to him at the Academy. I didn't understand how he hit some of the shots he hit, but he was comfortable in how he played.'

Cowan soon saw that there was more to him than met the eye. 'He was a little person but even at the Academy he squatted huge weights. He was a strong bugger, and he was fit, and he wanted success. He snuck under people's guards because of his laidback attitude, but he wanted to be the best.'

The 2007 tour to India, Cowan says, was 'my first understanding of his hunger to score runs. A lot of kids are talented, but he had a mind for it. It was hot but not stupidly hot, you-couldn't-step-outside hot. But it was testing, and he made this absolutely beautiful hundred. It was so enjoyable seeing someone really special coming through.'

Wade still marvels at the Chennai century. 'I'd never seen a player play some of the shots he played.'

But by leading the AIS team to a win in the match, Phillip had created a problem. Based on the results achieved by previous intakes, the young Australians would not have been expected to make the final of the tournament, so Cricket Australia had booked their flight home between the semifinal and the final. But this year was a particularly strong one. Due largely to the 170-run stand between Phillip and Cowan, they had made the final against Mumbai, but were scheduled to fly out first. A meeting was held and, says Wade, 'We were out of there. But we had to forfeit the final.'

At that stage the Centre of Excellence was very much a finishing school for first-class players, so Phillip, who had only played grade and underage cricket, had been taken in for his potential rather than his experience. It was growing clear that even though he had only made one Sydney first-grade century, he was in the NSW selectors' sights. He only had to produce runs to get his chance.

The 2007–08 summer would be one of changing landscapes in Australian cricket. Shane Warne, Justin Langer, Damien Martyn and Glenn McGrath had retired from the Test team the previous summer, and Adam Gilchrist was soon to follow. The effects would ripple through state cricket. While promoting new candidates into their Test places, a concerned hierarchy was keen to search for the next generation of Test batsmen to follow the experienced incumbents such as Ricky Ponting, Hayden, Mike Hussey and Simon Katich. Rising batsmen were at a premium, most of all if they were young.

Phillip started the season with a flurry of runs that saw him promoted to the level immediately below Sheffield Shield. His 221 runs in six innings helped the Sydney Central team to the final of the State League Cup, a combined-club tournament where he played alongside Daniel Smith and Day, among others, and first came into competitive contact with many future teammates and friends including Peter Forrest, David Warner, Steve O'Keefe, Tom Cooper, Ben Rohrer, Trent Copeland and Beau Casson.

Casson, the left-arm wrist-spinner who would, within months, be the Australian selectors' choice to fill the gap left by Shane Warne, has a strong memory of bowling to Phillip in the State League Cup and offers an insight into a left-arm wrist-spinner's dilemma. Spinning the ball away from the left-hander with his stock ball, Casson worried that he might be feeding the Hughes cut shot.

'His hours and hours of practice gave him a fearless personal belief. Playing against him, you felt that. I tried to bowl straighter and make him play against the spin. I thought I was half a chance with his slog sweep. History shows I wasn't! If I erred to leg, he hit me. I'd float one up and think, "That's not a bad ball", but he'd hit it over mid-wicket with that slog sweep. But if I went wider, it was his bread and butter.

'He cut me a lot. Because of his height, the ball didn't have to be that short for him to cut you. He brought back the back cut. He just tapped it on the head rather than hit it hard. I tried to cramp him up, but I didn't have the pace. He was so quick on his feet, my margin for error was small. He gave himself room to hit through the off-side, even when we'd packed the field. That made me question what I was doing, and when he's got me at that point he's won half the battle.'

131

'That's the difference between the great players and the rest of us – they know things without needing to think. He knew his game from an early age, a thing you don't usually see until players are in their late twenties' – BEN ROHRER

Casson was one of an increasing band of frustrated first-class and Test bowlers. Soon they included the touring Sri Lankans, against whom Hughes made 49 for a Cricket Australia Chairman's XI in Adelaide, before being stumped off the world record holder Muttiah Muralitharan.

The match that announced his readiness for first-class cricket came a few days later, against a Victorian Second XI attack that included past and future Australian representatives Mick Lewis, Clint McKay and Michael Beer. Aaron Finch, who had remained close with Phillip since the Centre of Excellence, was telling his teammates in the Victorian Second XI, 'Watch out, this kid's a genius.' On a soft, difficult wicket at Hurstville Oval in Sydney's south, Hughes stood vigil for 51 in more than three hours in the first innings – seventh man out in a total of 182 – before hitting a more aggressive 137 in the second. The Victorians were more than a match for Steve Smith, who made a pair down the order. 'They didn't believe me after the first innings,' Finch says, 'but they did after the second.'

'It was an interesting game,' says Rohrer, who was seeing Hughes bat at length for the first time.

Right-arm Victorian quick Cameron Huckett was no-balled out of the game in his first over for bowling two beamers at Hughes. That was an accident, but the frustration from the experienced Victorians was intriguing.

'The funniest part was watching opposition teams trying to counter his cutting,' Rohrer says. 'They'd put in a couple of points and a gully and he found his way through there. They'd drop men back and he'd get it past them to the fence. He rarely hit the point fielder. He had an uncanny knack of knowing where they were and where they weren't. He had something subconsciously where he just knew. That's the difference between the great players and the rest of us – they know things without needing to think. He knew his game from an early age, a thing you don't usually see until players are in their late twenties.'

Steve O'Keefe saw him bat and thought, 'He's ready to go. I hadn't seen anything like that.'

Those two innings, Daniel Smith recalls, were 'the first time people sat up and thought this

Phillip receives his baggy blue cap from ex-Test opener John Dyson, ahead of his NSW debut on 20 November 2007.

kid could play. To be a young punk against a team whose bowlers played for Australia, and Second XI cricket at that time was very strong, showed he was a first-class player.'

The NSW Sheffield Shield side had a new coach looking for new talent. Matthew Mott, a former Victorian and Queensland Shield batsman, had been assistant for two years to Trevor Bayliss, who in 2007 accepted an offer to coach Sri Lanka. Seeking information on Phillip Hughes, Mott spoke to Daniel Smith, whom he rated a very good judge of a cricketer.

Mott asked, 'What do you know about this kid?'

'He knows how to score runs,' Smith said. 'He might not look orthodox, but he knows how.'

'What about the next level?'

'If Second XI runs mean anything, he'll be right.'

The state team had already played three Sheffield Shield games. With Phil Jaques opening the batting in the Australian Test team, NSW had been using Grant Lambert, the Fairfield all-rounder, as a makeshift top-order partner for Cowan.

Phillip knew, through Daniel Smith, that he was in the running. His main rival, as he saw it, was his old sparring partner, Usman Khawaja. Who would the state choose?

The complicating factor for Khawaja was that he was finishing a tertiary degree in aviation and had his end-of-year exams coming up. Hughes knew that Khawaja sometimes took time off from cricket to study.

He called Khawaja and said quietly, 'Are you playing this week?'

Khawaja said no: he had exams.

The path was clear. Education had come to Phillip's rescue.

'From there,' says Daniel Smith, 'it went a million miles an hour for him.'

> 'He knows how to score runs,' Smith said. 'He might not look orthodox, but he knows how'

TEN

A LEAGUE OF HIS OWN

The night Phillip Hughes was selected for NSW, he celebrated in the Palace Hotel with Matt Day and the locals who had adopted him as their favourite son.

HE RECEIVED A TEXT message from Simon Katich, the Test batsman who had been brought to Sydney from Western Australia and installed as state captain when he did not make the Australian team.

'Congratulations mate, looking forward to it, can't wait to play with you.'

Meanwhile, Neil D'Costa, while thrilled for Phillip and his family, harboured some quiet doubts about the upcoming Shield match. Was Phillip ready? He was still a month from his nineteenth birthday and had struggled for runs until the end of the previous first-grade season. His Centre of Excellence winter stint had done him good, but the step up to Sheffield Shield cricket, intense competition with the best adult players in the country, had undone more talented young cricketers than could be counted.

'I didn't think he was ready when he was eighteen,' D'Costa admits. 'I thought he might go well at the start but then they'd work him out and he'd be stuck.'

For Phillip, D'Costa had stepped into the gap left by not living with Greg. Like a father, the coach was nervous when he went to the SCG on 20 November 2007.

Greg, Virginia and Megan Hughes drove down from Macksville, Megan taking some days off school, and Jason was at the game too.

'We drove down all the time, with Mum and Dad in the front and me in the back,' Megan says. 'I loved that atmosphere when he played state cricket. He was so happy being in that NSW team . . . We were all so proud of him. The whole family shared his joy.'

Katich won the toss and decided to bat, which meant Phillip would be in the game immediately, opening with Cowan against Tasmania's Ben Hilfenhaus and Brett Geeves, both future Australian representatives. In the SCG home changing room, coach Matthew Mott was confident in Phillip.

'It's funny, my first impression had been how small he was. From what people had said about his batting, I'd had this picture of a big, strong, power hitter, but he looked like a little left-handed battler. But in the way he prepared, he showed this steely resolve and he just wanted to score runs.'

Another, smaller thing impressed Mott upon their first meeting. 'He had great manners. He looked you in the eye, shook your hand firmly.'

Katich had only seen Phillip play once, in a recent club match, in which Randwick–Petersham's right-arm paceman Burt Cockley had troubled him with awkward short-pitched bowling into his ribs. But when Phillip came into the Sheffield Shield group, Katich says, 'He was a happy-go-lucky young bloke. You can see young guys that get really overwhelmed with coming up to that level and it is all about how they perform, but that was never an issue with him.'

Phillip's shy cheerfulness was needed during the baggy blue cap presentation, made by former NSW Test opener John Dyson beside the SCG nets. Throughout a stirring speech about what it meant to play for NSW, Dyson was steadily looking Ed Cowan in the eye. Finally, Dyson stepped forward to present the cap – to Cowan, who said, 'Actually, it's this bloke'. Phillip, who had been hiding behind someone taller, emerged, amid great laughter, with a bashful grin to accept his cap.

This was the SCG, the home ground of Trumper and Bradman, Simpson and Walters, the Waugh brothers and Clarke; the Test arena where Neil Harvey, Greg Chappell and Ricky Ponting had produced their very best for Australia. For the 18-year-old Phillip Hughes, it was simply a place to go out and do his business. He felt at home. When he arrived at the wicket he greeted a familiar face: Darren Goodger, a north-coast umpire who was also making his Sheffield Shield debut. Goodger had umpired Phillip through

Right: Phillip and his mum. Greg and Virginia were often in the SCG Members Pavillion for Phillip's first season as a NSW Blue.

the ranks and says, 'He always knew you, always. He had an unselfconscious ease in recognising all and sundry. That was the country boy in him: it never worried him saying g'day to a fat umpire. He was raised by a gentleman to be a gentleman.' Goodger remembers it as a special day 'because people came down to see Phil on debut and got the bonus of seeing me!'

The first overs were uneasy. Phillip faced a maiden from Geeves before Cowan, on two, fell to Hilfenhaus. Phillip was then joined by Peter Forrest, a stylish 22-year-old right-hander from the Hawkesbury club north of Sydney. Forrest was playing his fifth first-class match. He had observed Phillip's batting in club and Second XI cricket, but felt that 'he played low-percentage cricket. You felt he couldn't keep playing like that without nicking off. But everyone was talking about him, they had such big raps on him. I didn't know whether to enjoy it or to see him as an upstart who might take my spot.'

Cricket is an unusual game, being a series of individual battles within the context of a team sport. It is not unusual for teammates to be competitive with each other and sometimes jealous of each other's success, fearing what it will mean for themselves. Cricketers must all deal with this cross-purpose in their own way, and Phillip was seeing this as he rose through the ranks. He and Usman Khawaja had always engaged in friendly competitive banter, partially testing themselves against each other even when in the same team.

Forrest, that day in November 2007, fell in love with Phillip as a teammate. 'I was in really good nick and felt comfortable,' Forrest says. 'In that first innings, he played a lot differently from what I'd seen. He let a lot of balls go. Every now and then he'd play an unbelievable cover-drive. He was a solid, typical opening batsman.'

What Forrest soon enjoyed was the bowlers' inability to work his partner out. 'They thought he'd get himself out, but they didn't realise just how strong he was outside off-stump and how he backed himself.'

Trumper. Bradman. Morris. Walters. Waugh. Clarke … Hughes. Phillip's place in the SCG dressing rooms found him walking in the footsteps of NSW's greatest ever batsmen.

'He looked sensational. He hadn't changed anything. We'd been preparing for that day the whole time. He was mentally clear, ready to play' – NEIL D'COSTA

Before long, Forrest was 'standing at the other end thinking, "You're too good for this." He was so strong in the areas where bowlers were told to bowl'.

Phillip and Forrest batted out the first session. From the changing room, Katich saw that the wicket was spinning early and that right-arm off-spinner Jason Krejza, soon to make his Test debut, turning the ball sharply away, had two slips to the left-handed Phillip.

'He played it like he'd been playing them for five years,' Katich recalls. 'There were no nerves, he played proper shots. Hilfy was in a good patch, but Hughesy made him look like a medium-pacer.'

Hilfenhaus was a bowler Phillip admired greatly, and he later told Matt Day that the highlight of his game was making runs against Hilfy. The other opening

bowler, Geeves, remembers, 'He was only 18 and we just assumed we would get him out at some stage. He played incorrect cricket, I guess: anything on the stumps he cut the hell out of, and anything straight he stodged around.'

D'Costa, watching emotionally, saw the innings differently. His reservations about Phillip's readiness for this level began to fall away, although he knew that greater challenges were yet to come. On this day, however, D'Costa says, 'He looked sensational. He hadn't changed anything. We'd been preparing for that day the whole time. He was mentally clear, ready to play.'

At lunch, Phillip came in unbeaten on 34.

'I think he couldn't believe where he was at,' D'Costa says. 'It had been so easy. He looked like he'd played a hundred first-class games. He'd let go, let go, let go, hit a four – beautiful!'

After the break, Phillip accelerated, moving to 51 and taking the partnership with Forrest to 112. Then Krejza bowled a long-hop and Phillip's eyes lit up.

'It was one of those balls he could do anything with,' says Forrest, 'and he got it horribly wrong.'

His cut shot slewed to backward point, where Geeves held the catch.

When Phillip came off, he was devastated at getting out when he was set.

Coach Mott observed his reaction approvingly. 'In your first game, your first thought is just not getting a duck,' Mott says. 'When he got out for 51, he had this pure disappointment, he was not happy. Some players pretend to be disappointed when they've made 50, but he was genuinely upset.'

Forrest went on to 177, a maiden century, Brad Haddin added 100 and Katich declared on the second day at seven for 512. Tasmania struggled to nine for 214 before Phillip enjoyed his first fielding landmark. Beau Casson was bowling to the Tasmanian tail-ender Brendan Drew.

'I'd like to say it was a lovely delivery,' Casson says, 'but it wasn't. Drew swept it quite hard to deep backward square leg.'

Nobody, including the bowler and the batsman, saw Phillip fielding in the deep. Phillip, always the butt of jokes over his height, emerged from 'below grass height', his teammates said, before taking the catch.

'The boys had a joke that he popped up out of the ground,' Casson says. 'He had this ability to wait right till the end and catch the ball just before it hit the ground. It was quite funny. I didn't know he was out there. Happy days!'

NSW won the match by an innings, and Phillip was hooked on Sheffield Shield cricket. High quality, combative and yet friendly, without the scrutiny of close-up television coverage, in an atmosphere of hard-edged mateship on both sides, it was made for him and he for it.

Mott was right, however; the one person who was not impressed by his first half-century was Phillip himself. He went back to the Activate Cricket Centre and said to his friend Ash Squire, 'These guys are too good for me. I have to work harder.'

Over the next two months, he made a seamless transition into interstate cricket, bringing the extraordinary run-scoring consistency of his junior years straight into the first-class game. It was incredible, and yet he had promised that he was ready for this. Now everyone believed him.

He played four Sheffield Shield games by mid-January, making half-centuries in all four. He also scored 68 in his one-day domestic debut in the 50-over Ford Ranger Cup against Victoria at the Melbourne Cricket Ground, and was selected in invitation teams playing one-dayers against the touring New Zealanders and Sri Lankans, gaining a taste of international adult cricket.

His impact on the NSW Sheffield Shield campaign was immediate. His second match put him squarely into the kiln of hard first-class cricket. NSW batted first, and he was out for a duck. Victoria's first innings ended with an altercation over a catch taken by Katich off the 34-year-old Victorian fast bowler Shane Harwood. When he came off and changed into his bowling gear, Harwood was steaming.

Matthew Wade, who was keeping wicket for Victoria, remembers: 'Hughesy had to open the batting against a very angry man, who was a big guy and bowling very well. Harwood hit him in the helmet and the ribs, but then Hughesy started smacking him everywhere. The faster Harwood bowled, the harder he hit him.'

He made another 51, in a partnership of 101 with Greg Mail, to see NSW out of trouble.

The grown men were coming at Phillip Hughes. These weren't north coast A-graders, but the most hardened professional cricketers in the country. In his third match, against Queensland on a juicy Gabba pitch, Phillip batted in the middle-order after the selectors preferred Phil

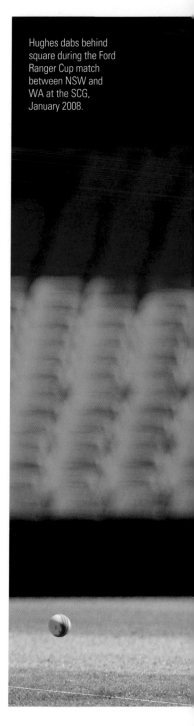

Hughes dabs behind square during the Ford Ranger Cup match between NSW and WA at the SCG, January 2008.

Jaques and Mail as openers. Coming in at four for 124, he batted with Katich and, for the first time in state cricket, his good mate Daniel Smith.

'You'd turn around and there was [Jimmy] Maher, [Shane] Watson, [Chris] Hartley, [Michael] Kasprowicz – I was in awe of what these guys had done in the game,' Smith says. 'For a young kid from the country to walk out onto a spicy wicket and get 50 or 60, it didn't surprise me, but he batted like he didn't have a worry in the world.'

'He didn't play reputations or lie down for big egos,' says Matthew Mott.

Out in the middle, the running commentary from the slips cordon and others in the field was incessant and belittling.

'The Queenslanders got stuck into him to find out if he had what it takes,' recalls Smith. 'He'd just smile and I took it upon myself to stand up for my mate. The little guy always gets picked on. I don't think it was personal. The Australian way, the NSW way, was to stick up for each other; it's two against eleven out there.'

At stumps, they had both been dismissed: Phillip for 53 and Smith for 42.

'He got out before me and I had a crack at him at the end of the day thinking we were going

The grown men were coming at Phillip Hughes. These weren't north coast A-graders, but the most hardened professional cricketers in the country

to get big scores,' Smith says. 'But I got out not long after him.'

By the end of January, Phillip, flying high, had helped NSW to the top of the Shield ladder. Expecting to hold his place for the remainder of the season, he was resistant when Cricket Australia asked him to join the Australian team for the Under-19 World Cup in Malaysia.

'He was disappointed at having to miss Shield games and potentially giving his spot to someone else,' says Day. 'Also, he'd been captain in his last year of NSW Under-17s and Under-19s, and he was quite disappointed that he wasn't captain in the Under-19 World Cup.'

The tournament was not a good one for Australia who, despite having players the calibre of Phillip, Steve Smith, Josh Hazlewood, James Faulkner and James Pattinson, failed to make the semifinals. Playing as a batsman-wicket-keeper, Phillip's highest score in four matches was 46.

Having kept wicket through his junior career, Phillip was less keen to practise now, giving almost all of his skills-training time to batting. Daniel Smith, himself a keeper, says that Phillip 'had ability, and being three-foot-one always helped. He had nice hands and a good understanding of it. But he didn't really love it. Cricket was about batting'.

Phillip was back with the rest of the NSW team on his return to the Sheffield Shield, where he resumed his astonishing consistency with 73 and 58 not out against Tasmania in Hobart and 35 against South Australia in Sydney. NSW would host Victoria in the Sheffield Shield final a week later. Even though all of their Test stars were back, including Michael Clarke, Brett Lee, Stuart MacGill and Stuart Clark, Phillip retained his place at the top of the order with Jaques.

The match was a showcase for Katich (86 and 82), Lee (five wickets and a vital second-innings 97), Casson (89 and four wickets to bring the match home), and Victoria's Peter Siddle, who took five for 66 and four for 101. In a high-quality, tense affair, the star performers were present and future Australian Test players; but only one batsman from either side made a century. Phillip was out for six in the first innings, caught by David Hussey off Siddle, and the match was on an edge, NSW leading by 65, when he started his second innings.

Phillip would start it in pain, having sprained his ankle earlier in the match. 'It was very tender, and at night he was having physio treatment,' Greg Hughes recalls. 'We didn't know if he'd be able to get back out there, but he was so determined to help the team out.'

Over the next four hours, with Jaques and Katich playing second fiddle, Phillip took the game out of Victoria's reach. It was a vital moment, Katich recalls. 'The SCG gets flatter as the match gets on and . . . we had a bit of work to do.'

The Victorians, having dismissed Phillip cheaply on day one, were flummoxed and eventually frustrated. David Hussey remembers that 'the whole of Australia's cricketing world was watching and waiting for a big performance from him. We had all these plans in place for him in the second innings, and he just seemed to find a way of getting out of trouble. We thought early on that he didn't move his feet very well, so we were going to bowl really full and try to get him to drive on the off with the ball shaping away from him to bring the slips into play.

> **'Bowling to him was a battle. He played spin with real aggression and wanted to dominate. It was on from the first ball'**
> **– BRYCE McGAIN**

'That worked ever so well in the first innings, but he raced to about 30 from 15 balls in the second innings and it was, "Oh no, he's off to a flier". Then we started the leg-stump line, like the old Bodyline theory with six on the leg side, but he found a way to get the ball really fine. So we put in a really fine fine leg and then he pulled one past square leg with the full face of the bat and we were like, "How are we going to get this guy out now?"'

They turned to spin, through the leg-spinner Bryce McGain, who was bowling well enough to bring himself a Test debut at age 36 a year later.

'We'd keep hearing about some young kid,' McGain says, 'and as you usually do, you just plan to bounce the crap out of him and get him out, but it wasn't that easy when it came to the Shield final. What struck us was that he was in for the fight, and don't worry, we gave him absolutely everything. He copped it and we were going hard at him because we wanted to get into the middle order, but he batted really, really well. He was so impressive.

'Bowling to him was a battle. He played spin with real aggression and wanted to dominate. It was on from the first ball, he was liable just to run down and belt you over your head. He didn't seem concerned with the consequences of the way he played, he always wanted to be on top. He slog-swept me, but he was pretty patient. He wasn't just flaying the ball around, which we found out later that he could do. He was pretty patient, did what was required, played to the conditions and put away the bad ball.'

Watching Phillip deal with McGain, Katich was lost in admiration. 'All lefties have challenges facing spin at the SCG, where you've got rough and orthos firing it in there, or a leggie. Bryce is a very good bowler, and he was coming around the wicket into the rough. It was spinning, but Hughesy treated it as another little challenge. He played him beautifully, he wasn't afraid to go down the wicket and hit it over their head or slog-sweep them, or hit out of the rough through cover, which was one of the hardest shots you can play as a leftie. None of it worried him at all.'

After Phillip hit McGain out of the attack, the Victorians returned to pace and gave him, Hussey says, 'a bouncer barrage' as he got close to his century.

'He cut us for fun into the stands as well. It was a case of us executing our skills poorly or him keeping a step ahead of us and playing better. We tried to get into his head but nothing ever fazed him. Maybe he was like a duck on a pond paddling madly away under water, but on the surface he stayed very calm. With that cheeky grin, he seemed in complete control, which was all the more frustrating as an opposition player.'

Pay television was broadcasting the final, and in his office at Macquarie Bank, Matt Day could see his mate getting close to a century. 'When he was on 90, I sneaked out of work

two hours early to get to the ground.' He got there just in time.

Phillip's celebration when he passed 100 is, Katich says, 'still talked about to this day'.

Jaques says Phillip 'nearly leapt into orbit. I haven't seen such passion from anyone on making a hundred in my career. He was so pumped, he loved playing for NSW.'

Katich, who was at the other end, recalls, 'It was great to be there. He went crazy, and it was fantastic to see that sheer joy and excitement because it was that exciting for him. I don't think I have seen a celebration as excited as Hughesy's that day, not in my whole career, and I have seen some pretty good ones.

'Growing up, I saw Michael Slater at Lord's and plenty in between, but in terms of excitement and sheer jubilation, probably none better. He ran down the wicket, massive big punch and jumped in the air and just kept running. The boys thought he was going to run into the crowd like Pat Cash at Wimbledon . . . Eventually when he came back we had a big hug.'

Even one Victorian was cheering for him. Wade, who had been dropped as wicketkeeper for Adam Crosthwaite for the final, watched on television. 'I was supporting Victoria but was really happy he had done what he'd done. Everybody else was seeing what we already knew.'

With Katich, Clarke, Casson and Lee making half-centuries, NSW were able to declare more than 600 runs ahead. The game was safe, though Phillip was not finished. Victoria's champion batsman, Brad Hodge, came in at number three to face MacGill. He cracked his first ball to mid-wicket, where Phillip was positioned.

'It was a brilliant catch,' Katich says. 'It bounced out of his hands and he spun around and got it on the second grab.'

The post-match celebrations, after Casson spun out the last four wickets, were for the team achievement, but there was a special focus

Phillip goes 'into orbit' becoming the youngest player to reach a century in a Sheffield Shield final, at the SCG, March 2008.

NSW	7 / 531	SpeedBlitz Blues (2nd Inns)		R	BF	FOW
Vic TRAIL BY	596	Jaques	lbw b McGain	23	69	75
Bracken	0	Hughes	c McGain b White	116	175	220
Lee	82	Katich (c)	run out (McDonald)	92	177	302
Extras	40	Clarke	cw Crosthwaite b Siddle	64	77	320
OVER 75(155)	REM 31	Haddin (+)	b Siddle	4	3	324
Vic -1st	216	Thornely	b Siddle	21	41	355
NSW -1st	281	Casson	b McGain	89	202	531
McGain	2/98(35)	Clark				
. wk		MacGill				
OVER RATE	+7	Cameron (12th)	NSW 281 Vic 216			

'I don't think I have seen
a celebration as excited
as Hughesy's that day,
not in my whole career'
– SIMON KATICH

on the teenager who had finished his first Shield season with 559 runs at 62.11.

'Any time a kid of that age makes a hundred in a Shield final you know he is special,' Katich says. 'He was the youngest to do it, I think. Whenever someone does something like that you know natural progression will lead to higher honours. Experience with their raw talent will get them there.'

David Hussey was among the Victorians who visited the NSW rooms, and went about getting to know Phillip a bit better. Hussey was drinking with Katich, telling him, 'Everyone thinks this kid is going to be a hundred-Test player, and if he keeps playing this way, look out, world.'

Phillip joined them.

'Congratulations,' Hussey said, 'and make sure you never forget how you played and when you do start playing Test cricket remember how you scored these runs.'

Megan Hughes remembers, 'After the crowd went home, he walked down the SCG steps from the dressing rooms and waved to us and called us over. We always waited for when he was free and we were about to go home, but he said, "Come! Come in!" That was the first time we got to meet his new peers and to soak up that he was really doing this. That was the time I remember thinking, "My brother is going to make something out of this".'

Casson's parents were also inside, and he says he will 'never forget our parents sharing that experience. I remember Phil sitting there with the NSW flag around him and a massive smile on his face. The only ones in our team who hadn't played for Australia were Phil, me and Dom Thornely, and part of me wanted to have my autograph book out.'

Casson would be playing for Australia within a month, on the Test tour to the West Indies. Phillip would only have to wait another year.

●

JASON HUGHES HAD MOVED permanently to Sydney, registered with the Western Suburbs club and started working for a credit union. He and Phillip moved into another unit in Mortlake,

the suburb adjoining Breakfast Point, behind the Palace Hotel, and maintained their little colony with Day, Daniel Smith, Andrews, Gosh Daher (known in rugby league as 'the Phantom Siren') and Wests players including Phillips, Ash Squire, Manjot Singh and, when he was not on tour, Michael Clarke.

Phillip had turned his circle of friends into a surrogate family, filling the space left by the absence of his parents. 'He always wanted to instil "home" wherever he was,' Squire says. 'He'd regularly come to stay at my place when I was living with my parents. My dad, Ross, was cooking. Phil loved that. I'd go to bed and he'd sit up late talking with Dad.'

'He was always calling us,' Andrews says. 'It was our little mixed family: we'd take the piss out of each other, just like family members, and always look out for each other.'

Sometimes when he was playing at the SCG, they would go to watch after a flurry of texts. 'How much is he on?' 'He's going to make a hundred!'

Phillip enjoyed female company as much as any of his mates. Nino Ramunno remembers a surprise twenty-first birthday party for his cousin in late 2009 at Hurricanes, a restaurant in Bondi. Needing to think of a pretext to invite Phillip, Nino tried unsuccessfully for two days. Phillip didn't want to go. Then Nino said there would be lots of girls.

'Zoom!' Nino laughs. 'He was there straightaway.'

●

IN AUGUST 2008, PHILLIP was off to India for an Australia A tour comprising two first-class and five one-day matches. Having been there twice, he was growing more comfortable in India, but he had a disappointing return of 48 runs in three first-class innings. He did somewhat better in the one-dayers, averaging 50.66 with a highest score of 49 not out. Katich, his captain, says Phillip 'got knocked over by quicks bringing the ball back in to him, but that was just an experience thing'.

Opponents still took notice of him, however. Among them was Virat Kohli, the young Indian star who had played against Phillip in the Under-15s and Under-19s but first got to know him off the field during the 2008 A tour.

'Straightaway I found out he was one of those mischievous, chirpy type of lads,' Kohli says, 'and he would want to talk to people he admired or liked their game and that is when we had a bit of conversation about the bats and where the bats are made and all that sort of stuff. That was my first proper interaction with him.'

Phillip's own teammates from other states were getting to know him better as well. David Hussey remembers that Phillip 'was rooming with Shaun Tait, and he was hanging on to Shaun Tait's pocket wherever he went. We drank eight coffees a day because it was that boring, but he was very good company. He always had that wicked grin and something funny to say, and he would laugh and laugh.'

No matter what happened on the field, Hussey recalls that Phillip 'was always very consis-

tent – he would put his bat down and reflect on the innings and then get on with it, just enjoy everyone's company in the dressing room'.

As well as Tait, Phillip roomed with Brett Geeves on the tour. Since Phillip's Shield performances against Tasmania in his first year, Geeves had the utmost respect for him.

'To see an 18-year-old come in and dominate the game and to be spoken about in the same way we were talking about Simon Katich in his first year is a remarkable thing,' Geeves says.

Due to bomb threats, the team spent long days cloistered in their hotels and got to know each other better. Phillip bantered about his Italian background, calling himself a 'wog'.

'All those things that have been said about Phil are really true,' Geeves says. 'He was a simple, humble country kid and he would not have had an enemy in domestic cricket.'

If Phillip had caused ripples in his first year with NSW, in his second he made crashing waves. Still a teenager, he finished the season third in the Sheffield Shield aggregates and averages with 891 runs at 74.25. Meanwhile, Matthew Hayden struggled with his form and Phil Jaques with a chronic back injury as Australia suffered a home Test series defeat against South Africa, its first since Phillip Hughes was four years old and playing with his Tonka trucks.

On his return from India, Phillip did not immediately build momentum towards the chance of Australian selection. Adapting from the low wickets of Chennai to the early-season WACA proved beyond him, and three failures in Perth were followed by two more in the Ford Ranger Cup against Queensland and South Australia.

Neil D'Costa, having moved to India to head the Vidarbha Cricket Association's academy program, was not nearby, and Phillip prepared for the Sheffield Shield match in Adelaide under a cloud, having had a moderate Indian tour and then 24 runs in his first five innings in Australia.

South Australia made 313 on the first day, and then, on the seventh ball of the NSW innings, Phillip ran out his partner Greg Mail. He was joined by Peter Forrest.

'Facing Shaun Tait for the first time, we were pretty nervous,' Forrest remembers. 'Or I was. Hughesy might have been.'

They survived the new ball and found their flow, taking the score to 112 by the break. While Forrest was outscoring Phillip, 67 to 43, he says it was Phillip's quiet maturity that helped him shed his own nerves.

'He'd give you nothing in your chats between overs. There's guys who chew your ear off, and you can't wait to get up the other end. Not him. He didn't say much, but he had that belief that he was better than anyone he was facing. He had this steel in his eyes, an inner drive. He was *so* competitive.'

The partnership blossomed after lunch, the pair adding 134 in the afternoon session and both passing their centuries.

'He was so much fun to bat with,' Forrest says. The South Australian bowlers 'saw this tiny kid playing shots, and they got more and more angry and irritated, they didn't know where to bowl to him'.

Forrest fell that evening for 135, but Phillip batted into the next day until he was caught behind off Mark Cleary for 198. It was 'a special innings again', says Daniel Smith. NSW could not force a win in the game, but Phillip had ignited his season.

He followed up with first-class half-centuries against Victoria and the touring New Zealanders and some

Right: At a poultry show in Maitland. Phillip never missed an opportunity to drive up from Sydney for family time

Left: A day at the races with Jason. The brothers were still incredibly close.

useful runs in the Ford Ranger Cup. Five weeks after his Adelaide innings, he produced one of the greatest batting performances in the Sheffield Shield's then 116-year history, a match that is still talked about with wonder by those who played in it.

Before the NSW team flew to Hobart to play the strong Tasmanian side, the boxer Shannon Briggs, who was a friend and former rugby league teammate of Phillip's, phoned his mate Damien Wright, the long-serving Tasmanian opening bowler.

'Phil Hughes is coming down to play you guys and he's going to score a hundred for sure,' Briggs said.

Wright – who would not be playing in the game – responded, 'Not a chance in hell. We'll sledge the hell out of him and let him know what it's all about.'

Among first-class bowlers, this was a common response to the sight of a teenage opening batsman.

On the trip down, as usual Daniel Smith made an advance phone call to the team hotel.

'We'd become really close by then,' says Smith, 'and were always roommates. We rang the hotel, and if they didn't have us together we'd change the rooms. We got there and went to our room. The night before that game, he said, "I'm on tomorrow, I'm going to score some runs". I'd have loved to be a betting man, because when he said that, he almost always did.'

Throughout his career, Phillip had this uncanny knack of forecasting a big score.

Ash Squire recalls: 'The first time I really knew how good he was, the day before a first-grade game against North Sydney, I fed him balls for a long time and I'd never seen anyone hit the ball so badly. He said, "I'm going to make a hundred tomorrow." He went out and got 112. He had this amazing mental strength.'

Wary players wandered out to the Bellerive Oval wicket to inspect it or, in this case, to see if they could find it. It was, says Smith, 'the greenest I've ever seen, even more than the Gabba'.

Ed Cowan says it 'looked like a jungle'. Usman Khawaja, who would be opening with Phillip, says 'it was so green, it looked like the outfield'. And then the NSW captain, Dom

Left: Out the back at East Street for Christmas.

Thornely, deputising for Katich and Haddin, who were in the Australian Test team, lost the toss.

Geeves and Hilfenhaus opened the bowling. By lunch, NSW had lost Khawaja, Forrest, Cowan and Thornely for 75. Phillip was 51 not out.

'His attack was premeditated,' says Matthew Mott. 'The boys had gone and taken a look at the wicket, and [Phillip] thought a ball would come along with his name on it, so his view was, "I'd better get them before they get me. I'm not going to get out nicking off, I'm going to take them on". He was going to live by his plan.'

Khawaja had settled on a different plan – to try to dig in and survive – but was caught behind off Geeves after an agonising, almost scoreless half-hour. He sat on the sidelines to watch. Forrest joined him a few balls later.

'We were watching Hughesy and saying, "I don't know what's going on here",' Khawaja says. 'They couldn't stop him and didn't know how to stop him. He got smashed in the helmet by Geeves, and then he slogged the next ball through mid-wicket for four. I loved his bravado.'

On the edge of the ground, Daniel Smith was 'a bit worried' about Phillip. 'The wicket had a bit of pace in it, and he was just a young kid. But after half an hour I thought, 'I'll sit back and enjoy this – and hope I don't have to go out and bat!"

It was a wondrous innings, stunning everyone who was watching, no matter what their vantage point.

Cowan, who laboured at the other end for 47 minutes before being caught behind off Gerard Denton, recalls, 'He was hitting balls from the top of middle and off stump with power for four. They didn't know where to bowl to him because he had a knack of hitting balls that others would think of as good bowling for four, backward of point, consistently smacking them off the middle of the bat. These were balls I would leave, but he thought that most of the balls go here and he could hit a fair number of them for four. They'd have two slips and two fly slips and he kept finding the gap. He put pressure on bowlers to do something differently. And he wasn't just an off-side player. I thought he had a great leg-side game. He had a good pull shot for when they bowled it up in his ribs.'

Steve Smith and Moisés Henriques came and went, and Phillip was the seventh man out, for 93, when Geeves trapped him lbw. The score was 163 and the next three wickets fell for nine.

By lunch on the second day, Tasmania were all out for 127 in the 47th over. Aside from Denton's 48 at number nine, the next highest score was 25. After lunch, NSW resumed, and so did the pattern of the match, with the bowlers bossing everyone but Phillip.

In the second innings, Khawaja made 0, Forrest 3 and Cowan 1. When Thornely was fourth man out for 0, NSW had 51 runs on the board and Phillip had scored all but four of them.

'He dominated from ball one,' Daniel Smith says. 'Brett Geeves was bowling quick. Geevesy had been around for a while and was getting all the assistance from the wicket, and a little kid is doing this to you, you're frustrated. Phil just smirked and smiled and kept swatting him to the boundary. People say Phil couldn't play the short ball, but he dominated. Unorthodox pulls, down-on-one-knee sweep-pulls. Those two innings showed us that this kid had what it took on all surfaces all around the world.'

Steve Smith helped Phillip to a century partnership. His second innings was even more remarkable than his first.

'It was an incredible day,' Cowan says. 'It wasn't just that he got them, he got them at a clip. Everyone was playing forward defences and nicking them. He'd have seen five slips and two gullies and thought, "Bugger it, I'll go for them". Conditions were irrelevant to him.'

On the Tasmanian side, there was shock, frustration, anger – and not a little admiration. Phillip's former Australian Under-15 teammate Brady Jones, who lived in Tasmania, was watching him play first-class cricket for the first time.

'In the change rooms during breaks, Geevesy was saying, "We're bowling a good length and he is putting his front foot to square leg and hitting us behind point". Half of me wanted to see him knocked over, but I enjoyed that day, he was too good.'

Geeves's frustration boiled over, and when he brought his roomie banter from India to the middle of Bellerive, Phillip responded with his bat.

'There were guys we came up against in domestic cricket that were just too good for us,' Geeves says. 'When you had the ball in the hand you knew you weren't going to get them out. Simon Katich, Matthew Elliott and Phil Hughes were [my] three guys . . . We just never looked like getting him out. Hilf is a very competitive bloke and a great bowler but we were at a loss, at an absolute loss as to how to go about bowling to him. He was just too good for us.

'That day, the wicket was green so we thought we'd get one in the right spot and it would nibble and he would inevitably nick one. But he scored all those runs and he was outstanding. In the second innings we went really hard at him – we were quite aggressive verbally, and in terms of our lines and lengths. Before we knew, we had both gone for 30-odd. We felt like we were in the game the whole time because he was getting it through the gaps and over fielders and at no stage did I think the score was racing to where it was, and we looked up after ten overs and they were 70. It was, "How did this happen?"

'He was unbelievable. Our plan was to target his body and he just found a way of cutting everything: balls that were at him on the leg stump he had the time to create room with three gullies and four slips, or he would get it over the top and you would put the man back in the hope he would spoon one and he would get it squarer. It was like catching practice

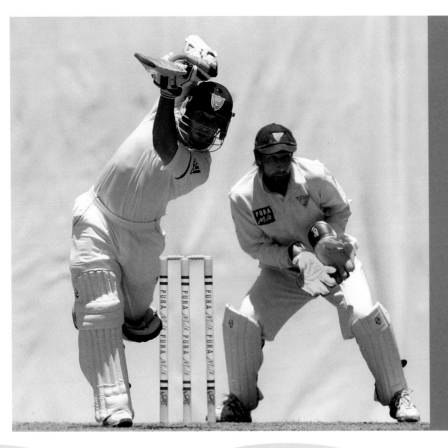

'Phil just smirked and smiled and kept swatting him to the boundary ... this kid had what it took on all surfaces all around the world'
– DANIEL SMITH

into the zones where there were no fielders! It was almost like he was mocking what we were trying to do.'

Meanwhile, Damien Wright was on the phone to a gleeful Shannon Briggs.

'He's the real deal,' Wright conceded. 'The more they sledged him, the better he got.'

Phillip later said to his cousin Nino Ramunno, 'Some of the things they were calling me! I had to look down or away because I didn't want to laugh.' Instead, he scored 108.

Phillip's contribution in his two innings, 201 runs out of his team's 345, broke a record set by Don Bradman. Chasing 221 to win, Tasmania lost five wickets for 90 but the wicket was settling by the third day, enabling Dan Marsh and Tim Paine to secure a three-wicket win. George Bailey, who scored five and eight for Tasmania, says 'the wicket was hideous ... After that game the Tasmanian batsmen spoke as a group about changing our mind-sets on that wicket. Hughesy had proved scoring runs on it was achievable if you committed to a plan.'

As a story about Phillip's chutzpah and skill, the game was instantly entering the realm of myth. At the end of the match, Geeves and Daniel Smith sat down for a beer.

Geeves admitted, 'I had no answers. Didn't matter what I did. Round the wicket, over the wicket ... He was too good.'

'You often hear about a country boy who's going to be a superstar, and they were right about him' – BEN ROHRER

Ben Rohrer, NSW Sheffield Shield player 706 to Phillip's 707, was chosen for the one-day match to follow and arrived on the last day of the first-class match. He found his teammates abuzz, saying Phillip was 'playing a different game to everyone else. Grant Lambert [who scored two and one] loved Hughesy and still tells me about that game all the time.'

Rohrer was instrumental in Phillip's next century, which came in his next Sheffield Shield game two weeks later. Batting first against South Australia at the SCG, Phillip and Greg Mail endured a torturous half-hour before Phillip again ran his senior partner out.

'I don't know if he was a good runner between wickets to start with,' Cowan says. 'He ran Maily out a few times. Phil was in the Michael Slater mould – "If it comes out of the middle, I deserve a run". To be fair, it takes time to get used to the standard of fielding in first-class cricket. Coming from where he came from, it took him a while to realise that not every good shot produces runs.'

Phillip began to find his rhythm, but Forrest missed out and Rohrer joined him at two for 46. Although he had made his debut before Phillip, Rohrer had not played much with him until then.

'I'd heard a lot of the stories before he came to Sydney. You often hear about a country boy who's going to be a superstar, and they were right about him. He played at this level and looked like that's all he should have been playing.'

Off-field, Rohrer had felt the instant bond with Phillip that so many others did. 'From when he was in the squad, he made you feel like what you had to say was the most important thing to him at that time. He was really curious about what you did outside cricket and where you came from. We'd chat about that sort of stuff. He'd talk about the farm and the cows. I don't know which was a bigger passion, that or batting.'

When Rohrer joined him in the middle in the South Australia game, he was nervous, but the little teenager reassured him from the first ball.

'He was so laidback and relaxed out there, you'd have friendly chats in the middle. He knew where he was going to score and where he was going to be targeted. He picked that up as quick as anyone I've seen, with the exception maybe of Steve Smith.'

The left-handers put on 50 in a brisk eight overs before lunch, and then another 120 before Phillip was out for 114. Rohrer notched his maiden first-class century, out soon after Phillip.

'It was a great experience to look back on,' Rohrer says. 'I played a lot through point as well, and learnt a lot from him in terms of selectiveness in shot-making. He knew which lengths and lines he could cut, and which ones he couldn't go near. He helped me drill where my

Phillip had emerged like no other batting talent since Ponting

off-stump was and knowing which ones to hit, which was amazing in that he was eight years younger and I was learning off him. That's how good he was.'

It was a matter of time before the National Selection Panel, chaired by South Australian former Test opener Andrew Hilditch, verified what was being said in Sheffield Shield cricket. Phillip had emerged like no teenage batting talent since Ponting. He might not have the textbook technique but he was making runs in all conditions, against elite bowlers, at a time when Australia was growing desperate for its next generation of top-order batsmen.

Nothing seemed beyond Phillip that summer. The Sheffield Shield went into recess after Christmas to allow a window for the then state-based Twenty20 Big Bash League. Phillip was successful straightaway in the abbreviated format, topping the aggregates and averages for NSW, his highlights an 88-run opening stand in eight overs with David Warner in Adelaide and an unbeaten 80 off 60 balls to chase down 162 runs at the Gabba. 'I sat back and let him have the strike,' Warner recalls. 'They bowled well to both of us, but to him they were feeding the cut shot. We saw a different side to Hughesy, how he could play the short-form game.'

By then, Mott was observing, 'He scored a lot of tough runs. If we had tricky chases, he'd play an uncompromising cover-drive from the first ball of the innings and it settled everyone down.'

By the time the Shield resumed, Phillip was in the Australian selectors' sights for the upcoming South African tour. Hayden had announced his retirement, and the mooted candidates to partner Katich in the Test series were Phillip and his state teammate Jaques. One of the unluckier Australian cricketers in that period, the left-hander nicknamed 'Pro' had scored three centuries in his 11 Test matches between 2005 and 2008, averaging 47.47. He would have been locked in for a prosperous international career but for an ongoing back injury that often left him unable to run, let alone bat.

The late-January Shield match between NSW and Tasmania at Newcastle No 1 Sports Ground was billed as a 'bat-off' between Phillip and Jaques. The national media had converged on Phillip for the first time, and he was lapping up the attention. He drove with Forrest from Sydney to Newcastle, and Forrest recalls that the media build-up made it 'like a showdown'.

Two nights before the match, Phillip was to stay with his father, who had driven to Newcastle from Macksville.

An excited Phillip said to Greg, 'Have you seen the papers? Ponting says they're going to go with experience in South Africa. I'm going to show the bastards!'

Jaques was also competitive, in his measured way, but was under extreme duress. 'My back was no good, so I spent a lot of time on the floor of the change room trying to get it right. To be honest, I had rushed back because I could see a really good young player who was going to be there for a long time, and I wanted to make it as hard for him as possible. That's part of being a competitor.'

The next morning Katich, back from Test duty, won the toss and decided to bat. In cricket's dual individual–team nature, Jaques and Phillip, in a contest for the Australian opening spot, went out to face the new ball together.

Ten years Phillip's senior, despite knowing what was at stake, Jaques could not help liking his confident young partner/rival.

'All the guys were excited about him coming into the team at first, and when he came in, the thing I was most impressed with is that there was no ego to him, no arrogance, just a country kid who enjoyed his cricket and loved making hundreds,' Jaques says. 'He was very respectful of the older guys in the squad and was really eager to learn and improve his game and get to where he wanted to go. He was very focused on playing for Australia and he had that aura of self-belief about him, but without arrogance, and that was refreshing for the older players.'

Whatever eventuated with the so-called 'bat-off', the first thing to ensure was that they did not run each other out.

Phillip said to Greg, 'Ponting says they're going to go with experience in South Africa, I'm going to show those bastards!'

Right: A proud-as-punch Hughes family at the Steve Waugh Medal with Phillip's Rising Star Award.

'As long as we didn't have to run between wickets we were fine,' Jaques jokes. 'We got out a few times over the years that way, he got me a few times and I got him a few times. As long as we were hitting to the boundary, we were fine.'

The wicket was good, and Jaques's attitude on the day was generous, almost paternal. 'I always talked a lot in the middle, particularly batting with the younger guys, but he was very self-assured, he knew what he was trying to do and it was just a matter of keeping him focused and not getting too excited. He always had a really good plan on how he was going to play and didn't need too much advice. I gave it out a bit, and he would nod respectfully and get on with his work.'

Geeves and Denton opened the bowling. As they chatted between overs, Jaques told Phillip to get over the top of his cut shots 'and hit them to the boundary every time they give us a bit of width'.

The contest was a non-event. Jaques and Phillip got a flying start, clubbing 23 off the first 23 balls before Jaques was bowled by Denton. Phillip, in partnerships of 116 with Forrest and 104 with Katich, made his way to a well-paced 151, surely the innings of a Test opening batsman.

'It was chalk and cheese,' says Katich, who scored 143 while Thornely made 110, setting up a big NSW win.

Phillip, having made his point in the first innings, flayed a celebratory 82 in the second. Jaques scored 12. 'Hughesy was in prime form and Jaquesy couldn't move,' Katich says. 'Hughesy was playing a different game. He just smoked them. He kept cutting the hell out of Krejza and they ended up having three or four points to stop it, so he ended up going the other way – hitting them through deep mid-wicket. He had an amazing eye, which is a huge advantage as a batsman. Throw in technique, and you have a double weapon.'

Left and right: 'As long as we didn't have to run between wickets we were fine,' Jaques jokes. His 'bat-off' with Hughes in January was a showdown to determine who would open for Australia in South Africa. Phillip's 151 left no doubt.

The Tasmanians were getting a familiar feeling. George Bailey recalls 'an enormous amount of cut shots. With two points, an extra gully and a deep point, it seemed almost a game to Hughesy to see how tantalising he could make it for the fielders while drawing us closer and closer to despair.'

Geeves was finding Phillip 'impossible to bowl to. My natural line and length had served me well, and I was coming off my only good summers at that time. I was bowling at my best, and he made me look stupid'.

After NSW's 114-run win, with Phillip's selection for the South African tour now a formality, Jaques was proud of his partner. 'I couldn't have been happier for him. While it was personally disappointing to miss out, it was great to see your mates there. As long as there's a blue cap, there was never any trouble. As it turns out, Phil was the better man and got the runs on the board.'

Beau Casson, a quiet student of the game, was twelfth man in Newcastle. He celebrated the team's success in the usual way, but was also observing Phillip.

'A lot of people, if they get close to international cricket, it consumes their thoughts,' Casson says. 'I was amazed at how he put that aside and did what he did really well. He must have realised he was a chance, but he was the same lad in the changing room and knew his job was to make runs. To do it at his age shows how much belief in his processes he had.'

The only process Phillip had in mind now was how to get down to Sydney and continue the celebrations. He drove home with Forrest, quietly smiling.

'So,' Forrest said, 'is first-class cricket what you thought it would be?'

Phillip continued to offer nothing but a smile.

'Maybe you're too good for it?' Forrest said.

Phillip Hughes was in the Australian squad as Simon Katich's opening partner. Barring the unforeseen, three weeks later in Johannesburg, he would become Australian Test player number 408

Phillip said, 'No, no!'

'But he had this cheeky grin,' Forrest says, 'like he knew he was ready for Test cricket.'

Phillip was at home with Jason in Mortlake when a call came at 8.30 pm. He listened quietly, said a few words, then hung up and went outside to the barbecue area.

Jason said, 'Anything happened?'

'No, nothing.' Then, after a pause: 'I'm going to South Africa!!'

The brothers 'jumped about and took our shirts off and celebrated and did what two young blokes would do', Jason says.

In a later interview, Phillip said, 'I couldn't stop running around the house, I was just that pumped.'

Up in Macksville, the rest of the family were 'ecstatic', Greg says. 'This was his dream, the culmination of all his hard work. We were so proud.' Greg flew down to Sydney the next night to join Phillip's inner circle, who converged at the Palace Hotel.

'We certainly celebrated,' says Daniel Smith. 'Pretty much the whole pub was celebrating on his behalf. Even though he'd only been here a short time he was like a local, because he'd walk in and buy a beer and have a chat with anybody. We got that out of the way and then he was down to business, ready to play.'

Phillip Hughes was in the Australian squad as Simon Katich's opening partner. Barring the unforeseen, three weeks later in Johannesburg, he would become Australian Test player number 408.

Above: Phillip's prodigal son status was confirmed before his Test debut, winning the Bradman Young Cricketer of the Year award at the 2008 Allan Border Medal.

ELEVEN

ON THE WORLD STAGE

It was a long way from Macksville, but on the morning of 26 February 2009, a bare 18 days after Phillip Hughes was batting for Australian selection on the Newcastle No 1 Sports Ground, Greg, Virginia, Jason and Megan took their seats in the Wanderers Stadium in Johannesburg. Virginia had an Australian flag in her lap. She couldn't see many others in the ground.

THEY WOULD NOT HAVE to wait long to see their boy bat. Ricky Ponting had won the toss for the first Test match and decided to bat. The Wanderers has a small playing surface, known as 'The Bullring' for the nearness and height of the grandstands, some of them packed with corporate boxes and seeming to rise vertically above the players. It generates an atmosphere far noisier than its 34,000 capacity.

An hour before the start of play, the Hughes family looked on as Ponting presented new caps to Phillip, Ben Hilfenhaus and Marcus North.

'I couldn't tell you one word that [Ponting] said,' Phillip confessed later. 'I was that pumped, very nervous but I was just that pumped, and that happy. The cameras were going wild and the guys were coming over shaking my hand, giving me a hug. It was just amazing really, I put it on straightaway and we did the warm-up and I don't think I've ever done a warm-up like it before, I was just running around, it was just crazy.'

The Hughes family watched, also a little crazy with nerves, as the South Africans took the field behind Graeme Smith. They had a

Above: Phillip, Marcus North and Ben Hilfenhaus try on their new baggy green caps before the first Test in South Africa at Wanderers Stadium, February 2009.

Left: North, Hughes and Hilfenhaus become Australian Test cricketers numbers 409, 408 and 407, respectively.

bird's-eye view down the length of the pitch. Then Phillip followed Simon Katich down the long race, sheathed in clear perspex, joining the changing rooms to the field. He had been so nervous he had started to kit up too early and Katich had to settle him in the changing room and tell him, 'Slow down, enjoy it'.

Phillip said later, 'I was trying to think to myself, "I'm just going out to play cricket, enjoy it, enjoy it", but it was that big of a stage and I was very, very nervous.'

When they got near the end of the race, Katich turned and said, 'Hughesy, you go first', and let his junior partner run onto the field ahead of him.

Suddenly, the weight of the moment hit Virginia and she grabbed Greg by the arm.

In the story of the Australian Test team that summer, Phillip Hughes was a character entering halfway through. Australia, trying to rebuild on the run after the departures of its nucleus of great players, was in flux. The South Africans had stormed to victory in contrasting Test matches in Perth and Melbourne, bouncing back from a Mitchell Johnson onslaught to stage a record fourth-innings chase at the WACA and then recovering from an impossible position to break Australian hearts in the Boxing Day Test match. But the hosts fought back, again behind Johnson's speed and hostility, to win in Sydney and leave a sense of unfinished business.

But there are other ways of telling the story, and for the Hughes family and Phillip's close friends, this was not the halfway point but the beginning. This was when the prodigy of Macksville and NSW was to arrive on the world stage and show that he was indeed the boy wonder, the future champion to follow in the footsteps of Clarke, Ponting, Greg Chappell, Doug Walters and the long line of precocious Australian cricketing heroes.

In the Palace Hotel and at the Activate Cricket Centre in Breakfast Point, Phillip's crew gathered to watch on television. Macksville homes with pay-TV were packed out. The Star Hotel was putting on free beers for the length of Phillip's first innings. On his lounge in Brisbane, his mate Peter Forrest was feeling the nerves, as were teammates and cricket friends throughout Australia.

Within the Australian team, the snowball of Phillip Hughes's gift for friendship had been gathering new mates.

'He adapted to whatever way of life, whatever characters he met,' Katich says. 'They might have been the complete opposite of him, but he got on well with everyone. I certainly never heard anyone say a bad word about him . . . That's unusual in a cricket team – there's always going to be differences in personalities and opinions, some guys are closer with others, but there aren't too many who are universally loved like he was.'

Katich had, in the changing room after the Sydney Test match a month earlier, had a notorious stoush with Clarke. Typically, Phillip was good mates with both of them.

Before leaving home, the Australian squad had staged a short camp in Brisbane, which served as a getting-to-know-you session between the established players and the debutants Phillip, Hilfenhaus, McGain and North.

Mike Hussey, three years into his Test career but now vaulted into senior-batsman ranks by the retirements of Hayden, Langer, Martyn and Gilchrist, had never met Phillip, but he was close to Katich, who had been best man at his wedding.

'Kato had been saying to me for a while, we've got someone really special here,' Hussey recalls. 'When Kato says that, you listen. The thing that struck me about Hughesy was that he was a very respectful person from the start. He wasn't cocky, just quiet and respectful of the older guys. There was something different about him. None of the overconfidence and brashness of some of the younger guys.'

Having suffered from the old-style hazing of junior players by their elders in his early years, Hussey was intent on doing things differently, seeking out Phillip for conversations about his background and his family.

'I knew what it felt like and the emotions he was going through, so my one-on-one talks were just along the lines of, "Play your way, stick to your game, you don't want to change".'

When Hussey had made his Test debut in 2005, Shane Warne had said those words to him, and he never forgot.

McGain, though 16 years older than Phillip, enjoyed the camaraderie as debutants who were equally wide-eyed despite the age difference. McGain missed the flight to South Africa, and once he arrived Phillip kept saying cheekily, 'Make sure you set your alarm' at the end of every day.

The first tour fixture, six days before the Johannesburg Test match, was at Senwes Park in the town of Potchefstroom, a university town some 1350 metres above sea level. As the team warmed up, some were struggling for breath in the thin air.

McGain was stretching when Phillip came to him and said, 'You a bit cooked, old man?'

McGain said, 'I think we all are, mate.'

Phillip was quiet for a few seconds before saying, 'You know what? You're old enough to be my dad.'

He punched McGain on the arm and broke into laughter.

'He was always laughing,' McGain says. 'I guess it was his country upbringing. He didn't care who you were or how old you were, everyone was a mate and he was there to have a good time and make the most of it. He was certainly doing that on that trip.'

Phillip tuned up for the Test match with 24 and 53 (retired). Katich said to him, 'You're in', not that there was any real doubt.

But there remained the critical matter of where he would field. Being in the firing line and under the helmet at short leg is, traditionally, the lowest rung on the ladder and the place where a debutant batsman is sent to field.

As Australia prepared to bowl in the Potchefstroom game, Katich picked up the short-leg pads and said to Ponting, 'You want me to hand these over to Hughesy?'

Katich then joked that Phillip, at his height, was 'built for short leg and won't even have to squat'.

Ponting, however, had adopted Phillip as his 'personal project'. He says now, 'I saw a lot of myself at the same age in Hughesy. He wanted to soak everything up and learn.'

The captain fixed Katich with emotionless dark eyes. 'No, champ, you're still doing it.'

Katich couldn't believe it. Meanwhile Phillip was sitting next to Ponting, cackling to himself.

'Only he could get away with that,' Katich says now. 'If it had been anyone else I might have got the fire going, but because I was so close to him I let the cheeky little bugger get away with it.'

Phillip had got away with it at NSW as well, slipping into second slip without paying his dues at short leg. State teammates joke that he deliberately fumbled and bumbled at short leg so he could get moved out, but nobody can remember him asking permission to move; he simply materialised in the slips cordon one day.

Katich wasn't buying that in the Australian team, but he accepted Phillip's craftiness in avoiding the dreaded position. 'You had to congratulate him on being a smart player.'

Play your way, stick to your game, you don't want to change

'Oh well, what's the worst thing that could happen in your first Test innings? You could jump a metre in the air and try and hit a cut shot over slips for six and get out for a duck. I've got that out of the way now, I can get on with it'

But Katich had a surprise in store. As they readied for the big day at the Wanderers, he said to Phillip, 'Well, if I'm fielding short leg, the least you can do for me, youngster, is face the first ball.'

That ball would be delivered by Dale Steyn, then a 25-year-old small-town boy but who had swiftly won a place among the world's fastest and most feared bowlers. Steyn was no giant, but his athletic, smooth action generated great pace and swing, and he bristled with hostile intent. In an interview before the Test match, Steyn was asked how he was going to deal with Phillip.

'We don't need to put pressure on him,' Steyn said with his irrepressible smirk. 'I think trying to replace Matthew Hayden and fill those massive shoes will place enough weight on his shoulders.'

Virginia Hughes waved her Australian flag. She had eyes only for Phillip, who took his guard and scratched out his mark. His studs dug into soft, dark, wet earth. He exchanged nods with Katich, who had often told him, 'There'll be two wogs opening for Australia soon.' And now there were.

As Steyn ran in, with his clean, fluid 400-metre runner's stride, Phillip tapped his bat in his characteristic gentle manner and raised it from his cocked wrists. The first ball was a good one, pitched just outside off-stump and nipping away, and Phillip confidently left it. Back in Brisbane, Peter Forrest thought, 'Phew, he's got through that one!' A nation of cricket followers was holding its breath.

To the second ball, Phillip gained the reassuring feel of wood on leather, fending to mid-wicket. The third he left, and the fourth was in his zone, short and wide of off-stump, meat and drink since he was ten years old. He went for a high cut shot, his feet leaving the turf with the thrust of his bat. This was the first-ever Test match in which a video referral system was used, but there was no doubt about this one: the sound of the nick carried clearly around the ground.

Greg and Virginia sat stock still. The Palace Hotel groaned. In Macksville, the Star Hotel had saved a lot of free beer. In Brisbane, Peter Forrest thought, 'Well, that didn't look very good!' Neil D'Costa, Ash Squire and Lloyd Andrews, watching at the Activate Cricket Centre, sat in silence.

'He was such a kid,' Squire says. 'We were shitting ourselves just watching from here, and he was facing it! There was no hiding for a very young man.'

When he eventually returned to Sydney, Phillip would give his batting gloves from that day to Squire, telling them they had been 'bad luck'.

Daniel Smith was shattered. 'This wasn't how it was supposed to be. I thought, "It's gone", straightaway. You could say, "Jeez that's a terrible shot", but that's the way he played. It was in his zone. He just didn't execute it. That's if you knew him. But what were other people going to think?'

Phillip left the field, removed his gear and sat alone in the changing room for a few minutes. He took a shower and went onto the balcony to join his teammates.

'I just knew it's not going to be my only duck,' he said later. 'It's going to happen again. I'd like it not to, but that's just a part of cricket.'

Watching the play, Phillip sat next to McGain. Both were feeling tense, for different reasons: Phillip over his dismissal, McGain over the prospect of a collapse and having to go out and bat against Steyn. Periodically, the television screen in the players' area recapped the dismissals, and Phillip had to suffer seeing his, over and over.

He finally blurted out, 'why do they keep showing that?' Then he turned to McGain and said, 'Oh well, what's the worst thing that could happen in your first Test innings? You could jump a metre in the air and try and hit a cut shot over slips for six and get out for a duck. I've got that out of the way now, I can get on with it.'

McGain felt that that summed him up: even at this level, he took his medicine and moved on. By day's end, Australia were five for 254, having fought back from the early loss of Phillip, Katich and Hussey through solid contributions from Ponting, Clarke, Haddin and North.

After stumps, Daniel Smith texted Phillip with commiserations. Phillip texted back, 'It's fine, that's the way it goes, that's Test cricket.'

Smith laughs at the recollection.

Above and right: The Hughes family's view of the Wanderers Stadium in Johannesburg for Phillip's first Test. A second-innings 75 fortified Phillip's self-belief.

'I thought, "How would you know? You've only been there five minutes!" But you could tell that he was happy to be there and he knew he'd have another chance.'

That evening, Phillip caught up with his family, who found him in an upbeat mood. 'He got as disappointed as anyone, but he was able to pick himself up again really quickly,' Greg says. 'He was saying, "That's cricket, there's another innings, I'm going to contribute. The game's still in progress."'

North's century on debut and a spanking unbeaten 96 from Johnson gave Australia a first innings of 466 and an eventual lead of 246. Towards the end of South Africa's first innings, an incident occurred that some teammates would remember for years.

On the first evening, Steyn did a television interview on the Wanderers outfield. Asked about Phillip's dismissal, Steyn chuckled that his only regret was to have got him out fourth ball; he would have preferred to keep Phillip batting for longer, so he could hit him on the body a few times.

Unbeknown to Steyn, Peter Siddle was walking past, listening in. Siddle was boiling, but kept it to himself, and no other teammates saw the interview. By the third day, when Steyn walked out to bat at eight for 156, Siddle was ready for him. He bowled two fierce bouncers in Steyn's four balls before lunch. On the resumption, Siddle tore in and bowled the fastest series of bouncers to Steyn that anyone had seen Siddle bowl. Between deliveries, he stood on the wicket and screamed, 'You want to hit my mate? I'll hit you!'

Hussey, watching from gully, thought, 'Wow, this Phil Hughes must be a great guy, everyone's sticking up for him like this!'

Hussey says he and the team were 'pumped' to see Siddle taking the personal risk of attacking Steyn on the youngster's behalf.

Thanks to century-maker AB de Villiers, South Africa added 64 runs for their last two wickets. Ponting, who had played in Calcutta in 2001 when Australia had enforced the follow-on only to be trounced by India, decided to bat a second time, which gave Phillip the chance to clear his first innings out of his system. He took the first ball again, from Steyn, and in the next over Makhaya Ntini bowled him a short steepler outside his off stump, not unlike the ball that had got him out two days earlier. This time he slapped it behind backward point to the boundary: a cut shot for four, his first runs as a Test cricketer.

As thunderclouds massed around the Wanderers, Phillip cracked seven boundaries through the off-side, five of them off the back foot. Greg recalls the tension. 'The match was evenly poised, and it was very dark.' The South Africans snarled, 'You're no Matthew Hayden', but Phillip responded with a grin. He survived an appeal for a leg-side catch off Morne Morkel on 21 – had the South Africans called for the video, it might have shown a touch to the glove

– and the loss of Katich to be unbeaten on 36 when the storms closed in. The next morning, he played in a more settled fashion. The South Africans kept pouring in with short bowling and verbal abuse, but, Phillip said, 'I like to smile at them'.

Seeing Ponting, Hussey and Clarke depart in the space of four balls and North an over later, Phillip compiled a mature 75 before falling to a stunning de Villiers catch at leg-slip.

Katich is full of admiration for that innings. 'There was so much talk in the media about the way he got out in the first innings, but for a young guy to put that aside and come back, that was his huge mental strength, to overcome being on a pair and trust his game.'

Greg Hughes rated the innings 'as good as any cricket I'd seen him play. It was under lights, with South Africa coming at him, with Ponting at the other end. It showed how gutsy he was and how he belonged in Test cricket'

Beau Casson, watching in Sydney, says, 'He understood himself better than anyone his age. You'd have thought he was a 35-year-old veteran of 150 Test matches.'

At the Wanderers, Greg Hughes rated the innings 'as good as any cricket I'd seen him play. It was under lights, with South Africa coming at him, with Ponting at the other end. It showed how gutsy he was and how he belonged in Test cricket.'

Johnson and Siddle ensured a 162-run Australian win, and Phillip got to sing the team song led by Hussey and to share the joy with his family. His second-innings 75 fortified his self-belief for the second Test match in Durban starting four days later. He belonged.

After being invited into the dressing room to celebrate, Greg and the family flew home, Phillip's quiet reassurance still in their ears. Even more than the Wanderers, the Kingsmead pitch at coastal Durban had a name for assisting fast bowlers. The 'Green Mamba', as it was called, was supposed to grow damp and dangerous as the tide rose from the Indian Ocean, a short flat walk away. For the second Test match, hot-spot technology was added to the video umpire's arsenal, the players were wearing black armbands to honour those who had died in the recent terrorist attack on Sri Lankan and Pakistani cricketers in Lahore, but two things never changed: the Durban humidity was extreme, and Ponting, upon winning the toss, looked at the grassy damp wicket and said to Graeme Smith, 'We'll have a bat.'

The pitch was not even flat: it had a ridge running through it. Through the combined first innings of both sides, 14 players would be dismissed for single-figure scores, six of them for ducks, and the South African captain would retire hurt for two. Amid this carnage, the 'two wogs' were an anomaly.

Hughes swats Paul Harris for six during the second Test match against South Africa in March 2009.

He jumped out to a flighted fifth ball and hoisted it over the long-on rope to go to 99. If that took guts, he was not going to wait another over to see if the mood would return

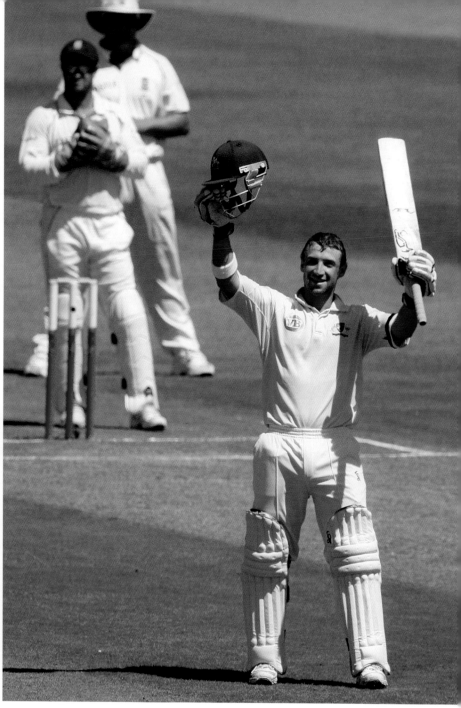

Hughes celebrates his
century during day one of
the second Test between
South Africa and Australia
at Kingsmead Stadium,
South Africa in March 2009.

A prodigy, a patriot.
Hughes kisses the
Australian crest to
celebrate his first ton at
Kingsmead Stadium,
March 2009.

Katich felt that he had bonded well with Phillip at NSW, though they had not opened the batting together. 'A lot of the time, once we were both out, he would be sitting beside me and we would chat and watch the other boys bat,' Katich says. 'Obviously he was a farm boy and I consider myself a farm boy, growing up on 12 acres. We had that little bit in common, growing up around animals. I would always ask him about his bulls and cows and things like that. Everyone knew he loved them – it was one thing you could always talk to him about, it was something that he was more passionate about than other things you would expect young blokes to be passionate about at that time of life.

'The other thing that stood out for me was his work ethic. That doesn't surprise me, growing up where he did and helping his dad . . . The boys loved him, the whole group loved him. He was funny, and he was consistent. Normally you did sense when somebody got down, but if he got down he hid it well, because I never saw it.'

Together, they put together a remarkable first session against Steyn, Ntini, Morkel and left-arm spinner Paul Harris. Katich proceeded steadily to 36, while Phillip hit an extraordinary 14 fours before lunch. This time, the South Africans were not feeding his cut shot. They adapted, bowling fuller and on his pads, and most of his boundaries were clips through the on-side.

Phillip was 'really laidback' to bat with, Katich recalls. 'We didn't really say too much at mid-pitch, just 'How ya going?' He was pretty cruisey, he didn't get too fussed if the ball was doing a bit or whatever. Having a joke helps with a top-order batsman. You can get too intense and worried about what it's doing and you get tentative, but that's the beauty of youth too: they don't have that bank of experience that holds you back a little bit.'

Australia's 0/119 at lunch was just the entrée. An over after the resumption, Phillip survived an lbw video referral, but he had edged his sweep off Harris into his pad. The poor referral was a clear sign of Smith's desperation to get him out. Phillip began to target Harris, skipping down the wicket and trusting himself to hit across the line. Nine overs after lunch, he was on 89, with Katich 51.

Harris was bowling without the assistance of any rough. Phillip thought, 'I'm going him.'

Ponting says, 'He reminded me of Gilly at his best. His power on the off-side was as good as I had seen from a young cricketer. The more fielders they put in the off-side, the more runs he would score.' Hughesy had just announced his arrival

'Australia's youngest centurion since Doug Walters in 1965, a happy, history-making Hughes leaves Kingsmead, March 2009.

Above: After witnessing Phillip's fourth ball duck and 75 on debut, Greg and the family missed their son's twin tons in the second Test but Phillip said, 'The first phone call, I'll call those guys.'

Ball one, he got underneath a full-length delivery and scooped it over long-on for a one-bounce four. Balls two, three and four he blocked. By ball five, Phillip thought, 'Why bother blocking? If the ball's there, I'm going to go for it.'

He jumped out to a flighted fifth ball and hoisted it over the long-on rope to go to 99. If that took guts, he was not going to wait another over to see if the mood would return. Harris gave ball six some air. Phillip took a step and a half forward, then crouched into a sweeping position and threw his bat at the ball. He connected perfectly, launching it onto the grass bank wide of mid-on.

'After the first six, they brought the guy up from the fence and there were gaps there if I wanted to go,' Phillip said later. 'He threw it up so I thought I'll go again and it just happened. It happened to be my day.'

Fans and friends around the world were letting loose. In Macksville, Phillip's family, watching on television, had suffered a 'nerve-racking time' as he took on Harris in this 90s. Greg says, 'I was thinking, "Just take your time!" But he had such control of his game.' In Brisbane, Peter Forrest was 'jumping in the air celebrating'. In Breakfast Point, Daniel Smith cried for the second and last time watching cricket. Matt Day was on his feet with the locals at the Palace Hotel. In Hobart, Brett Geeves was watching Steyn and Morkel 'going down the same path as Hilf and me. They thought they would get him next time, but it didn't work.

Dale Steyn has 15 kmh of pace on me and seeing him go down made me feel good about myself as a cricketer, and he is possibly my favourite fast bowler. To watch Phil do that to him was extraordinary.'

The scene was no less jubilant in the Australian changing room at Kingsmead, Ponting and Clarke leading the cheers.

Ponting says, 'He reminded me of Gilly at his best. His power on the off-side was as good as I had seen from a young cricketer. The more fielders they put in the off-side, the more runs he would score.' Hughesy had just announced his arrival.

For Clarke, who had known him as the keen little sparrow who had flown into the Western Suburbs club only three years earlier, it was a moment of high emotion. 'I had seen how good he was and had all the faith in the world that he would be successful,' Clarke says. 'I felt so much emotional attachment, I was *willing* him to success. I was as pumped as if I'd scored a hundred.'

For those who did not know Phillip so well, it felt like a major new discovery that comes along once in a lifetime.

Mike Hussey reflects, 'I was a bit in disbelief. This guy was playing a different game. He hit balls you wouldn't expect, from the top of off-stump through point. I thought, "Crikey, that's a bit of a risk, but well played!" There was a ridge on the pitch, it wasn't good to bat on. I had a terrible time there, but Hughesy and Kato made it look like they were playing on a road.'

After celebrating, Phillip became, if anything, even more fearless, thrashing Jacques Kallis for boundaries on both sides of the wicket. Kallis was still stunned the next over when Phillip offered him a sharp chance at slip off Morkel, and it went down. Kallis had his revenge soon after, when Phillip cut him to gully and Neil McKenzie was unable to get out of the way, putting his hands in front of his face to take the catch. The scoreboard showed a scarcely believable 115 off 146 balls for Phillip, and it was not even tea yet.

After celebrating, Phillip became, if anything, even more fearless, thrashing Jacques Kallis for boundaries on both sides of the wicket. The scoreboard showed a scarcely believable 115 off 146 balls for Phillip, and it was not even tea yet

He wasn't finished with the South African bowlers, but he would have to wait a day or two. Katich went on to a courageous 108, Hussey battled to 50, admitting to Steyn in a heated on-pitch exchange that he was terrified, and the South Africans underscored the dangerousness of the pitch by capitulating for 138, a deficit of 214 runs.

Again Ponting batted a second time, a blessing for Phillip. On an improving wicket, he played an innings of a completely different character, hitting the boundary 15 times over six hours as he resolutely steered Australia to an unbeatable lead. Katich and Ponting both outscored him in their partnerships, but Phillip could not be accused of riding his luck this time. He waited for Ponting to take the lead and, from the stands, Tim Nielsen observed that 'when Punter hit a ball back over the bowler's head after they'd been batting for a while, it was like the signal for Hughesy: "We're getting on top of them here".'

Phillip was 97 when Ponting was dismissed for 81. His new partner was a fretful Hussey, who was enduring a difficult tour after being targeted by the South African bowlers.

'My chat in the middle was about the next ball,' Hussey says. 'I certainly didn't detect any nerves from him. I was more stressed about my own game. He just said, "Stay positive". It was calming, batting with him.'

Hughes had become the youngest batsman in the 132 years of Test cricket to make two centuries in a Test match

Being calmed by a partner 13 years his junior felt entirely natural.

For five overs, Phillip fed Hussey the strike. Finally, Morkel offered an irresistible ball wide of off-stump, which Phillip slashed over gully. He removed his helmet and raised his bat. Hussey walked up to him and bowed, as if in worship. Phillip looked tired now, but was far from satisfied: he would bat for another two hours and take his score to 160. The South Africans kept at him with the verbal taunts, and he kept responding with a grin. One of the bowlers finally exclaimed: 'Is he deaf?'

Watching on television, Neil D'Costa was seeing what he had seen for years, only on a bigger stage. 'When he got in, he was hard to get out. He didn't play stupid shots. He had brilliant risk management. If there was open space, he hit it in the air, but if there wasn't, he'd hit it along the ground or hit it somewhere else. Another player would get a start and lose concentration in the middle of the innings. Phil didn't. He was like Muhammad Ali. If he hurt you, he'd knock you out.'

Shortly after Phillip was dismissed, Ponting declared 545 runs in front. Phillip Hughes had become the youngest batsman in the 132 years of Test cricket to make two centuries in a Test match, beating a record set before World War II by the so-called 'black Bradman', the West Indian George Headley. Not that Phillip knew that. When he looked at the honour board of Test centurions at Kingsmead that he was about to join, his eyes skated over the older Australian names of Stan McCabe and Neil Harvey, recognised Mark Waugh and Ponting, but took especial satisfaction from one in particular. He might be no Matthew Hayden, but his name was going to be up on that board forever.

His comments, when he met the media at the end of the day, were low-key and humble. His first thoughts were for his parents, who had 'come over for a fourth-ball duck'.

'It was a special time to have my Mum and Dad at my first Test,' he continued, 'but they've flown back home and they were definitely watching on TV. The first phone call, I'll call those guys.'

A proud Greg remembers that perhaps the people of Macksville were the only ones in the cricket world who were not too surprised. 'The town was going wild. In his younger days, playing above his age group, he'd always deserved to go up to higher levels. Then he'd dominated Test bowlers for those 18 months in the Shield. He always believed he was an Australian Test cricketer. And now he'd shown everyone else.'

TWELVE

OUT IN THE WILDERNESS

The South Africans regained some face with a win in the third Test match in Cape Town – Phillip scoring a brace of 30s – but the Australians were already in celebratory mode before leaving Durban.

'ONE OF MY BIGGEST regrets is staying home and not going out with them,' coach Tim Nielsen says. 'They had a ripping night: I remember the camaraderie, the gleam in their eyes, and Hughesy was right in the middle of it.'

Ponting ranked the 2–1 series win among the best of his seven-year Test captaincy and, given his inexperienced personnel, the location away from home, and the quality of an opponent who had so recently beaten Australia in Australia, he would be justified in placing this on a pedestal above the Ashes whitewash of 2006–07.

Much of the attention in what appeared a sudden and unexpected Australian renewal was focused on Johnson, who was named the ICC Cricketer of the Year, and Phillip. Both had unusual techniques and, in both cases, the praise would be mixed with a picking-apart of their styles and a rising debate over whether they would succeed on the coming Ashes tour of England. Phillip was set for a rigorous examination by bowlers and commentators alike.

His defenders rallied in advance. Justin Langer still rates Phillip's batting in South Africa in 2009 as one of the best achievements he has seen in cricket. 'They were saying he couldn't play the short ball ahead of the second Test in South Africa, and he got those hundreds.

In his first county championship game, at Lord's against Glamorgan, he struck 118 from 169 balls in the first innings and an unbeaten 65 off 72 in the second. No Australian 20-year-old had hit England with such figures since Bradman

Unbelievable: he just kept grinning at them. They were baiting him in the press conference before the game and at him out there, but he just kept grinning. They were the best fast bowling attack in the world and he got a hundred in both innings. That was freakish. Seriously mate, that is Muhammad Ali stuff.'

Clarke says, 'He loved that they thought they had seen a weakness. Scoring runs was in his genes, in his blood, and he adapted to anything and didn't care what he looked like.'

But others did care, so much so that 'experts' on technique viewed Phillip's achievements as something of a fluke, disregarding that he had been piling up runs in this style all his cricketing life. As debate grew, the *Australian*'s Malcolm Conn approached the high priest of correct batting technique, Greg Chappell, who gave a stern rebuff to questions about Phillip's footwork against fast short-pitched bowling.

'It's the way Bradman countered Bodyline,' Chappell said. 'There's no right way or wrong way. Have a look at the scoreboard and tell me that he's played badly. He doesn't comply with the coaching manual, but the coaching manual should have been burnt before it was even published, because it's been the greatest impediment to exploring batting in its fullness that's ever been perpetrated on the game of cricket. The better players have not necessarily fitted the coaching manual. To focus on replicating the perfect cover-drive actually misses the point of what batting's all about. You don't want to hit the ball in the same way and in the same area all the time. Phillip has his own method and who's to argue with it?'

A gleeful D'Costa told journalists, 'I can show you a player that the traditionalists would love. He's averaging 21 in grade cricket.'

Six years on, D'Costa still adheres to the view that the discussion of Phillip's technique was irrelevant. 'My job was to get out of his way, keep the road clear for him and keep other people out of his way. He was a batting genius. You just had to set the right environment, a few tips, and keep people out of his way.'

In his post–South Africa interview with Mike Coward, Phillip explained: 'You get a few coaches who like to change a lot of different things, but my own personal coach, Neil D'Costa, he's been great. Obviously we're always working on my game and keep improving it . . . but overall you'll keep what you've been natural at.'

Tim Nielsen, who had overall charge of Phillip as Australian head coach, says that nothing was said to him during the tour by the coaching staff about his technique, and that the sanctum of his personal relationship with D'Costa was respected.

'People had always spoken about him playing differently,' Nielsen says. 'Our biggest thing was, "Don't doubt yourself, mate, you've played this way to get here". The thing is, all players are going to be on their own when they're out in the middle. Our approach was to get them thinking about things that might happen, so that when they are confronted with it it's not the first time they've thought of it. So when the South Africans set him nine gullies, eight slips and a couple of deep backward points, he'd anticipated that. He'd always had it. And they still couldn't get him.'

Phillip came home and visited family and friends in Sydney and Macksville, where an award for a promising young local cricketer was named in his honour. He prepared to leave for England, not for the Ashes yet, but instead for a one-month county stint with the Lord's-based Middlesex club, where he would reunite with his former underage teammate Sam Robson.

Middlesex's director of cricket, former Test bowler Angus Fraser, had signed Phillip before the South African tour as cover for the county's Indian overseas player, Murali Kartik.

'It was seen as a left-field signing at first,' Robson recalls. 'Often overseas players had been Test players, so he was an unusual signing.'

Although he had not played in England since the NSW Youth tour in 2006, Phillip adapted with stunning speed. In his first county championship game, at Lord's against Glamorgan, he struck

118 from 169 balls in the first innings and an unbeaten 65 off 72 in the second. His other county innings were 139 against Leicestershire, and 195 and 57 against Surrey: a return of 574 runs at 143.5. No Australian 20-year-old had hit England with such figures since Bradman. Phillip was less successful in the limited-overs format, but finished his stay with a one-day century and a 50 at Lord's.

'Everyone was in awe of the way he played,' says Robson, who was in the Middlesex Seconds, having elected to pursue his future as an England player. 'But he was just the same as ever. We hung out together like nothing had changed.'

Phillip came back to Australia to prepare for the Ashes, and impressed his teammates with how little he *had* changed. He had been preparing for this since such a young age. The low-key maturity – telling Daniel Smith 'That's Test cricket' when he had only played one innings – now seemed to make perfect sense.

'Some days I still wake up and think to myself how good it's been,' he told Mike Coward. 'It has been a dream, it has happened very fast. But it's something I've always planned for too.'

What happened next was certainly not part of the plan. In retrospect, his first stint in Test cricket seems to have been played in fast-forward: the fourth-ball duck, the plundering of the South African bowlers, and then the downfall. While the suddenness of Phillip's success at Test level set new records and captivated the cricket world, the rapidity of his demotion was equally stunning.

In the way memory warps perceptions of time, observers will recount how Phillip lost his way against around-the-wicket, short-pitched fast bowling in England in 2009, before being put out of his misery by merciful selectors. The fact is that Phillip did not have any prolonged form slump. He only played five matches over the course of four weeks on that tour. In the first, he made 15 and 78 against Sussex. He then had two single-figure scores against the England Lions at Worcester, where the awkward high action of Test bowler Steve Harmison made his dismissals look ugly.

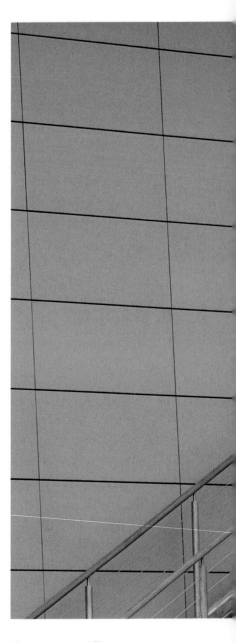

Above: Hughes and Simon Katich take the pavillion steps to the turf in the warm-up match between England Lions and Australia in Worcester, July 2009.

While the suddenness of Phillip's success at Test level set new records and captivated the cricket world, the rapidity of his demotion was equally stunning

'I remember bowling to him and I thought, "My God, this guy has got his game sorted." Everything hit the middle of his bat – defence, attack, everything' – SHANE WATSON

Teammate Shane Watson, who had only seen Hughes from across state lines in the Sheffield Shield, recalls that Hughes was still batting well in the nets. 'I remember bowling to him and I thought, "My God, this guy has got his game sorted." Everything hit the middle of his bat – defence, attack, everything.'

In the first Test match at Cardiff, he made 36 in an hour, and in the second, at Lord's, a match in which only Clarke mastered the England bowlers, he scored four and 17. His family went to England to watch those two Test matches. In the second innings at Lord's, Greg remembers Phillip surviving for 45 minutes against Flintoff before edging the ball just short of Andrew Strauss at first slip. 'The television replays showed that it didn't carry, and Ricky Ponting was begging the umpires to go upstairs for a review, but they wouldn't.' Immediately, Greg's phone began to fill with outraged texts from friends. 'We were all disappointed. It shouldn't have been given out, and if it hadn't, who knows how many he'd have scored?'

The umpiring error proved to be a turning point in Phillip's life. In the next match against Northamptonshire he scored ten and 68. He was not setting the world alight, but he had every right to expect to play in the third Test match at Edgbaston. He had planned for this very game, hitting a hundred at the ground for Middlesex, as he had planned ahead by playing Surrey at the Oval, the venue of the fifth Test match.

The day before the Edgbaston Test match, duty selector Jamie Cox knocked on Phillip's hotel-room door. 'It was a short conversation,' Cox recalls. 'I told him the reasons we were leaving him out of the Test. We had concerns about the way Harmison and Flintoff had got him out, and it wasn't a decision we'd taken lightly. He was fine – obviously disappointed, but he wasn't going to drop his lip.'

Phillip had been dumped. The outside world learnt just as abruptly, via the social-networking site Twitter.

'Disappointed not to be on the field today,' D'Costa, on Phillip's behalf, posted on match morning. 'Will be supporting the guys, it's a BIG test match 4 us. Thanks 4 all the support!'

Here, too, Phillip was a ground-breaker. Not knowing that the team was not yet publicly announced, he was reprimanded for the breach of protocol and was responsible for a ban on such use of social media by players. There was an irony in this, as Hughes was not a

'The selection panel was thinking about the long-term impact it could have on him. When he'd made runs on the tour, the execution wasn't convincing' – TIM NIELSEN

social-media devotee, and rarely sent emails. A brief but affectionate note to D'Costa in 2011 was, he wrote, the 'first email I have ever sent mate hahahahahaha'.

When Ponting and Nielsen explained Phillip's omission (though neither was a selector), they offered him a number of interpretations. There was a desire to protect him from a prolonged working-over. He found Flintoff's action from around the wicket particularly difficult, as had other left-handers including Adam Gilchrist, Justin Langer and Matthew Hayden. There was a belief among selectors that Phillip's confidence was brittle, and that he needed to be shielded from the trauma of being picked apart in England. Nielsen, who consulted Cox before a phone hook-up with chairman Hilditch in Australia, says, 'The selection panel was thinking about the long-term impact it could have on him. When he'd made runs on the tour, the execution wasn't convincing.'

'Sometimes,' Cox says, 'it's important to find the right time to take them out.'

The immediate reasons were also pragmatic. In Cardiff, Australia had failed to close out a win from a dominant position, allowing England to escape with a draw that was as good as a win. At Lord's, Johnson and the other pacemen had lost their heads on the first day and

Australia had imploded. Ponting felt that he needed more bowling options. The selectors wanted a more experienced player of fast bowling at the top of the order.

Not for the first or last time, Shane Watson was seen as the solution. His Test batting average was 19.76 and he had never batted higher than number six, but he had excelled as a one-day international opener.

'It was no blight on Hughesy,' says Nielsen, 'more that we needed to make a change to counter what England were throwing at us.'

Watson took Phillip's place, and to his credit Watson proved the most stable of the Australian top order in the three remaining Ashes Test matches, scoring 240 runs in five innings, three of which were half-centuries. Watson himself still remembers Phillip's fall from favour as 'the biggest surprise of those Ashes'. He only bowled eight wicketless overs. But although Australia's batsmen scored eight centuries to England's two and they had the three top wicket-taking bowlers (Hilfenhaus, Johnson and Siddle), they lost the 'big' moments at Lord's and the Oval, and surrendered the urn.

Some of Phillip's teammates were, and still are, perplexed by his omission. There was an orthodox idea about young players needing time in the wilderness to work on their game and build their resilience to suffering. It had worked for the nucleus of the recent great era in Ponting, Clarke, Hayden, Langer and Martyn. It had worked for Steve Waugh and Ian Chappell, and it had even been used (for one Test match) to harden up Don Bradman.

Ponting says the decision was one of the most difficult during his captaincy, but supported the selectors' reasoning and experience, and agreed with the view that Hughes's confidence might be even more damaged by a prolonged exposure to the skilful English pacemen. He felt Hughes's pain, but says, 'We had all been there before, many of us at an older age. I had no doubt he would bounce back.'

It was a proven formula. But in this case, was it necessary?

Mike Hussey doesn't think so. 'I personally was disappointed for him. I have never liked that selection policy of giving a young player time in the wilderness, because it shows everyone how quickly selectors can lose confidence in you. I was worried about how he would cope in the short term, and in the long term I was worried about how it would affect the team to see someone that good get dropped so quickly.'

Hussey has an explanation for why, in 2009 and also later, Phillip was so often the man to be dropped when selectors were faced with line-ball decisions. 'His technique might have made him an easy guy to drop. There's this story they can tell about going back to first-class cricket to fix up aspects of your technique, and when it came to a choice between Hughesy and another guy, they might have thought it was easier to tell that story to him.'

Katich is blunt in his disagreement with the decision. 'He copped Flintoff at the peak of his powers, particularly in Cardiff. I can remember him bowling absolute pace with the new ball. It was as quick a spell as I have faced, and then at Lord's once again . . . on a quicker wicket. Hughesy wasn't the only one to miss out at Lord's, and that was the last time Freddie bowled at that pace. I thought [it was unfair] because you are looking at a guy who a couple of Tests before had won us a Test series with the way he played at that game in Durban. To be dropped after three innings, to give the side a change in balance, was hard to take from his point of view. I thought it was tough at the time . . . He paid the price for us not being able to finish the job at Cardiff, a Test we should have won and didn't, through no fault of his. I understand why they did it – he was the fall guy because we needed another bowling option and the other bats were pretty entrenched.'

'I thought [it was unfair] because you are looking at a guy who a couple of Tests before had won us a Test series with the way he played at that game in Durban' – SIMON KATICH

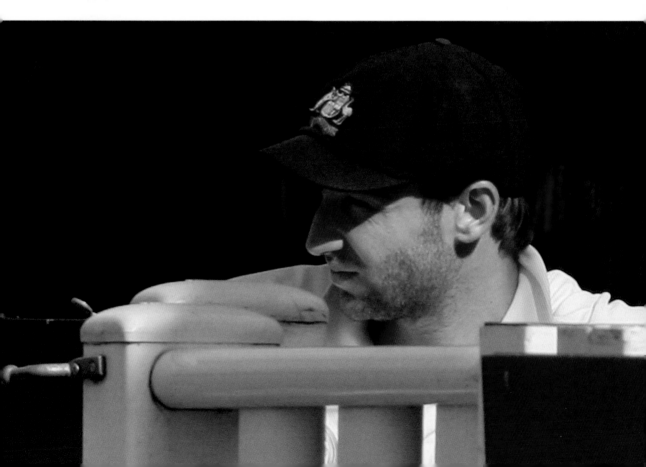

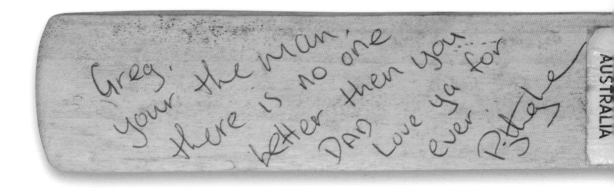

Greg,
your the man,
there is no one
better then you...
Dan Love ya for
ever. Pitale

Phillip did not parade his disappointment publicly or to many teammates. Cox recalls spending extra time talking with Phillip to reassure him that 'we thought he was a beauty, he would play an enormous amount of Test cricket. To me, he was quiet but very professional in understanding what I was saying.'

Hussey says, 'He never really showed how hurt he was. Running drinks, he was cheerful, and he was helpful in the dressing room, which showed really good character.'

Even to close friends back home, Phillip was staying bright. He exchanged texts with Peter Forrest, but, says Forrest, 'I never heard him whinge. I think it was the first time he had been dropped from any team. Right or wrong, it's hard to take. It's on the big stage, there's so much media hype in England, it's a lot to go through, but he didn't show much disappointment to me.'

But privately, on the tour, a different story was unfolding.

'The guys who aren't playing, you try to spend a little more time with them,' Nielsen says. 'I'm sure that he was smiling through gritted teeth. We trusted our senior players a lot and encouraged them to take younger players under their wings.'

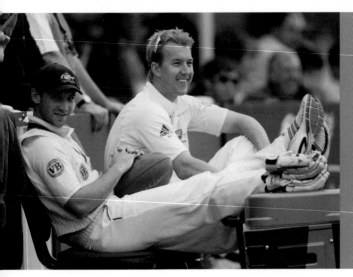

For a player entirely focused on winning, Phillip was doubly disappointed by the loss of the Ashes. The selectors had gambled by leaving him out, and had lost both ways, losing the series and leaving him with a wound

Through late nights in hotel rooms, Phillip shared his devastation and confusion with the senior teammate he most trusted, Michael Clarke.

'Being vice-captain, I had to do what's best for the team and act like I had made the decision myself, even if I didn't agree with it,' Clarke says. 'I had to be very careful. Being so close to Hughesy, I couldn't say, "Yeah, I can't believe they did that". I said things more like, "What do you want to do now? If you need a shoulder to cry on, if you want balls thrown at you, if you want to go out to a bar, whatever you want, I'll be there for you". It was more about moving forward than going over the selectors' decision.'

Katich took a similar view. Like Clarke, he could offer sympathy and understanding but was mindful of the need to steer him away from bitterness.

'He took it hard. I said, "If you need to get it off your chest, come to me", because I had been through it myself and if anyone understood, it would be me. We did talk, and I understood where he was coming from, the frustration of feeling like he hadn't done too much wrong . . . I think through that period he went out for a few drinks to let off steam, which is fine. That was his way of dealing with it, which is what most blokes do.'

For a player entirely focused on winning, Phillip was doubly disappointed by the loss of the Ashes. The selectors had gambled by leaving him out, and had lost both ways, losing the series and leaving him with a wound that, Katich says, 'stayed with him'.

When Phillip arrived back in Australia, he found plenty of support, and the solace of friends who could let loose their own anger.

D'Costa picked him up from Sydney Airport and says, 'it's the only time I've ever seen him upset. This was his dream. To live it and get it taken away so quickly, to see how people changed their opinions of him so quickly, was eating him.'

D'Costa said the experience changed Phillip, not just because he was out of the Test team so soon after his success but because of the difficulty, for a young man who lived and breathed cricket, of spending the last five weeks on a cricket tour not playing matches.

'He had too much free time after they dropped him. He needed to be kept busy. That 2009 tour, he went weeks without playing. He'd gone from being a star to being a pauper.'

Even in the car leaving the airport, D'Costa set about building Phillip back up, reminding

Back with the Blues, still king of the kids, Phillip signs autographs at Newcastle Sports Ground, December 2009.

him that he had broken more of Don Bradman's records than anyone, that he was the youngest player to score twin Test centuries, and that he was the youngest to make a hundred in a Shield final.

'If he'd been Indian,' D'Costa says now, 'he'd have played every Test and never been dropped, they'd have found a way. It was a disgrace what they did to him.'

In the days after his return, Phillip reconnected with his closest friends. Some tried to steer the talk away from his omission.

Daniel Smith says, 'If we were at a pub or cafe, we were talking about life, not cricket selections. He had that segregation between the two. He was a deep thinker about the game, but didn't harp on it 24/7. I saw my role as getting him thinking about something different instead of dwelling on why he'd been dropped. That would only make it worse. I knew he was hurting, but I also knew he was going to get back up and score a lot of runs.'

After an introduction through Brett Lee, Phillip had also begun to seek the counsel and mentoring of radio announcer and former rugby coach Alan Jones. They would communicate by text, Jones sending motivational messages, and sometimes Phillip would drop over at Jones's waterfront apartment overlooking Sydney's Circular Quay.

'Even if I was busy, he would happily sit on the veranda with his form guide saying he was "trying to pick a winner in Muswellbrook,"' Jones says. 'Of course, Muswellbrook was a metaphor for trying to pick a winner anywhere.'

As their friendship grew over the years, Jones would find Phillip an inquisitive young man who 'wanted you to open up and do the talking. He loved to ask questions. I can still see him standing on the veranda. He was fascinated by so many things – he wanted to be worldly and couldn't learn fast enough. They were precious times.'

When they talked cricket after the 2009 Ashes tour and during the next few years, Jones would pump Phillip up by saying, 'Worry about the next one, not the last one,' or relating stories of unorthodox geniuses such as the great left-handed Test opener Arthur Morris. 'I think he trusted me because I'd had some success on the coaching front,' Jones says. 'I'd just say, "You can't play contrary to your personality." Or when there was criticism, I'd say, "You've got two ears. Let it go in one and out the other." I think he was happy to hear that.'

Jones urged Phillip not to change his style in response to being dropped. 'As a sportsman, he was not conventional,' Jones says. 'By dropping him, they made the risk of telling him that the way back was by becoming more conventional. I just said, 'It's served you in the past, it will serve you in the future.'

Phillip made light of his troubles in his inimitable way. Inviting his close friends to his home to cook for him, he would re-enact games in his lounge room, his bat waving around like a sword. He said that facing Andrew Flintoff had been like having your back against the fence and someone playing brandings, hurling balls at you. He turned the experience into a high-spirited comic routine, making his friends laugh by exaggerating the scenario.

'I looked at Kato for help and he gave me nothing – he just looked the other way, and when I wanted to run, he wouldn't back up!'

Already, Phillip was thinking about forcing his way back in. He spoke to his state coach, Matthew Mott, and expressed his disappointment. There was a lot of talk about international bowlers 'working him out' and denying him balls to cut, but Phillip had not been in any prolonged streak of bad form.

'It's toughest when you get dropped and you feel like you're going OK,' Mott says. 'Flintoff's bowling had put the spotlight on his technique. He started to question his own method for a while.'

Dave O'Neil, his club president at Wests, met him for coffee at Concord and suggested that he talk with Ponting.

'He was dropped about three times early in his Test career.'

Phillip wasn't sure about approaching the captain.

O'Neil said, 'Wait till you play Tassie and talk to him then, but in the meantime just put your head down and make runs.'

Which was exactly what he did.

First, though, he needed to go to Macksville and rally with Greg, Virginia, Jason and Megan, and with his close friends in the town. He said to Smith, 'Braz, I'm going home to play with the cows a bit.'

THIRTEEN

BUMPER SEASON

In the wake of the 2009 Ashes tour, and indeed after each time he was dropped by Australia, Phillip Hughes lived two lives. The face that he showed the public and many friends and teammates was that of a young man who was admirably unaffected by setbacks. He continued scoring runs and loving batting, he revelled in his social life, and the snowball of his friendship continued rolling on and picking up new mates.

YET THE PRIVATE PHILLIP was also trying to outpace the shadow of disappointment. He would be in and out of the Australian Test team another three times by 2012, and in private the mask came off. He could not understand why he was not in the Test team. Nor could he understand why the national selectors seemed to have pigeonholed him as a 'Test player', if that, but not picking him for one-day and Twenty20 internationals. His inner circle and family saw and shared the disappointment, and it eventually affected his cricket relations with his club and his state.

On the home front, he kept things solid, with family at the centre. A new Cricket Australia deal gave him some financial freedom after his Test debut, and he bought a two-level penthouse apartment on the eighth floor of a building in Breakfast Point in May 2009. He didn't want to live alone, however.

'Even when we weren't living together, we were at each other's place every night and he always wanted you to sleep over,' says Matt Day.

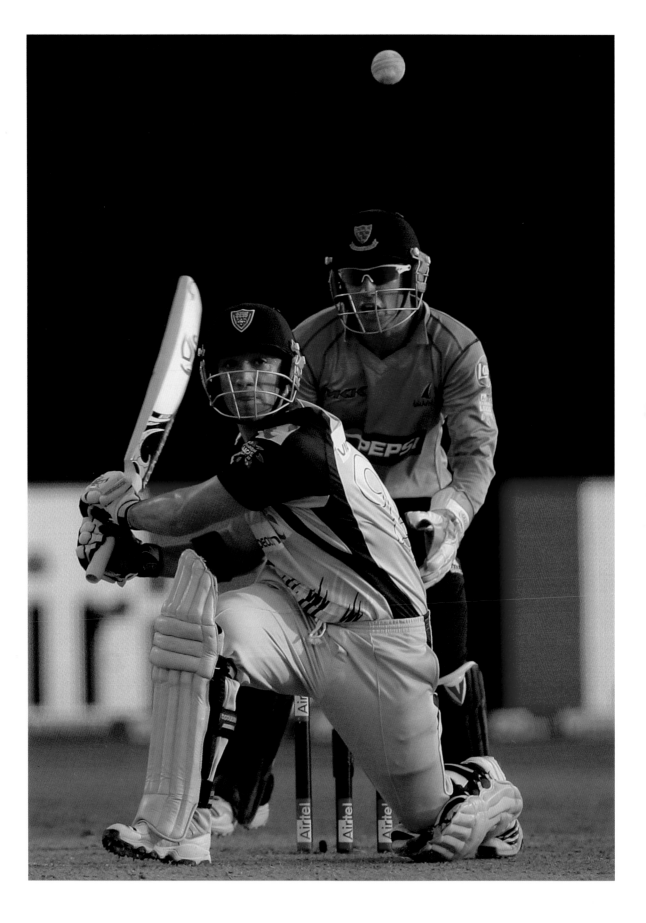

But by 2009, Day had shifted to Tasmania to push for a first-class career, and Phillip insisted that his brother Jason move in with him.

'I wasn't sure, because he might want his space, but he was definite about it,' Jason says.

The unit had a beautiful view over the Parramatta River towards the Sydney Harbour Bridge. Phillip occasionally grumbled that he wanted 'a single-floor unit on the ground floor', that he hated waiting for the lift and running up and down the stairs between the bedroom and the living area, but he was showing signs of domesticity.

To christen his new table, he invited friends over and said he was going to cook dinner. They traipsed down to the Breakfast Point IGA and bought a roast chicken, a loaf of white bread, balsamic vinegar, a Spanish onion, tomatoes and lettuce. In the unit, Phillip made chicken salad sandwiches and proudly served them on his new table: the one meal his mates can remember him ever 'cooking'.

●

Two months had passed since his previous cricket match when he padded up for a pair of NSW trial matches in Lismore in late September 2009. His teammates included Simon Keen, his former Under-19s captain who now played with the Campbelltown club and had represented NSW in Twenty20 cricket. Keen had also worked with D'Costa, who 'always wanted me to watch everything Hughesy did'.

Their careers had gone in different directions, but when Keen came into the NSW squad he found that Phillip was no different, 'always asking about my family, about what I was doing, far more interested in hearing about my life than talking about his'.

Knowing that Phillip loved boxing, Keen gave him some training mitts.

'It was like Christmas – he was so appreciative to be given something. He could afford mitts by then – he was in the Australian team! – but that was his caring side, to show how much it meant to him.'

The previous summer, Keen had been dropped for the final of the Big Bash League (BBL), when NSW had parachuted the New Zealand star, Brendon McCullum, into the side. At a moment when Keen was feeling quite low, he says, 'Phil made me feel such a part of it, and he went out of his way to make my parents part of it too.'

As BBL finalists, NSW had qualified for the Twenty20 Champions League in India in October 2009, which would be Phillip's first serious cricket since his axing from the Australian Test team. Twenty20 cricket was still in its infancy. The Indian Premier League had started in 2008, and the Australian team had only played a sum total of 25 matches in the format since their first effort, an exhibition game against New Zealand in 2005. The Champions League would bring together the top two teams from domestic Twenty20 tournaments throughout the cricket world. With his flamboyant style and fast run rate, Phillip would appear made for Twenty20, and he certainly thought so, even if the national selectors were preferring Shane Watson and David Warner as their opening batsmen.

Warner, in contrast to Phillip, was in danger of being pigeonholed as a Twenty20 slugger. A classmate of Phillip's at the Centre of Excellence in 2007, Warner had made his Australian Twenty20 debut in January 2009 at the MCG, marking the night match against South Africa by manhandling Dale Steyn, Makhaya Ntini and Morne Morkel, crashing an unforgettable 89 off 43 balls. But Warner had still only played one first-class match, coincidentally in the same week Phillip had scored his twin centuries in Durban. Amid the excitement of Phillip's batting in South Africa, Warner's Sheffield Shield debut went unnoticed by the wider cricket world.

As opening partners in Twenty20 cricket, Phillip and Warner meshed instantly. Having guided NSW to victory in the BBL, they now took on international attacks on one of the lowest and most fiendish Indian wickets, at the Feroz Shah Kotla Stadium in Delhi, and a faster surface at the Rajiv Gandhi International Stadium in Hyderabad, where NSW defeated the Diamond Eagles of South Africa, Sussex, Somerset and Victoria to advance to the final against Trinidad and Tobago, the only team to conquer them in the preliminary rounds. For the Champions League tournament, Phillip topped the NSW averages and Warner the aggregates. Phillip's strike rate of 108.02 would not be high by today's standards, but each of his significant innings was perfectly paced to put his team in a winning position.

'Between him and Davey, and Binga [Brett Lee] was outstanding, they won the tournament for us,' says Daniel Smith, who batted in the middle order.

D'Costa, who travelled to matches from his Vidarbha Academy base in Jaipur, says simply, 'He won the Champions League on bad wickets. He found a way. He won it for NSW.'

Predictably, many of the stories that emerged from the tour had Phillip Hughes somewhere involved. On the field, where Indian tours can get particularly frustrating, Phillip was amusing his teammates with his idiosyncratic catching technique

Team coach Matthew Mott was intrigued by how quickly and accurately Phillip and Warner could assess conditions. Their cricket brains were instrumental in NSW's success.

'They were foundation players of the T20 game, deeply into tactics,' Mott says. 'A coach is thinking it's necessary to get off to a flier, but they're sending messages back that a score of 130 or 140 is par – and they were always right.'

Warner smiles at the memory. 'A few people said Hughesy and I weren't the sharpest tools in the shed, and it was funny, every time we sent a message back, the guys had to second-guess us. They weren't sure if we were being sensible or not.'

As a combination, Mott says, they succeeded because 'They never seemed to try to outdo each other. Ego got taken out of it. They fed each other the strike when the other was going well, and they hit in such different areas. A good ball to Davey was in Hughesy's hitting arc, and vice versa. It really tested the bowlers.'

Ben Rohrer watched their batting with the security of knowing that he would mostly enter the game upon a sound platform built by the openers.

'As an opening batter, Phil was also hard to get out. It was amazing to watch some of the shots he and Davey played when nobody else could time it. Phil could cut low balls, I don't know how, get balls past point. Davey hit more straight, so they were hard to bowl to.'

Daniel Smith, jokingly, has a different explanation for their success. 'On that wicket in Delhi that wouldn't bounce over knee-high, it was lucky having a couple of midgets opening the batting. It was ankle-high for us, but good pace and bounce for them! But seriously, they got together and got the job done.'

Phillip and Warner failed to fire in the final, but NSW defeated the Trinidadians by 41 runs, Lee and Steve Smith starring with both bat and ball. When Phillip caught Dave Mohammed off Stuart Clark, the celebrations could begin.

Those who played in that NSW team echo Daniel Smith's assessment that it was 'one of the best tours I've ever been on'. Mott says 'it was such a novel idea, it freed everyone up. I've never had a better time with a bunch of players'.

Predictably, many of the stories that emerged from the tour had Phillip Hughes somewhere involved. On the field, where Indian tours can get particularly frustrating, Phillip was amusing his teammates with his idiosyncratic catching technique.

'He had a really good set of hands,' says Mott, 'but he had this habit of pointing his fingers up even on low catches. The boys would imitate that, going lower and lower while still keeping their fingers pointed up. But when he took a catch, he celebrated like he'd scored a century.'

Mott recalls the day when Phillip and Warner were practising together and Warner was hitting a supply of new balls out of the ground, one after another.

Seeing hundreds of dollars' worth of cricket balls disappearing, Mott rushed up and said, 'Stop it, it's killing my budget!'

Phillip was surprised. 'Do you *have* a budget, Matty?'

'Yeah.'

With a grin, Phillip said, 'You get on well with Gilbo – you can sort it!'

Mott laughs not only about Phillip's naïve optimism about the coach explaining his budget problem to the NSW chief executive, but because 'he called Dave Gilbert "Gilbo", and he called me "Matty". Nobody else called us that. He just made up these nicknames and ran with them'.

In the card games that fill the hours on an Indian tour, Phillip was a keen participant, without noticing how eager his teammates were to include him.

'He was a better cricketer than a punter,' Mott says. 'I think they used him to line their pockets.'

But all of Phillip's teammates enjoyed getting to know him. The tour went for three weeks and comprised six evenings of cricket, so there was ample downtime. At the end of a travel day, Rohrer and Moisés Henriques were having a quiet drink in their hotel bar when Phillip joined them at two in the morning. He was only drinking coffee, but he drank it prodigiously, sitting up and chatting until the sun was rising.

●

REFRESHED BY THE CHAMPIONS League tour, Phillip launched himself into another bumper season for NSW, reaping 953 Sheffield Shield runs at 56.05, another 221 at 27.62 in the Ford Ranger Cup, and topping the NSW averages in the BBL. In his demeanour and his output, he gave teammates no indication that he was suffering over his omission from the Australian team, which was playing three-Test home series against the West Indies and Pakistan. Watson and Katich were entrenched as the Test openers, but Phillip was doing precisely what was expected of him: consistently scoring runs and piling them up at the selectors' gate until it fell in.

In all but one of NSW's five Sheffield Shield matches before Christmas, Phillip scored at least a half-century, forming a reliable opening partnership with Phil Jaques. Nothing was mentioned about the 'bat-off' the previous year. Both were striving to make it back into the Australian team, but Jaques, who roomed with Phillip when Daniel Smith was not in the team, knew he was ceding the ground.

'I did everything I could to help him get where he wanted to go. If a person turns out to be better than you and takes your spot, then that is part of the natural progression of the game.'

In the last Shield fixture before the mid-season hiatus for the BBL, Phillip scored a timely 122 against Victoria in Newcastle. His ally for a 120-run partnership was Rohrer, who admired Phillip's apparent inability to hold a grudge over his stalled Test career.

'Even after getting dropped, you wouldn't have known. I can't remember a day when he didn't have a smile on his face around the group. He was always the same cheeky little bugger, he never acted cranky. Some guys are up and down, but Phil, you wouldn't know what was

Phillip launched himself into another bumper season for NSW, reaping 953 Sheffield Shield runs at 56.05. He gave teammates no indication that he was suffering over his omission from the Australian team

happening from his mood, because he was always on that level. I think that had a lot to do with why he was always able to score runs.'

The national selectors let him know that he was in their sights, calling him up for the second Test match of the series at the SCG, in place of the injured Katich. He knew he was in as a replacement, but a good performance would get him on the coming tour to New Zealand, and if he got there, the opportunity to regain his place might arise. He couldn't wish Katich or Watson to fail, but if they did, he could make sure he was next man up.

Australia was one–nil up in the series with Pakistan, but any hopes Phillip had of posting a big first-innings score were dented by his own captain. Never having forgotten the price he had paid for sending England in to bat at Edgbaston in 2005, Ponting abided by the old W.G. Grace orthodoxy of 'When winning the toss, bat first. Very occasionally consider bowling – and then bat first'.

On a humid morning under skies dark enough to require the SCG floodlights, Ponting walked out to toss with Mohammad Yousuf. In the changing room, one of the Australian players said, 'Surely he's not going to bat.'

Mike Hussey replied, 'He batted first on a pitch like plasticine in Johannesburg.'

Ponting won the toss, and batted.

Phillip was the first to go, and Ponting was out a ball later. Australia lasted a mere 44.2 overs

as Mohammed Sami and Mohammed Asif ran through them with high-quality swing and seam bowling. Pakistan led by 206 runs when Phillip and Watson went in again on the third morning. Phillip scored 37, laying a foundation for Australia's 381, which was enhanced when Hussey and Siddle took advantage of some bizarre field placings to add 123 for the ninth wicket and give Pakistan 176 to chase. They collapsed, and such was the past behaviour of Pakistan teams and the subsequent claims of a convicted criminal bookmaker, Australia's dramatic 36-run win had an asterisk against it.

With his duck and 37, Phillip might not have done enough to book his ticket to New Zealand as a reserve batsman, but he did so on NSW's southern tour, scoring 149 against Victoria at the MCG and 192 against South Australia at the Adelaide Oval.

Now in his third year as a Sheffield Shield player, he was welcoming new state teammates from his junior days. Khawaja, who had first batted with him as a schoolboy, was cementing a place at number three and re-establishing their friendship on and off the field.

The national selectors let him know that he was in their sights, calling him up for the second Test match of the series at the SCG, in place of the injured Katich. He knew he was in as a replacement, but a good performance would get him on the coming tour to New Zealand

'We'd both get to the SCG for games really early,' Khawaja says, 'because we had a long way to travel and we didn't want to risk getting caught in traffic. We both loved our sleep, and when we got there, we'd go into the back of the changing rooms and take a nap. We called it the bat cave.'

Another reunion was with medium-fast bowler Trent Copeland who, like Khawaja, had first played with Phillip for Combined High Schools. Hailing from the central coast and having risen outside the network of elite junior development, Copeland, then 23, played his first Shield match against Queensland at the SCG three weeks after the Test match. He recalls that Phillip 'was one of the first guys to come up and make you feel part of it. He knew in his own mind what it was like to come from the country and try to make it in the city.'

Practising for the match, Copeland bowled in the SCG nets to Phillip and Katich.

'I was thinking how good they were, they were just so different. I remember thinking, "I just can't bowl the way I bowl in grade cricket". Katich walked across and anything I bowled on the stumps, he hit to leg. To Hughesy, it was hit the other way.'

The next day, Katich sent Queensland in to bat on a green wicket. Bowling first change, Copeland struggled to break through initially. 'I thought I bowled all right, but I was none-for in my first spell and I thought, "Jeez, this could be a long day". But every time Hughesy came up to me, he would say, "Not bad, are you, bruzzy?"'

Copeland began to believe in himself and the wickets began to fall. He took eight in Queensland's innings, three caught behind by Daniel Smith and one in slips by Phillip.

'Every time I got a wicket, he gave me his handshake that finished with a click of the fingers, and he would say, "You're here, aren't you bruz, you are here!"'

A fortnight later, Phillip enjoyed a vintage southern swing. Against Victoria, with NSW

Familiar surroundings, unfamiliar shirt. Phillip was such a late call-up to the side to play New Zealand at the SCG, he had to wear Michael Clarke's number 389 all match.

trailing by 193 on the first innings and three early wickets down in the second, he put on a blazing five-runs-per-over partnership with Steve Smith to give his team fleeting hope. Eventual defeat in that game had NSW struggling to make the Shield final, but in Adelaide Phillip did his best to get them there. Jaques and Katich fell in the first session, before Phillip and Forrest put on 265 in even time.

'I remember him cutting the second ball of the game for six,' says Forrest, who had batted with Phillip when he made 198 on the oval the previous summer. 'He was on.'

After tea, Phillip gave an example of what colleagues were seeing as an irrepressible independence of mind. During the break, with NSW two for 214, Mott sat down with Phillip and Forrest and said, 'OK, do the hard work now and get to the end of the day.'

The coach could see that on a flat wicket, NSW's best hope of winning was batting just once and amassing a huge total over two days. After listening to Mott's directions, Phillip and Forrest walked quietly to the wicket. The first ball after tea, from left-armer Gary Putland, Phillip hoicked over mid-wicket.

A disbelieving Forrest walked up. 'What are you doing?'

Phillip grinned. 'I'm going him, braz.'

'The wicket suited us,' Forrest says, 'and I thought, "Surely he's going to make 200 today".'

'They didn't think like your normal opening batsmen. They thought, "What do bowlers *not* want us to do?"' – TRENT COPELAND

But on 192, Phillip was bowled by left-arm spinner Aaron O'Brien. 'I thought, "A 200 must be hard to get if Hughesy can't get one,"' Forrest says.

Forrest and Rohrer brought up centuries to enable Katich to declare at six for 565 on the second day, but Josh Hazlewood, the teenaged right-arm paceman from Tamworth, had broken down in the nets and coach Mott called on Steve O'Keefe to take the new ball with Copeland.

Four years older than Phillip, the left-arm spinner and handy lower-order batsman had been in the NSW system for nearly a decade. O'Keefe had played in countless emerging players' teams and NSW Second XIs (including with Phillip in 2007) but until that season had only managed a single Sheffield Shield game in 2005–06. O'Keefe was always amused by Phillip's self-confidence. In Phillip's rookie year, O'Keefe had given him a lift home from training and

advised him, with the hard-won knowledge of one who had met many frustrations, 'Mate, it takes a couple of years to find your feet, but be patient'.

'I was just trying to pass on a bit of knowledge,' O'Keefe says. 'He didn't say much, I don't think he believed me anyway. Six months later he'd scored a hundred in a Shield final to beat the Vics. He had just gone flying past me.'

Now, in late 2009, O'Keefe had been recalled by NSW but was hanging on to his place by his fingernails. Feeling the pressure of opening the bowling against South Australia, he toiled through some 25 overs to finish the day wicketless.

'I completely had my head up my bum,' O'Keefe says. 'I thought, "You have completely stuffed your career as a spinner, you're never gonna make it now. This was your one shot and you've blown it".'

After the NSW team sat down in the changing room, O'Keefe was on his own, beating himself up. Phillip sat next to him and said, 'You did a good job today, eh, bruzzy?'

'Not that long before, I was trying to give him advice,' O'Keefe says, 'and here he was, looking out for me. Next morning, I kept going and I was bowling to Aaron O'Brien outside the footmarks. He cut a couple for four so I started to bowl them straight. Hughesy comes up to me and says, "Bruzzy, not straight, he can't keep cutting them, eh? Just keep putting it there".

'The very next over, O'Brien went to cut one out of the rough, it hit his handle, caught and bowled. Hughesy came up, didn't say anything, but just gave me his little flick handshake.'

O'Keefe went on to take three wickets in each innings, helping NSW to a convincing win.

From Adelaide they travelled to Hobart, where Phillip's first order of business was to make contact with Matt Day, who was trying to crack the Tasmanian team.

'He'd make me come and eat with him and sleep at the hotel, or he'd stay at my place,' Day says.

The game also brought Ed Cowan back into contact with Phillip, this time as an opponent. Cowan had moved to Tasmania to gain more regular state cricket than he could manage in the congested NSW top order and had drifted out of regular contact with Phillip.

'Playing against him, I saw the other side of the coin. He loved his teammates. You might have been his friend, but you weren't his great mate if you weren't on his team. I'd send him texts if he was playing well, but it was a different relationship. And he always seemed to get runs against Tassie.'

NSW batted first, Phillip and Jaques putting on a masterclass on a damp wicket in the first session.

'It was one of those wickets where if you played down the line, eventually there would be a ball with your name on it,' Copeland says. 'They both had this attitude where they attacked, so that the bowlers had to try different lengths and take catchers out. When you are going hard at balls outside off, they fly further too. They didn't think like your normal opening batsmen. They thought, "What do the bowlers *not* want us to do?"'

O'Keefe agrees. 'That takes courage and wisdom. You would think a bloke would be thinking, "Just don't throw your wicket away and look stupid here". But he tended to just take it on.'

Phillip was out 25 minutes before lunch, having scored 58 off 80 balls. NSW had 115 on the board. The wicket had dried out, and Steve Smith would be able to use the opening partnership as a launchpad for his 177, a score he would never exceed in Phillip's lifetime. It was Smith's third first-class century. Phillip, also 21 years old, had scored thirteen.

NSW came home with a rush of four wins, but finished one win behind the second Shield finalist Queensland. Had NSW made the final, Phillip would have missed it in any case, as an injury to Watson triggered another call from the Australian selectors for the first Test match against New Zealand in Wellington.

Opening with Katich, Phillip scored 20 in the first innings of a game that is better remembered for Michael Clarke's unbeaten 168. Clarke had just borne the cost of his high public profile, when his break-up with his fiancée, model Lara Bingle, became tabloid fodder. Clarke had left the Australian team to sort out his personal life, and then returned for the match in which, supported by his teammates, he hit his then highest Test score.

Australia's five for 459 (declared) put them in a position to force New Zealand to bat twice. Left 106 to win, Phillip and Katich went out to bat late on the fourth afternoon. Phillip gritted his teeth, knowing that whatever he did, he would be omitted for the second Test, Watson having recovered.

Phillip survived an early chance and then thought, 'Stuff it, I'm going to motor'.

He blazed away, reminding the cricket world of what he had done in Durban just 12 months earlier, cracking a dozen fours and one six in a memorable hour and a half. In 75 balls, he scored 86 not out. Greg says, 'He was in great form and played his natural game. Even if he was going to get left out again, he knew that the best place to be was to be the next spare batsman in line.'

Katich, with 18 off 65 balls, was a delighted and somewhat bemused spectator. It didn't matter to Phillip either way. He was going to be dropped again, but he would leave them something to remember.

He blazed away, reminding the cricket world of what he had done in Durban just 12 months earlier, cracking a dozen fours and one six in a memorable hour and a half. In 75 balls, he scored 86 not out

coming

back

FOURTEEN

HARD WORK

While with the Australian team as cover for Katich for the third Test against Pakistan in Hobart, Phillip made an important career move. Aside from Neil D'Costa and his father Greg, Phillip had never had anyone act as his manager. On Michael Clarke's suggestion, Phillip approached James Henderson, CEO of DSEG, who managed Ricky Ponting. Clarke told Phillip that Henderson would be a perfect fit for him: Ponting was DSEG's only cricket client, and Henderson's experience and network could help Phillip while letting him focus on his cricket. Ponting was also strongly encouraging the link.

PHILLIP MET HENDERSON IN the Qantas Club at Sydney Airport a few weeks after the Hobart Test. 'Hughesy put me through the wringer,' Henderson says. 'It felt like my first ever job interview. But the longer we chatted, the more I wanted to work with him.'

They met again at at an east Sydney cafe later in the summer, Phillip bringing his cousin Nino along. 'By now,' Henderson says, 'I'd bought into Phillip Hughes hook, link and sinker. He was 21, but put me through a process far more complex than any CEO I'd done business with. All I wanted was the phone call to say he wanted me to manage him.' The call soon came and the two drew up a strategy that would give Hughes the momentum he needed to return to the Australian Test team. 'The plan highlighted the importance of continuous cricket, regular trips home to regenerate when tired and, above all, continuing to train and work hard on his cricket and control everything that was

There seemed no quick way back in. Watson was batting as well as he ever had, and Katich was Australia's most consistent player. Yet, as everyone kept reminding him, he was still 21. He had years ahead of him

under his control,' Henderson says. 'If he did this, then everything else would take care of itself.'

Hughes was suffering anguish from not being in the Australian team but knew he could only survive in the public eye if he could disguise his frustrations.

Tim Nielsen, who as Australian coach had seen Hughes in and out of the Test team three times within the year, admits, 'Doing it tough was not unique to Hughesy. We take away something they desperately want by not selecting them when they're screaming to play. We support them as much as we can. But I don't know what goes on when they go back to their bedroom or their family or their private place. Everyone's different. He was struggling in his own way. We hoped that that was all part of the process of developing the mental strength so he wouldn't go through this again.'

But Hughes was not letting the frustration show outside his inner circle. 'It didn't matter what form he was in or how he was going, he was always the same person, which was something I loved,' says Trent Copeland. 'He might have been down at home, but at training he was always the same. He always made you feel welcome.'

There seemed no quick way back in. Watson was batting as well as he ever had, and Katich was Australia's most consistent player. Yet, as everyone kept reminding him, he was still 21. He had years ahead of him.

He began preparing himself physically for an Australia A tour to Sri Lanka and, he hoped, Australia's next Test tour. Since the Lahore terrorist attack in 2009, Pakistan were playing their international matches on neutral territory, and their scheduled two-Test series against Australia in July 2010 would be played at Lord's and Headingley. Hughes hoped he would be taken as the reserve batsman, and looked forward to proving a point on English soil if the opportunity arose.

In May, Cricket NSW announced that Hughes had badly dislocated his shoulder in a training mishap. There was no cover-up about his having hurt himself while boxing, though the precise circumstances were kept quiet.

The truth was that Hughes's passion for boxing had struck again. When he was injured, he was with a group of mates, mucking around with boxing gloves and headgear. One of his friends was Nathan Brown, a talented young Western Suburbs cricketer and rugby league player four years Hughes's junior. Hughes had mentored Brown, giving him a cricket bat and welcoming him into his inner circle.

Brown was much bigger than Hughes. They were sparring, and Hughes threw a punch. He connected with Brown and his shoulder popped out. He lay on the ground, screaming in pain, 'Put it back in! Put it back in!'

His friends got him into a car and rushed him to Concord Hospital. He was operated on by top surgeon Greg Hoy, but the injury ruled him out of the Pakistan series and probably the tour after, to India in October. That is, if he was even a candidate; his schoolboy teammates Usman Khawaja and Steve Smith were now in line to take the junior batting slot for the trip to England.

A dark winter for Hughes at least gave him the chance to deepen his friendship with Clarke. Although close, Clarke and Hughes had been separated by age and geography, with Clarke's international cricket commitments limiting his time in the same place as Hughes. Since Hughes's arrival in Sydney, Clarke had invited him to house-sit when he lived in Breakfast Point and Lilli Pilli. Now Clarke lived in Bondi – alone, after his split with Bingle – and Hughes moved in with him for around a month.

'We were both going through personal problems and it was a good time for us to have company. Both of us were getting our anger and frustration out,' Clarke says. 'It wasn't planned that way, but that's how it was.'

Left: Teammates and, for a time, flatmates, Clarke and Hughes forged a close bond in adversity.

Right: Finding the warrior within. Hughes boxes with Australian batting coach and mentor Justin Langer during another arduous training session.

The friendship developed into a fraternal bond. Hughes offered what consolation he could about Clarke's failed engagement, and Clarke helped Hughes's rehabilitation. There was one incurable incompatibility – 'I don't drink coffee, so I wouldn't accept his 150 invitations a day,' Clarke laughs – but they bonded over food, cricket and nights out together. It was the start of a new phase of companionship between the Western Suburbs clubmates.

Clarke went to England with the Australian team in July, another reminder of where Hughes sat. Once he regained mobility in his shoulder, he signed a short-term contract with the Hampshire club, with whom Clarke and Shane Warne had played. It was a strategic move to be in England while the Test team was there, in case a call-up arose, and also to gain further experience in English conditions, but Hughes scored just 85 runs in three county matches and 33 runs in two 40-over games.

Off the field, Greg Hughes says, 'It didn't really work out. They were an older team, he said a lot of them were married with kids, and he didn't have a great time.'

Hughes went to India but did not play a game, which, says D'Costa, who was still coaching him from time to time, 'he didn't like at all'. Steve Smith had broken into the Test team in the middle-order, while Watson and Katich were the strongpoint of the Australian batting at the top.

India was Hughes's most miserable tour. After two weeks of watching, the one-day series started and he was sent home to play for NSW.

●

IN AN INTERVIEW LATE in 2010, Hughes said, 'I want to concentrate on playing for NSW and I want to dominate this season. I want to improve. I want to dominate more than I did last year and the year before and the year before that.'

It was strong talk, and reflected the mentoring he had been receiving from James Henderson and Justin Langer. Hughes had travelled to Perth during the spring to spend time at the Australian batting coach's home. With a Test career that amounted to 7696 runs at 45.27 in 105 matches, Langer had made the most of his gifts and then some.

Langer was a cricket workaholic. Mike Hussey recalls a Perth club match when Langer, after being dismissed, in full view of the players on the field, spent the afternoon running up and down a steep hill. For Langer, the answer to almost any problem in cricket was work. When that wasn't enough, the answer was more work.

Langer was an intriguing model for Hughes. Langer had come back from being omitted by Australia four times between his debut at 22 and his final return at 31, after which he played 64 Test matches. If anyone could teach Hughes about the long game on the field and in life, it was Langer.

Langer admits that he 'tried to smash him. I had just finished playing and I had this idea of setting up an academy, and I almost used him as a test case. I thought if I am going to do an academy, I am going to do it differently from everyone else. It had to be hardcore. I tried to break him to see what he had, but I couldn't do it.

'Before a Test, I used to run a hundred hundreds, a hundred singles, and I made him do it on City Beach on the sand, which is bloody hard. He did it and said, "OK, what's next?" I did boxing with him. I put him on the bowling machine and tested him with the short ball, but he handled that. I tried running him between batting sessions, and he just couldn't get enough of it. I thought he was crazy, but that was how I gained so much respect and affection for him, because I know that anyone who is that hungry will do well.'

'We needed him to learn to survive good bowling so he could then score his runs. Some openers are just surviving all the time, but he had the capacity to get through those tough periods and then up the tempo' – GREG CHAPPELL

Langer gained confirmation when he took Hughes for sessions with Bob Meuleman, who had been the batting coach for both Langer and Adam Gilchrist. Meuleman said to Langer afterwards that 'if there is anyone in Australian cricket I want to coach, it's Phil Hughes'.

Langer and his family developed a strong affection for Hughes.

'Women's instinct is very strong,' Langer says, and his wife Sue 'absolutely loved him. He's in our house with two teenage girls and two younger ones . . . The whole family adored him, and that said a lot to me. We were discussing him marrying one of the girls or adoption! We wanted him as either a son or a son-in-law.'

One facet of Hughes's personality that the Langers discovered, in unusual circumstances, was his love of sleep.

One night while Hughes was at the Langers', a candle started a fire in their kitchen. Langer got up and put it out, but 'there was smoke everywhere, the girls were all up and screaming and panicking'. A fire engine arrived. 'Hughesy didn't even know. He was absolutely oblivious to everything that was going on, he'd slept right through it.'

Strengthened by his time with Langer, confident in the plan he had developed with Henderson, and hardened by the winter's frustrations, Hughes began the season determined to dominate. But something was not clicking. After three low scores in domestic one-day matches, he made just 56 runs in his first three Shield innings. Picked for an Australia A team to play Andrew Strauss's touring Englishmen in Hobart, he was out to the towering Chris Tremlett for two in the first innings, but made a steady 81 in the second, figuring in a big partnership with Victoria's Cameron White, as England ground towards an ominous ten-wicket win.

That would be Hughes's only half-century in first-class cricket before February. While this was his leanest season so far, the landscape was tilting his way. At the beginning of the season, Greg Chappell was appointed to the national selection panel. The former Test captain and batting great publicly stated his advocacy for youth, and took some credit in his earlier stint as an Australian selector for the promotion of then-unproven young players such as Craig McDermott, Steve Waugh and Ian Healy. Chappell believed that selectors should be looking for champions, and, as nearly all of the Australian champions in history had emerged while very young, they should be looking not for journeymen and stopgaps but for young players of potential greatness. Although Chappell was working as a selector under Andrew Hilditch's chairmanship, there was little doubting his influence.

'We were only waiting for him to give us an excuse to pick him,' says Chappell, who had observed Hughes at close range at the Centre of Excellence. 'I knew of him before I knew him because he stood out so much for his immense talent. He knew how to make runs and adapted to every level he played at. You knew he was going to be a good international player.'

Chappell does not disapprove of the then-selectors' treatment of Hughes in 2009. 'When they run into their first big setback, they sometimes need time to get away. Most of our best players have needed that early in their career, and have come back with their games improved.'

That said, he had absolute faith in Hughes's future. 'We had no doubt that at some point he was going to be a very, very, good international player in the long term. He was always going to be hungry enough to make it work. When he scored runs, he scored big runs. That was another reason we liked him. He scored his runs quickly, but we needed him to learn to survive good bowling so he could then score his runs. Some openers are just surviving all the time, but he had the capacity to get through those tough periods and then up the tempo.'

As selector, Chappell also brought a forceful view that would work in Hughes's favour. 'A thing that is often overlooked is that to be a good Test cricketer, you have to play Test cricket. There's no other way to learn. Whether you've played ten or 110 first-class games, it will take you time to adjust to Test cricket.'

Sweeping changes were demanded after England's heavy win, and Hughes was recalled for the third Test match in Perth

Chappell and the other selectors gained their chance when Katich tore his Achilles tendon in the second Ashes Test match in Adelaide. Sweeping changes were demanded after England's heavy win, and Hughes was recalled for the third Test match in Perth, along with Steve Smith, Mitchell Johnson and Ben Hilfenhaus.

While some state players had noticed a more subdued Hughes during the spring and suspected that the scars were beginning to show, once he was in the Australian set-up he was his normal ebullient self.

'He hadn't changed much as a bloke,' says Nielsen. 'He was still confident about taking the opposition on. All the best players in the world have had to reflect on their games in some time away. He'd probably reflected on the difference between Shield and Test cricket, on how you might have one very good bowler to face in a Shield team whereas in Test cricket you have four. It's unrelenting.'

Mike Hussey, whose middle-order resistance had held Australia's batting together in the Ashes Tests in Brisbane and Adelaide, noticed 'small changes in Hughesy's technique' when he came back, but 'his work ethic was outstanding, as it always had been. He loved training, he took being dropped on the chin, he just asked, "What do I need to do to get better?"'

With another Hussey century and destructive bowling from Johnson and Ryan Harris, Australia crushed England by 267 runs at the WACA. Hughes scored two and 12, finding the bounce as hard to handle as the Englishmen did.

Hughes crashes a boundary in 2011. A bright spot in a rough patch.

The Australians spent Christmas in a mood of febrile confidence. They were brought to earth at the MCG, a calamitous first day leading to an innings defeat that left the Ashes in England's hands. Another one-sided loss followed in Sydney, where Clarke was Australian Test captain for the first time in Ponting's injury-enforced absence and Khawaja made a highly praised debut.

In each of his four innings in Melbourne and Sydney, Hughes had made starts (16, 23, 31 and 13). Uncharacteristically, he could not go on. The English seam bowlers James Anderson, Tim Bresnan and Tremlett were troubling all of the Australian batsmen, but Hughes was annoyed by his inability to produce a match-turning innings, and at home during and after that period, his brother Jason noticed a growing moodiness.

'People always said how cheerful he was, but some days he didn't want to play. It was hard for him.'

Henderson was also aware of how flat Hughes had become and started speaking to a number of influential administrators, players and coaches – including Michael Brown (Cricket Australia's Head of Cricket) and Greg Chappell – to gather as much information as possible to give

Hughes targets to work towards.

Just as hard for Hughes was not being considered for the ICC World Cup on the subcontinent in early 2011. But his recent domestic one-day form did not warrant selection, and he knew he had to work hard in the remaining four Sheffield Shield matches to keep his Test spot for Australia's next series in Sri Lanka later that year.

At the SCG, Hughes was working with Mott and the state batting coach, the former 100-Test England left-hander Graham Thorpe.

'He was a low-maintenance player who didn't need a lot of coaching and always put the team first,' Mott says. 'He was always clear that Neil D'Costa was his confidant, so we would be careful not to talk too technically with Hughesy, but Graham Thorpe was unbelievably good in talking about Test cricket and the lengths they would bowl and the mindset that was needed.' Even in his low times, Mott says, Hughes had an 'infectious attitude towards scoring runs. Every session had a real clear purpose. He always wanted to get something out of it.'

> 'Phillip carved up the Tassie attack. It was the best innings I had ever seen him play live and he was sending another message to the selectors that he was a run-scoring machine'
> — JAMES HENDERSON

Results came belatedly that summer. Opening with Warner against Western Australia at the SCG in March, Hughes spanked 54 in the first innings and, in front of Test selector Chappell, played a measured, match-winning knock of 122 in the second. He was back to his best.

NSW, chasing 251 to win, lost Warner and Jaques late on the third day and wicketkeeper–batsman Peter Nevill on the third ball of the last day. Hughes put on 76 runs with Katich before sealing the victory with a century partnership with Ben Rohrer, who recalls, 'When it was properly on the line, he always made runs'.

It was on the line again the next week, when NSW travelled to Hobart for the Sheffield Shield final. As usual, he contacted Matt Day before the match: friendship first, Shield final second, even though Day was a reserve fieldsman for Tasmania. Hughes missed a ride on the team bus so that he could give Day a hit in the nets. 'Even mid-game, he fed me balls, even though I was on the opposing team,' Day says. 'That's the kind of guy he was.'

His generosity, says Day, remained unchanged. 'Whenever he had new bats, he'd say, "Come and get a bat". If I happened to pick the one that was his favourite, he'd say, "Don't worry, just take it".'

On the first day of the final, the conditions at Bellerive were overcast and moist, so

Hughes celebrates his century during day one of the Sheffield Shield final match in Hobart, March 2011. He was out for 138, his best innings all season.

Tasmanian captain George Bailey sent NSW in. 'Tassie were content to wear us down but Phil threw down the gauntlet,' Mott says.

Warner made a bright 47, but he, Khawaja and Jaques were out in quick succession before Hughes put on a positive, initiative-seizing 180 runs that afternoon with Katich. Matt Day was on the field for one over, 'the over he brought up his century'. In the shadow of stumps, Hughes was out for 138, his best innings of the season.

Henderson, who was born in Tasmania and still has close ties with the state, watched Hughes make that century from the Chairman's Lounge. 'I had never ever barracked against my home state,' he says, 'but I did that day as Phillip carved up the Tassie attack. It was the best innings I had ever seen him play live and he was sending another message to the selectors that he was a run-scoring machine. I think I actually led a standing ovation from the Tassie faithful as he left the field that night.'

 **Hughes already had a four-year goal to make the Australian one-day team for the 2015 World Cup on home soil. He flew to Harare for the final of the Tri Series. There were no playing outfits for him, so he had to wear Maddinson's, which were a couple of sizes too big**

Thanks to Hughes, NSW made 440 in their first innings at nearly four an over. But Tasmania only needed a draw in the five-day match to win the Shield, and Ed Cowan dug in for a seven-hour 133. The Tasmanians took two days to eke out 453, but when Hughes went back out with Warner on the fourth morning, there was still hope if NSW could put on 250 to 300 runs and declare late that day.

Instead, Warner and Khawaja fell in Hilfenhaus's second and third overs, and Hughes and Jaques were forced to consolidate. They added 181, but their run rate of three an over was falling behind the clock if they were to get Tasmania back in. Their scoring was restricted by tight bowling and Bailey's clever captaincy but, Bailey says, Hughes and Jaques 'batted so slowly that we had a couple of conversations about keeping them both in . . . We felt they lost sight of the fact they needed to win the game. It was the age-old cricketing dilemma. To my mind Hughesy was always about scoring runs, knowing that generally this was the best way to help the team. However, on this occasion we thought they got it wrong and were a little selfish. Fine line!'

Hughes made 93 off 178 balls, Jaques 94 off 156 – reasonable strike rates in normal circumstances – but Katich was only able to set a target of 203 and get four overs at the Tasmanian openers that evening. The hosts cruised home by six wickets on the last day.

Still, for Hughes a depressing home summer had ended on an upswing. Desperate to put his name forward as a one-day batsman, he went to the Centre of Excellence in Brisbane during the winter to work on his game with Khawaja. The pair were both in the Australia A team to tour Zimbabwe in July for three first-class matches, but they also wanted to press their claims for a one-day Tri Series, involving South Africa A, that would precede the main tour. Neither had been chosen in the limited-overs squad.

Early in the series, however, Matthew Wade who had been taken as a specialist batsman, and his roommate, up-and-coming NSW teenager Nic Maddinson, were both injured. Nielsen sat down with Hughes and Khawaja. To Khawaja, he said, 'We want you to do some more work before you go for the one-day games.' To Hughes, he said, 'You're going.'

Hughes already had a four-year goal to make the Australian one-day team for the 2015 World Cup on home soil. He flew to Harare for the final of the Tri Series. There were no playing outfits for him, so he had to wear Maddinson's, which were a couple of sizes too big.

Against a South Africa A attack including future Test bowlers Vernon Philander and Rory Kleinveldt, Hughes and Warner crashed 206 runs off 37.3 overs. Warner was first out for 120 off 127 balls, but Hughes exceeded him that day, steering Australia to 290 before missing a big hit off Philander. Warner recalls the joy of batting with Hughes in limited-overs cricket. 'We would always say, "You are on, cock!" when one of us hit a good shot. If I hit a six he would say, "You are on, brazzy!" We would have a laugh, it was funny.'

With 138 from 138 balls, Hughes's four-year plan had kicked off. And then, with a run-out and a catch, he helped Australia to victory by two runs.

Opening the batting with Warner in the first-class matches, Hughes was now a senior member of a team of his contemporaries led by Tasmanian wicketkeeper Tim Paine. Hughes's and Warner's lowest opening partnership in three innings was 58, and in the four-day match in Harare, Hughes made a patient five-hour 125 to set up an Australian win.

Khawaja remembers how Hughes always kept the mood light with his foibles. He played up his unworldliness in a canny way, and was smart enough to build friendships through humour.

At a lunch break on the Zimbabwean tour, a 'deer curry' was served.

'Phil was sitting there, staring at the curry, and at me, and back at the curry,' Khawaja says.

Finally, Hughes said, 'Are you going to eat it?'

Khawaja smiled. 'Don't you eat that in Macksville?'

'Just the Angus,' Hughes said. 'Just the Angus.'

Teammates were growing used to Hughes's unquenchable love for Angus cattle. Khawaja already knew of Hughes's keen knowledge of farm animals. 'When he came to my parents'

When Hughes and Warner were 'on' at the crease together, opposition teams took cover. On and off the field, they always had fun.

place in Sydney, he knew all the types of chickens in the back-yard, he loved them.'

But his love of cattle was something else. At times, Hughes would be proudly showing photos on his phone to someone, and a curious teammate would sidle up, expecting to see a girl-friend. Invariably Hughes was showing off his favourite cattle.

'He'd talk about an especially good-looking one,' Khawaja laughs. 'I had no idea what he was talking about!'

During the 2013 Ashes tour, the Australian team bus was on a long drive through the English countryside.

'Everyone was really tired, and we'd been driving for ages,' says Ashton Agar. 'Suddenly Hughesy stood up and called out, "Look left!" There were black cattle everywhere and he was so excited. Everyone was laughing so much they were crying.'

Hughes was also schooling his teammates in his unique method of cattle mathematics.

'On the sidelines at the cricket,' Steve O'Keefe says, 'he would measure money by cows. If it was a match payment of, say, $10,000 from Cricket Australia he'd say, "That's two cows, eh?"' When the NSW players were working out their individual shares of prize money from a Champions League, Hughes looked at Trent Copeland and said, 'That's got to be four cows, doesn't it?' Copeland didn't quite know how to reply.

Justin Langer loved it. 'Everyone else was talking about Mercedes Benzes and diamond earrings and shaving their legs. He was talking about cows, that's what made him so likable. He wanted to make a lot of runs so he could buy cows and retire on the farm.'

Soon Hughes would take steps to bring that dream to fruition.

'Suddenly Hughesy stood up and called out, "Look left!" There were black cattle everywhere and he was so excited. Everyone was laughing so much they were crying' – ASHTON AGAR

FIFTEEN

A CHANGE OF STATE

After the difficulties of 2010, the next year was turning into the one in which Phillip Hughes would make his big move. The stars were in alignment. Clarke had succeeded Ponting as captain after Australia's quarter-final exit from the World Cup, and a review into the game chaired by former banker Don Argus had recommended that the captain and coach become members of the national selection panel. With two panel members, Chappell and Clarke, as firm supporters, Hughes finally felt confident that he would be given a decent run in the Test team and press his claims for the short formats.

WHEN HE WAS PICKED for the August–September Sri Lankan tour, though, the moment was bittersweet. Hughes, along with Khawaja and West Australian Shaun Marsh, were chosen in a clear sign of generational change, but Katich, 36, had been sacrificed.

Justin Langer, as full-time Australian batting coach, did not take a firm hand in advising Hughes on his batting technique, reasoning that if the young man had already scored 16 first-class centuries, he must be doing something right. But Hughes wanted some fine-tuning, so he called Neil D'Costa before the tour and asked him to come to Australia for some work. For two weeks in the nets, the reunited pair worked on specific points that would soon bear fruit.

'Those two weeks with Neil had a profound effect on Phillip, and I sensed he had unlocked a few of the problems that were worrying him,' Henderson says.

His relationship with Langer was on a different plane. In Colombo, where the tourists arrived to prepare for a lead-up game at the P Sara Ground, the temperature was 42 degrees and the humidity 98 per cent when the Australians put in what Langer decided was a sub-standard fielding practice.

'It was so hot, it was hell, I had tingles all along my body,' Khawaja says.

At the end of the session, Langer called Hughes and Khawaja over.

'You boys want to score a hundred runs every time you bat?' Langer said. 'I want you to visualise it.'

Khawaja thought, 'I can visualise it back at the hotel.'

Then Langer started running up the wicket, and called for Hughes and Khawaja to follow. He ran a single, then a two, then a three, and then a four. Then he ran a four, a three, a two and a one.

Khawaja says, 'I was nowhere, it was so hard.'

At that point, Langer said, 'We're a quarter of the way through. We've got three-quarters to go.'

There is rarely just one version of a Phillip Hughes story, and here the recollections of Khawaja and Langer diverge. All Khawaja can remember is Langer driving them on in the heat, so that, at the end of the session, Hughes and Khawaja were 'lying on the changing room floor in our undies. I said, "Have you ever done anything as tough as that?" Phil said, "No way." I said, "What's he doing?" Phil said, "He's just trying to break us. Don't let him break you." He was so strong and serious about his cricket in that way.'

Langer recalls the second part of the session slightly differently. After the running, Langer says he saw that Khawaja was 'cooked', but it was Hughes who said to Langer, 'Come on, mate.'

'What?' Langer recalls saying.

'Come on, mate, let's go again.'

'You're crazy.'

'No, let's do it again, you won't break me, you have no chance of breaking me. Let's do another hundred.'

Whatever the version of the story, the moral is the same: Hughes was willing to go through every imaginable pain barrier to succeed for Australia.

Trent Copeland had been picked on the tour for his Australian debut after two outstanding seasons for NSW, and Hughes was among the first to get in touch to congratulate him and the most eager to make him feel part of the squad. Copeland took five for 47 in the first innings of the lead-up match, sealing a Test debut at Galle the following week.

In the practice match, Hughes went out to open the innings with Khawaja. In the third over, the fast–medium right-armer Dhammika Prasad dug the ball in short. Hughes ducked, but was hit very hard in the grille at the side of his helmet. Khawaja hastened down the pitch. Hughes had his helmet off and asked Khawaja if there was a mark on his head.

Khawaja looked at Hughes's head, near his ear, and saw a large lump swelling up.

'No, you're fine,' Khawaja said.

'Don't lie to me,' Hughes replied.

Knowing how much Hughes wanted to bat and make runs, and having witnessed his determination in training, Khawaja said nothing. They put on 153. Khawaja made a century and Hughes 76, passing the 5000-run mark in first-class cricket three months before his 23rd birthday.

The Test series would be a tour de force for Hussey, who was man of the match in all three games. Australia won in Galle and drew in Pallekele, but Hughes was again frustratedly unable to turn his starts into scores. When he made a duck in the first innings of the third Test match in Colombo, sections of the media were asking whether he would keep his place for Australia's next tour to South Africa for two Tests a month later. Marsh had made a century on debut, Watson was solid, and Khawaja had unluckily but temporarily lost his place through injury. There was little room at the top of the order.

Hughes responded. Australia were trailing by 157 runs on the first innings after an Angelo Mathews century, and nearly two days remained when Hughes and Watson walked onto the sweltering Sinhalese Sports Club ground. The left-arm spinner Rangana Herath came on early and trapped Watson lbw. Hughes batted with a grim, almost ferocious stubbornness. He lost Marsh and Ponting, but urged Clarke to stay with him until the end of the day. When he reached his third Test century, he performed the time-honoured ritual of giving the media box a defiant fist-pump. After five hours of batting he came off, having steadied Australia and taken them to a 52-run lead. Safety was in sight.

'That knock in Sri Lanka I remember very clearly,' says Hussey, who replaced Hughes the next morning when he was dismissed for 126. 'He was so determined and showed so much courage. It was a Justin Langer-type of innings. He might have felt it was his last chance, but he thought, "I'm going to take them on". He went to slog-sweep the off-spinner, and I thought, "Oh no, that's a low-percentage shot!" But he hit the ball out of the ground. It was one of those innings where I thought, "The selectors have to stick with him now".'

Australia secured the draw, and Hughes had a 'huge grin' during the celebrations.

'The pressure was off and he loved the team environment with the music blaring,' Hussey says. 'I remember his big beaming smile all night, he was so pumped about being back in the team.'

●

THE CHALLENGES KEPT COMING. As Nielsen had told him, Test cricket would be unrelenting and there was no such thing as security of tenure without consistent run-scoring to back it up. South Africa held fond memories for Hughes, but he was no longer the unchained spirit of 2009. He was a hardened young pro who gave up-yours to the press. He had undergone his share of suffering in those two-and-a-half years. And this time, Dale Steyn and Morne Morkel had made plans for him in advance that were more sophisticated than merely telling him he was no Matthew Hayden.

It was neither Steyn nor Morkel, however, who would give Hughes the most trouble. When it comes to bowlers, sometimes difficulty, like beauty, is in the eye of the beholder. Ever since Alec Bedser kept getting Arthur Morris out in the 1940s and 1950s, some bowlers have posed peculiar problems for some of the best batsmen. Glenn McGrath famously kept getting Mike Atherton and Brian Lara out, not just because he was the leading fast bowler of his time but because the idiosyncrasies of his action made their lives especially awkward.

Hughes had already encountered this with Andrew Flintoff, a bowler he found harder than any other. He was about to fall under a similar spell to two international bowlers,

When he reached his third Test century, he performed the time-honoured ritual of giving the media box a defiant fist-pump. After five hours of batting he came off, having steadied Australia and taken them to a 52-run lead. Safety was in sight

Vernon Philander and Chris Martin, and his failure to master them would cost him his Test place.

There was no disgrace in falling to Philander in late 2011. The Cape Town right-armer had risen steadily through the ranks and, at 26, was a fully mature exponent of fast-medium swing and seam. On his home wicket at Newlands, Philander had a dream debut, complementing Steyn and Morkel on the first day of the Test match to dismiss Australia for 284. Hughes nicked Philander on nine. Only Clarke prospered, playing arguably the best innings of his career to that point, a counter-punching 151 at nearly a run a ball.

The match took an extraordinary twist on the second day. It began with Australia batting in the first innings of the match and ended with South Africa well under way in the fourth. In between, 23 wickets fell. Ten South Africans went down for 96 and ten Australians for 47. Hughes's nine was the top score until Peter Siddle and Nathan Lyon rallied for a last-wicket partnership of 26.

As the wicket settled, South Africa won by eight wickets. In Johannesburg, Australia rallied after Hughes and Watson led off their batting with 88 apiece. Hughes was at his audacious best, striking 14 boundaries in his 111 balls. Disappointingly, he fell short of a century when he edged a drive off Philander to first slip. But the partnership of 174 in 161 minutes was a turning point for Australia, reasserting their belief in positive batsmanship after such an eviscerating collapse in Cape Town.

In their second innings, Australia had to score 310 runs, more than any last-innings chase on South African soil, to preserve their record of not losing a Test series there since 1969–70. The pursuit started disastrously, with Watson out to the second ball and Hughes, after cracking two fours and rekindling memories of 2009, edging Philander to second slip. He had lost his wicket to Philander three times in four outings, not the only Australian to find that bowler a handful, but it left a sour taste. Khawaja and Ponting would mount the recovery effort before fighting contributions from Haddin, Johnson and debutant Pat Cummins saw Australia home to a mighty win.

New Zealand's Chris Martin did not have a great deal in common with Philander, but he quickly became another bogeyman for Hughes. In truth, Hughes's run of dismissals in South Africa and Australia did not have exotic causes. Accurate, full-pitched bowling at middle and off stumps in helpful conditions will account for most batsmen. Bowling attacks had often departed from the fundamentals to counter Hughes. Martin, like Philander, discovered that the most dangerous plan was the most basic.

Batting on early-season wickets was no fun for anyone. In Brisbane and Hobart in the two Trans-Tasman Test matches, the top three batsmen in both teams struggled. Until the last innings in Hobart, the average score for Australia's top three (Hughes, Test debutant Warner and Khawaja) and New Zealand's top three (Brendon McCullum, Martin Guptill and Kane Williamson/Jesse Ryder) was a combined 11.5 runs. Only once the shine left the ball were runs possible. For Hughes, it was the repetition of his dismissals that caused most concern. In all four of his innings against New Zealand, which totalled 41 runs, he was caught edging the gangling Martin to second-slip Guptill. When batsmen keep getting out the same way to the same bowler, it is widely taken to signify some technical flaw.

In Brisbane, where Warner failed alongside him, Hughes kept things light for his state

New Zealand's Chris Martin became a
bogeyman for Hughes in the 2011–12 summer.

teammate's national debut. 'He came up to me after my first innings and we had a laugh,'
Warner says. 'We both said we didn't think we could play those cover-drives we like with
Martin bowling across us . . . He chuckled about those dismissals, he said, "Well, that's cricket,
we scored a lot of runs playing those shots and I'm not going to tuck them away".'

Warner reversed the tide on the last day in Hobart, carrying his bat for a masterful unbeat-
en 123, but otherwise it was a dismal series for the men at the top. Hughes was out of form
and had visible trouble with Martin, but he had scored 88 in Johannesburg two Tests earlier,
and 126 in Colombo two Tests before that. When his omission came for the first of four
home Test matches against India, it hit him with a hammer blow.

His place at the top of the order was taken by Cowan, who was making runs in irresistible
volumes for Tasmania, while Khawaja was also axed for Shaun Marsh. Interestingly, Cowan,
although he was the beneficiary, has reservations about Hughes's omission.

'Against New Zealand, it was just the one bowler,' Cowan says. 'If he'd played against India,
he'd have scored a lot of runs, I'm sure.'

Rod Marsh, who had come onto the national selection panel after the South African tour, says
the panel was in a bind over Hughes. 'We always knew that . . . what he needed was a long run at
Test cricket and he was going to be rewarded. But he had to get runs to stay in the side, and he
didn't get enough runs when he was in the side. It could be argued he didn't get enough time.'

247

Hughes was forced to watch as Warner, Cowan, Ponting, Hussey and particularly Clarke – all of the Australian batsmen except Marsh – plundered a timid Indian bowling attack through December and January. He remained the consummate team man, not complaining publicly about his omission and stating that he accepted the need to score runs to get back in – but there was little cricket to be played before February, and his actions soon showed that he had taken this latest setback harder than the earlier ones.

Set against his entire career, to be in and out of the Australian team four times in two years could have been psychologically crippling. He had only known success; the worst thing that had happened to him was being picked in the NSW Under-17s instead of the Under-19s. Since he was a child, he had been told that his cricketing home was the Australian team. He believed that, and at the age of 20 he had *proved* that.

But those two hard years had recast him as a 'fringe' player, a battler who could not quite hold his place. It was a tough hand to be dealt, and it challenged his fundamental sense of who he was.

His mate Matthew Wade, who was now the Australian wicketkeeper, says, 'We spent hours and hours talking about it. I just felt sorry for him, and also Steve Smith at the time. They got scrutinised like no-one who had ever played the game.'

For Hughes, cricket was the reliable cure for many of his woes. But there would be no first-class games for two months. He had signed with the Sydney Thunder in the new city-based Twenty20 Big Bash League, but after being dropped by Australia, he stood down.

'Following my performances over the last few months,' he said in a prepared statement, 'I have decided that, right now, I need to be completely focused on my first-class cricket career. I'm obviously disappointed that I haven't been able to score the runs in the last few Tests that I know I am capable of and I want to do everything I can to ensure that my game continues to develop.'

This was an easy decision, as the shorter form of the game was not going to help his drive to return to the Test team. It also gave him a break to go home and spend time with his family.

'Every time Phillip went home to Macksville, he returned a different person,' Henderson says. 'I sensed this trip was one of the most important trips home that he would ever make, as he needed to clear his head, go back to the real core values in his life and come back ready to do everything possible to play his best cricket.'

He was considering big career decisions, including the possibility of leaving NSW. His home state had made changes to its coaching set-up. Former Australian one-day international bowler Anthony Stuart became head coach when Mott left for an English county contract, and Sri Lanka's Chandika Hathurusingha took up the role of batting coach. Hughes had difficulty communicating with both, and felt that the state was not helping him with his overriding aim, which was to get back into the Australian team.

'I knew he was frustrated and needed a new challenge,' Mott says, 'but he was quite a private guy and wouldn't be harsh on individuals, so you couldn't sense how deep the frustration was.'

Hughes's ever-happy face in the NSW squad would have its flipside. His frustrations ran deep, but he did not let it show, and when he finally did, it caught his state by surprise.

Relations with NSW were already fractious. On his return from South Africa the previous November, Hughes had obeyed a Cricket Australia rule prohibiting cricketers from playing within 48 hours of long plane trips. This meant he missed an exhibition match at Hurstville Oval that had been heavily promoted with

> 'I sensed this trip was one of the most important trips home that he would ever make, as he needed to clear his head, go back to the real core values in his life and come back ready to do everything possible to play his best cricket'
> — JAMES HENDERSON

his name and image. Even though he was following the rules, his withdrawal from the match dismayed NSW officials. Dave O'Neil, his club president at Wests, says the state hierarchy 'never forgave him'.

Hughes was also less than content at Wests. Many of his friends had gone: Daniel Smith for a better deal at the Sydney Cricket Club, while Steve Phillips had moved to Newcastle. Matt Day had spent the last three summers in Tasmania, and when he returned to Sydney in early 2012, he decided to go back not to Wests but to Mosman.

Jason Hughes also began talking to Mosman about transferring. Phillip told Wests he was thinking of leaving.

'He wasn't upset with Wests,' Jason says, 'but he just thought he wanted to try a new club.' When Michael Clarke heard this, his response was firm.

'He knew how angry I would have been if he had left Western Suburbs,' Clarke says. 'I made it very clear to him. He might have had concerns with NSW, but we were Western Suburbs players and loyalty was extremely important to me.'

Tangled in conflicting emotions, Hughes found it hard to get motivated. Jason says his younger brother often didn't want to play club games during his break from first-class cricket. But with Jason, he had one last hurrah with Wests that season. Playing Mosman at Pratten Park, the brothers put on a memorable double-century stand, to which Jason contributed a half-century.

'Even to me, he didn't say much when we were batting,' Jason says. 'He was in his own world. He just said, "Take singles". He only wanted me to give him the strike, and he was hitting them everywhere. All I could think of to say back to him was, "Don't get out". He was a Test cricketer. What else could I say?'

When Wests bowled, as captain Hughes had the team he wanted, with two pacemen and Jason as the third bowler. He said to his brother, 'I want you to bowl ten [overs] straight.'

'I thought it was crazy,' Jason says. 'I never bowled ten straight. But I took five for 25 and it was the best day with the ball I ever had.'

The club captaincy was significant. Hughes wanted to be captain whenever he played for Wests, and wanted to be taken more seriously as a leadership contender at higher levels of the game. This surprised some, but his leadership qualities and ambitions were evident to those who had watched him closely.

For on-field tactical acumen, he had often proved his touch, most recently in a club Twenty20 final against Fairfield. Captain that day, Hughes batted deep into Wests' chase and hit the last ball for four to tie the game. This meant there would be a 'super over', and to universal surprise Hughes threw the ball to Andrew 'Flash' Gordon, a medium-pacer who did not play regular first-grade. But Gordon had Twenty20 experience from the Indigenous

Back in the 'burbs, Hughes captained Wests with the verve of a born leader.

competition, the Imparja Cup. Hughes saw something in him that was not apparent to others. In Gordon's over, Fairfield's main batsman, Ben Rohrer, hit a catch to Hughes at mid-wicket. Gordon took another wicket, and Fairfield managed only three runs, which Wests eclipsed easily. Hughes's decision was, says David O'Neil, 'a masterstroke'.

Hughes saw himself as a future Australian leader. He often discussed with Clarke the finer points of captaincy and leadership around the team. Hughes had also grown close to Ponting, mostly during the two years Ponting continued in the Australian team as a batsman under Clarke and since Henderson started managing him. Ponting was regularly on the receiving end of a Hughes text: 'coffee bruz?'

From their conversations about cricket, leadership and life, Ponting's respect for Hughes grew. 'He just blew me away how he kept working harder and harder every time he lost his place in the Australian team,' Ponting says. 'And he kept coming back – with even more domestic runs under his belt. It annoys me just how unlucky he was not to have played more international cricket.'

Hughes's captaincy potential was soon to be recognised outside NSW. His relationship with his home state, however, was about to implode.

●

WHENEVER HE WAS DISENCHANTED with cricket, Hughes found an outlet in his other passions: family, friends and cows.

'You could tell when he was struggling,' Daniel Smith says, 'because he'd get up and fly home for a couple of days. When he had to go, he had to go. He needed to talk with his

251

Left: Ricky Ponting helps Hughes with his batting technique at an Australian training session in 2011.

mum and dad and get away from the bright lights. It usually did the trick.'

Some of these trips home left his close friends with their happiest memories. Matt Day recalls Hughes's response to being left out of a cricket tour by the Australian selectors.

'He was shattered, but he said, "We'll have a good weekend anyway".'

Cattle was often the focus of these trips up north, and Hughes invited Lloyd Andrews and Ash Squire to the Macksville Show.

'Everything about him was relaxed,' Andrews says, 'but when it came to cricket and his cows he was like, "Game on". That Macksville Show, he and his family treated me and Ash like kings. Vin [Virginia] was, "Here's the fridge, here's the toilet, make yourselves at home, and let me know when you want me to pick you up at the pub". They were the family any kids would want. He got up at 4.30 in the morning for the show. We woke up and said, "Where is he?" He'd left his mum to take us to the show, and she did.'

The show, says Andrews, gave them a new insight into Hughes's approach to cattle.

'He had that look: "I'm going to win best cow". He was going to get it to stand just right, he was going to fix that one hair on its back that was out of place.'

An important part of many of Phillip's close relationships was that they did not talk about cricket, Andrews says.

Above: Pleased as punch, Hughes collects the spoils from the Kempsey Show with prize-winning Angus cow 'Vicky' in 2014. He and his cows won 'Supreme Beef Animal' three years straight.

'We talked cows – not that I knew what he was talking about – rugby league, and a lot about girls.'

Hughes attended the Andrews' wedding in Balmain. 'It was booked months in advance,' Andrews says, 'but he kept asking, "When is it? When is it?" There was all this suspense about is he going to be there, or is he going to be away playing cricket? Three days prior, he rang and said, "What do I wear?" He was always asking what he should be wearing.'

After the wedding, Hughes got back to the hotel in Drummoyne where he was staying with Day and his girlfriend in the early hours of the morning. Deciding he was hungry, he noticed a light on in a pie shop next door.

'He knocked and knocked until they let him in,' Day says. 'The next thing you know, he's sitting on a milk crate eating a pie, with a bag of sausage rolls to bring back to us. That was him through and through.'

During the time he was feeling most disillusioned with NSW in the summer of 2011–12, his surrogate family gave him one of his greatest thrills.

'Kat was pregnant that year,' Andrews says, 'and for the whole nine months he kept asking, "When's it coming?" I'd say, "I told you! It's nine months!" He was there the day Jackson was born. It was the best day.'

Hughes became unofficial godfather to little Jackson Andrews.

'He was always on the phone asking me to send photos. "What's he doing? Look how big he is. Is he running?" He was really the best . . . I'm always going to make sure Jackson knows who he was.'

●

NSW's SEASON RESUMED IN the first week of February 2012 with one-day and Sheffield Shield matches against Tasmania at Bellerive.

'Phil and I were both in a bad place, which is where you are when you're dropped by Australia,' says Khawaja. 'But we would expect to slot straight back into the domestic team.' Indeed, in their only match so far in that season's 50-over Ryobi Cup, Khawaja (116) and Hughes (96) had put on a record 212 for the first wicket against South Australia.

Khawaja continues, 'Just before play commenced in the Shield match [chairman of selectors] David Freedman said to Phil, "Sorry, you're not opening, Moisés [Henriques] is opening instead". It was a really bizarre decision.'

Henriques was out on the first ball of the match.

One NSW player feeling distinctly uncomfortable was Nic Maddinson. The 20-year-old South Coast left-hander had effectively taken the place of a mentor. 'I was in a strange situation, being the batter coming in when he was dropped,' Maddinson says.

Maddinson had become Hughes's regular roommate after Forrest left for Queensland and a finger injury put Daniel Smith out of the NSW team.

'He always called me "youngster", and he seemed like he'd played as much as the 30-year-olds, even though he was only two years older than me,' Maddinson says.

In an Adelaide Sheffield Shield match, Hughes helped Maddinson to an early success as his opening partner. As Maddinson loosened up in his innings, Hughes marched down the wicket and said, 'Come on, youngster, this is Shield cricket. This is the best chance you're going to get, so stop stuffing around, make sure you're still batting with me at the end of the day.'

'He was the hungriest player for runs. That's what I learned from him,' Maddinson says. So to be in the NSW team when Hughes was out was awkward. 'It was a strange dynamic, though I don't think he held it against me personally.'

He did not, but he did hold it against the NSW selectors. When Hughes rang Greg for his customary daily chat, he said his first reaction was that Freedman was 'taking the mickey', but once he realised the selectors were serious he said, 'That's OK, I can get a game somewhere else.'

Hughes had been courted by other states already. Darren Lehmann had approached Henderson on behalf of the Brisbane Heat Twenty20 franchise, which he coached, before

The Adelaide Oval had always suited Hughes's strengths square of the wicket, and he would be in a leadership role in all three teams

Hughes pulled out of the BBL. South Australia had shown interest, and players from Tasmania and Victoria had sounded Hughes out about a switch when they heard he was disenchanted with NSW. Henderson was particularly enthusiastic about the interest being shown by South Australia, and accelerated those discussions.

Word got back to the Cricket NSW chief executive, Dave Gilbert, who asked Hughes about his intentions. Hughes told Gilbert and the team that he just wanted to concentrate on a good finish to the season. In the final four Sheffield Shield matches, his form was patchy in a team that finished one place from the bottom of the table, although he scored an unbeaten 58 against Western Australia in the Ryobi Cup after he was reinstated.

By now Henderson had negotiated the framework of a deal that would see Hughes move to Adelaide to play for the South Australian Redbacks and the Adelaide Strikers. It was a compelling three-year deal that would deliver Hughes continuous cricket across the first-class, 50-over and Twenty20 formats. The Adelaide Oval had always suited Hughes's strengths square of the wicket, and he would be in a leadership role in all three teams. The slower-paced city of Adelaide would also sit well with Hughes's lifestyle and his training ethic.

Hughes went to Macksville, spent time with his family and considered his options.

Clarke contacted him and said, 'If you're not sure what to do, don't make a decision. But if you're certain, I'll back your judgement.'

Clarke says now, 'I was determined that if he was staying in Sydney, he should stay with Western Suburbs. But if he wasn't going to stay with NSW, that was his decision to make.'

South Australia's two top cricket administrators were state talent manager Tim Nielsen and manager of high performance, Jamie Cox.

'I knew how good a player he was and he was a bit on the outer,' says Nielsen. 'He was a pretty obvious choice.'

It so happened that as Australian team coach and national selector on duty respectively, Nielsen and Cox had been involved in that major turning point of Hughes's career, his omission during the 2009 Ashes tour. But, of his many admired qualities, one was that Hughes did not harbour grudges.

'I'd taken the time to talk to him when I saw him around the traps,' Cox says, 'and he was always so well prepared for his cricket, just a hard worker in the Justin Langer mould. It was during those years that I saw him as a guy who could bring back the level of preparation he'd seen through spending time with Ponting, Hussey, Clarke, those sorts of players, to South Australia where we had a void in that kind of leadership. His cricket by this stage looked like it needed a fresh start.'

Things moved quickly. Cox flew to Sydney with South Australia's coach, the former Victorian wicketkeeper Darren Berry, and met with Hughes at a hotel near Sydney Airport.

Berry, who was meeting Hughes for the first time, recalls, 'We had scoured a list of good names to recruit. We needed a player who was young, aspirational, who could be a leader in our group. We settled on Phillip, and within 15 minutes of meeting him I knew we couldn't leave until we had his signature. He had strong direction and purpose for a guy who was so young, and I saw a lot of similarities between us: country upbringing, love of family, steely resolve under a joking nature. And he was so respectful of others. It all came across in how he talked about what he wanted to do.'

Cox says, 'We sold it to him as an opportunity. He might benefit from having a new group to impress. It was, "You help us, we'll help you."' Cox came out of the meeting very excited, thinking, 'This might happen!'

Hughes's last performance for NSW was to score 22 and 0 in a defeat to Victoria at the MCG, the end of a poor 2011–12 season for both team and individual. His departure would have ramifications for Khawaja, who also left to pursue his future with Queensland, following Peter Forrest.

'That decision to drop him in Tasmania was massive for me,' Khawaja says. 'If they could do that to Hughesy, what was stopping them doing it to me? It took me a little while, but I came to the same decision.'

Ben Rohrer, who remained at NSW as one of its senior players, says, 'A lot of things fractured during that season, but I don't understand why we didn't do everything we could to keep Phil and Usman. Why wouldn't you move heaven and earth to keep them? We were told Phil was staying, and then we couldn't believe when he went to South Australia. But he thought it was the best thing for his cricket. It was a huge loss to us, for what he brought us on and off the field. We missed his personality.'

For Daniel Smith, who had lost his Sheffield Shield place to Peter Nevill but continued to play short-form representative cricket, Hughes's departure still rankles.

'He left for personal reasons and he had to go, because staying wouldn't have helped him get back into the Test team. I was sad as a mate, and I'm still a little bit dirty about it. He didn't have a choice because of how he was dealt with. Leaving him out of the one-day team was ludicrous in my opinion. He should have been a New South Welshman forever and a day.'

'We needed a player who was young, aspirational, who could be a leader in our group. We settled on Phillip, and within 15 minutes of meeting him I knew we couldn't leave until we had his signature'
– DARREN BERRY

Henderson believed that out of this disappointment, a new beginning was awaiting Hughes in Adelaide. He had also negotiated a 2012 county season deal with Worcestershire. For the first time since his international debut in March 2009, Hughes would have the opportunity to play a full uninterrupted season of all three forms of cricket.

SIXTEEN

IN AND OUT

Steve Rhodes, the former England and Yorkshire wicketkeeper who was now director of cricket at Worcestershire, had come to Australia in 2011–12 hoping to sign Ricky Ponting. Rhodes wanted a player 'who could get on a roll and score a mountain of runs in a short period of time'. Ponting was unavailable, but when Rhodes saw Phillip Hughes make runs at the SCG and the Adelaide Oval, he knew he had found what he was looking for.

IN A YOUNG TEAM at New Road, Hughes excelled in all three formats. He scored 111 in his first appearance, a 40-over fixture against Middlesex and between May and September, he scored nearly 1500 runs for the club, averaging 35 in county cricket, 83 in one-day cricket, and 100.50 in Twenty20 cricket.

His phone calls home were full of cheer.

'He really loved the Worcestershire guys and would have loved to go back there,' his father says. The club housed him in a flat by the River Severn, and he again caught up with Sam Robson, who had risen to the Middlesex First XI.

'He was such a brilliant, destructive player,' Robson recalls. In the century he hit against Middlesex, 'The guys found him so hard to stop. He hit balls to places others didn't hit them and made runs all the time.'

Off the field, Robson says, Hughes was immensely popular and generous. 'A mate of mine, Daniel Rootes, was playing league cricket in the area but Phil invited him to come and live with him for the summer because he wanted company. Phil was just one of those easy guys to be around.'

Rhodes says Hughes was ideally fitted to Worcestershire. 'He struck me as just the kind of player we wanted, a country boy himself, no ego, a guy who played with a smile on his face, a guy who wanted to have fun. At 22 or 23, he was the same age as a lot of our players. He immediately hit it off with all our lads. He was into his pedigree bulls, which was perfect for us in country Worcester. The whole place suited him as opposed to the bigger cities. He often called it his second home and we were very privileged to have him say that . . . he'd often comment on the animals when we were travelling around. He had a lot of pride in telling us about selling or buying a cow, he used to call it his life after cricket, it was something he was planning for and every time he got a spare $5,000 he would get a cow.'

'He struck me as just the kind of player we wanted, a country boy himself, no ego, a guy who played with a smile on his face, a guy who wanted to have fun' – STEVE RHODES

Although Hughes now did not have a central contract with Cricket Australia, having fallen out of the ruling body's list of top 25 players, in the back of his mind was that there would be an Ashes tour to England twelve months later. The Australian Test batting line-up seemed settled after winning series against India and the West Indies, with Cowan and Warner at the top of the order followed by Watson, Ponting, Clarke and Hussey. But he knew how quickly things could change and aimed to position himself again at the front of the queue.

The Australian selectors let him know they hadn't forgotten him by calling him up for a game for Australia A against the England Lions at Edgbaston in August. Though the game was mostly washed out, Hughes made a half-century batting at number four. That night at dinner Hughes told Henderson that he was feeling on top of his game, and that playing full-time cricket in England was 'the best thing we could have done. You get up and play or train every day and I reckon I now know much more about my game than ever before.'

Hughes hoped, also, that the Australian selectors had taken note of his superb form in limited-overs cricket. He was increasingly restless with the perception of him as a Test-match-only player.

'I knew I could make runs in the one-day and T20 games,' he told *The Australian* during his Worcestershire stint, 'but I suppose I needed to prove it to some people.'

He had no trouble proving it to Rhodes, who recalls, 'A lot of people talk about Worcester helping him with his game, but we didn't really, we gave him the platform. He'd already worked on his game, he'd done a hell of a lot of work with [Neil D'Costa]. He'd developed a leg-side game to go with his off-side game and he wasn't so restricted. He had a stronger bottom hand and he could pull well, so he was harder to bowl at. People knew they had to bowl a straight line to him or he'd cut them to ribbons or slash them through the off side but now he had a leg-side game he was a more all-round player and a better player. We got the benefit.'

•

AFTER SIGNING OFF WITH Worcestershire in mid-September, Hughes flew into Adelaide to join the Redbacks' squad less than a fortnight before their Sheffield Shield season started with a game against Queensland at the Gabba.

During the English season, he had crossed paths with South Australia's right-handed batsman Tom Cooper. Originally from Lismore, Cooper had played with Hughes in underage cricket on the north coast and for the NSW Second XI but, two years older, Cooper had not got to know him very well before moving to South Australia in 2008. When they met in England, Hughes asked Cooper about living in Adelaide, and during the next Australian summer he moved into Cooper's home. 'Us both being country NSW boys and him not knowing many people, everything we did was together,' Cooper says. 'Adelaide suited him. He had the stud in the ear, was into his nice clothes and all that stuff that you associate with a big city, but it became clear very soon after he shifted in that he was a country boy at heart. Whenever he got time off from training he would go home to the farm.'

With Cooper, Hughes soon got into his old habit of manipulating room-sharing arrangements while the state team was on tour. Cooper says, 'Everywhere we went we'd room together, because he would say, "I get homesick and I have to room with Coops," so he would make others change around.'

Above: Hughes's 2012 county stint developed his leg-side game and honed his talent for one-day and Twenty20 batting. The opportunity to play all three formats was key in his move to South Australia.

Hughes's effect on the South Australian playing group was immediate. 'His work ethic made everyone question what we had done in the past,' says Tim Ludeman, the South Australian wicketkeeper. 'It was what we'd been crying out for. We didn't have a lot of Australian representation, and so it wasn't just the young guys like Travis Head who he took under his wing, it was all of us, we all looked up to him.'

This was the impact Nielsen, Cox and Berry had been looking for when they recruited Hughes to the struggling state.

'It's really important to have guys who have played at the higher level, who bring back an increased intensity,' Nielsen says. 'He was a standout: as a leader, as a bloke, as a player.'

On the field, he took one match to make himself the cornerstone of the South Australian batting. The early-season Gabba wicket was challenging, but fast bowler Ben Cutting took the long handle to the Redbacks on the second day to clout a whirlwind century. Then James Hopes and Alister McDermott ripped through the South Australian top order, taking five wickets in a session. Only Hughes resisted.

'It was a tough wicket, but he made it look like something different,' says Ludeman, who joined him at five for 89 to put together South Australia's one respectable partnership. 'We were almost laughing at the way he fronted up to the bowlers like a boxer, with his footwork, and then played all these cuts and pulls. It was a great innings – but he played great innings pretty much every time he batted for us.'

Bringing back memories of his performance at Bellerive in 2008–09, Hughes was eighth man out for 95 when the score was 164. In the second innings he would be fourth out for 83, as South Australia skidded towards defeat.

'I thought, "Wow, we've got a special one here",' Darren Berry recalls. 'It was a green seamer, typical Gabba wicket, and he just willed us forward. It was like everyone else was on AM and he was on FM. It was all because of this power he had in his head.'

Hughes impressed Berry as much as the coach expected since their meeting in Sydney earlier in the year.

'He had a huge impact on me,' Berry says. 'I'm intense, organised, planned, thorough. Phil was always saying, "Chill, coach, it'll be all right". He was a fierce competitor, but he helped me a huge amount. He was a hard trainer but he could switch off and have a lot of fun.'

His attitude brought out the fun side of his coach, who nicknamed him 'Zorro' for his flashing blade and 'Little Man' for his stature.

'He'd have his gloves and bat lined up in the change room, his tools ready to go,' Berry says. 'He was meticulous with these things – although his clothing was all over the place, a mess. Before a game at the MCG, his bats were lined up, there was more wood than a forest. I stuck

some half-size bats among them, coaching bats, and took a photo. I titled it, "Hughesy getting ready for the game ahead".'

Greg Hughes says Phillip was relaying back his affection for Berry, who 'really backed Phillip one hundred per cent, a very forceful kind of guy'.

Berry says, 'Every time he played, as a coach I felt safe. We were a chance to win if he was in the team.'

He made 158 in that match in Melbourne, his maiden Sheffield Shield century for his new state, but in the springtime he was more outstanding in the shorter forms, scoring 37, 95 not out, 114 and 73 in his first four Ryobi Cup innings and 74 off 48 balls in his Twenty20 debut for the Adelaide Strikers. He had noticed a fretful Berry on the sidelines worrying over the

'He understood his own game so well. Sometimes you sense a feeling of confidence in a player. Even when he was out of form he seemed to play with confidence, which is an incredible skill'
— ED COWAN

Strikers' pursuit of the Perth Scorchers' 162. When he came off, with the match firmly in hand, he slung an arm around Berry's shoulder and said, 'Told you I had it sorted'.

Ed Cowan, who played a Sheffield Shield game against him in that early part of the season, noticed a new solidity in his forward defence.

'The ball was no longer trickling off to point, it was a full solid forward defence to mid-off,' Cowan remembers. 'He understood his own game so well. Sometimes you sense a feeling of confidence in a player. Even when he was out of form he seemed to play with confidence, which is an incredible skill.'

While Hughes was showing the way with South Australia, Cowan made his first Test century, against South Africa in Brisbane. Ponting reached the end of the line, retiring after the series, and the selectors' experiment with Victorian Rob Quiney at number three was shortlived. With Sri Lanka arriving for three Test matches, and the number-three position vacant, Hughes received his fifth national call-up, albeit out of his normal place in the batting order, for the first Test at Bellerive.

'He never cared about where he batted,' Clarke says. 'He just loved playing for Australia and I loved having him back.'

When Cowan spooned a pull shot in the sixth over, Hughes was as good as opening. He announced his return to Test cricket with a bristling cut shot to the boundary from his third ball. Through the morning session, he and Warner mastered the Sri Lankan medium-pacers until Warner ran himself out in the shadow of lunch, but Hughes proceeded patiently, with an escort from Watson, towards what seemed a certain hundred in the afternoon.

On 77, he nicked off to Chanaka Welegedara, but it was a clear no ball. All the stars seemed in alignment, and Stuart MacGill was tweeting to the world that Hughes would score 150. Watson played a loose drive to be out for 30, but Clarke, in the form of his life, accompanied Hughes, on 81, to the tea break.

It was a shock, then, when he chopped his first ball from Welegedara after tea onto his stumps.

'He was filthy,' Cowan says. 'He said he should have got 200, and was carrying on about them being pie throwers, which you didn't often hear from him. But Angelo Mathews was bowling first change, so it was a fair statement.'

Yet his 86 had something calm and assured about it that promised this would be his time, his chance for a long run in the Australian team.

Australia won the match on the last day, but not before Hughes was involved in one of cricket's curios. Of Australia's 32 wicketkeepers since 1877, only Rodney Marsh had ever bowled in a Test match, and that was in a pointless draw in Faisalabad, Pakistan. But as Clarke's team strained for a breakthrough on the last day, Matthew Wade pestered his captain for a bowl.

Although he had never rolled his arm over in first-class cricket, Wade had a high opinion of his medium-pacers – and so did his close mate Hughes who, sniffing something in the air, joined in, running up to Clarke between overs and saying, 'Give him a bowl, give him a bowl!'

Hughes had a mischievous agenda: he knew that if Wade bowled, he would keep wicket in a Test match.

'He had always bragged about how good he was as a keeper,' Clarke laughs. 'He thought he was better than Wadey.'

The over before tea, with Australia still needing six wickets to win, Clarke gave in: Wade would bowl to Thilan Samaraweera, well set on 38.

'His grin was the biggest I had ever seen,' Wade says of Hughes.

But Hughes hadn't thought things through. As Wade removed his pads and gloves, Hughes said, 'But I don't have any gear!'

'Just use mine,' Wade said.

Wade marked out his run, about eight steps, and wondered if the opposition, and the cricket world beyond, could take him seriously as a bowler.

'Then I looked up the other end, and thought, "How could they take anything seriously when Hughesy's behind the wicket?"'

Wade bowled a maiden to a careful Samaraweera, who blocked every ball before it could get to Hughes. In the television commentary box, Ian Healy was tearing strips off Hughes's technique.

But Clarke says, 'I reckon that was the happiest day of his life, when he got to keep for Australia. I made two people very happy that day.'

●

IN THE THREE TEST matches against Sri Lanka, only Hussey, Clarke and Wade made centuries for Australia. For the likes of Hughes, Cowan, Watson and Warner, opportunities were missed at every turn. In Melbourne, where Australia only needed to bat once, Hughes was run out for ten in a mix-up with Cowan.

'I hit it to the left of mid-wicket and called yes,' Cowan recalls. 'He hesitated, and didn't see the fielder pick it up. He was out by miles. It's so loud at the MCG. The noise in the middle, you can hardly hear the guy at the other end, you operate on sign language. Even with 30,000 there on day three, when Mitch Johnson was on a hat-trick it was like an F1 race was starting, it was so noisy. He didn't hear me, didn't respond. Afterwards, I said sorry and shook his hand and we got on with it.'

Another priceless opportunity against a weak attack went begging in Sydney, where Hughes,

It had puzzled him that he had never been chosen for one-day international cricket, but here was his chance

after a fluent 87 on the second day and a 130-run partnership with Warner, edged a cut off Rangana Herath. He was disappointed again at not going on, but was able to shed those feelings when Wade approached his second Test century later in the innings. When Wade slashed a boundary through cover to bring up his hundred, the first faces he saw in the SCG players' area were those of Hughes and Clarke.

'They were so happy for me, it blew me away,' Wade says. 'They were going bananas. Once you were tight as brothers, he took such happiness in your success.'

In the second innings, as Australia faced a nervous chase of 141 on a wearing wicket, Hughes steadied the ship with a quick 34. His 233 runs at 46.60 for the series kept his head above water, but more challenging times were to come, with Test tours to India and England during the winter.

A visit to Sydney always meant a chance to catch up with mates. Hughes still owned his Breakfast Point unit, where his former Western Suburbs teammate Nick Pryde had moved in (Hughes would sell the unit later in 2013). Hughes liked to go there with his friends to rekindle the old spirit. On one occasion, with Daniel Smith and Matt Day, he started an improvised game of golf. Hughes hated golf, asking, 'Why do you have to go get your own ball? In cricket, someone else has to get it!' Below the penthouse unit was the Breakfast Point country club. They saw a man trying to chip golf balls into a washing basket. Smith yelled out, 'Fore!' until the man saw them, and Smith said, 'Give us a go at a hole-in-one?'

From eight floors up, Hughes began lobbing golf balls to Smith, who hit them with his cricket bat, trying to land them in the man's basket. 'Not one of the greatest things we've ever done,' Smith comments.

In the meantime, with Hussey retiring, Watson injured and Clarke and Warner being rested, Hughes received the recognition he craved in one-day cricket, becoming Australian representative number 198 for the 11 January encounter with Sri Lanka at the MCG.

'He *hated* being pigeonholed,' Clarke says, and Hughes's pre-Christmas Ryobi Cup form, along with career statistics that bettered many of those who had played ahead of him, made his selection irresistible.

It had puzzled him that he had never been chosen for one-day international cricket, but here was his chance. The night before the match, he phoned Matt Day and said, 'I'm going to make a statement.'

Day needed no further convincing. 'He had a feeling for those big moments,' he says.

He spent time preparing with his opening partner, Aaron Finch, with whom he had remained extremely close since their time at the academy four years ago. 'His planning was meticulous, nothing left to chance,' Finch says. 'We talked about how to play Lasith Malinga. He said the only way Malinga could get him out lbw was if he struck his front pad out in front of the stumps, so he decided not to do that. Instead he'd trust himself to hit any straight balls. Easier said than done! But watching him, I learned so much about batting.'

His prophecies seldom failed. For a debutant, he put on a masterclass, dominating partnerships with Finch, fellow first-gamer Usman Khawaja and George Bailey to notch a hundred at just under a run a ball.

'It was something else,' says David Hussey, who followed Hughes in to bat when he was out for 112 in the 39th over. 'He smacked them to all parts.' Hughes had made history again as the first Australian to score a century on ODI debut.

The innings did not, however, open the floodgates. Along with his teammates, Hughes lost form over the next three matches, and Australia went to the final game of the five-match series in Hobart needing a win to tie 2–2 (the fourth match, in Sydney, had been a no-result after rain). Warner and Wade departed early and Hughes, batting number three, was pottering along until Bailey fell at three for 97 in the 27th over.

David Hussey, yet another who was battling for runs, walked out on the Bellerive wicket.

'How are you going out here, mate?' Hussey asked.

'I can't hit the ball off the square,' Hughes confessed.

'Well, let's just hang out here and have a bit of fun, eh?'

Suddenly they relaxed, and put on what would ultimately be a match-turning 98 runs before Hussey was out for 34. Hughes would steer Australia to five for 247, dominating the innings with an unbeaten 138 from 154 balls, giving the Australian bowlers the breathing space to shut Sri Lanka down.

But after the game, Hughes 'was fuming', Wade remembers.

'The selectors told him he had to go back to South Australia that night to start a Shield game the next day. He always seemed to be the bloke who got that gig; they always wanted more out of Hughesy. He was saying, "I'm doing everything I can!"'

Hussey had received the same tap on the shoulder: the Shield match was Victoria versus South Australia in Adelaide. He recalls: 'We were both working on a hangover when we got tapped on the shoulder and told we had to fly back to Adelaide to play in the Shield game against each other. I said, "But that starts tomorrow morning!" And they said, "Yeah, yeah, the flight's at 4 am." This was about 11 pm, and by the time we got into bed it was 2 am. Two hours' sleep before a Shield game is fantastic.'

Proving a point in his debut ODI series, Hughes smashed two memorable centuries, 112 in Melbourne and this unbeaten 138 in Hobart.

'The selectors told him he had to go back to South Australia that night to start a Shield game the next day. He always seemed to be the bloke who got that gig; they always wanted more out of Hughesy' – DAVID HUSSEY

The pair dragged themselves to the Adelaide Oval and were looking at each other when captains Johan Botha and Cameron White tossed the coin. It came down Victoria's way: Hussey would have to bat.

'I needed the runs and he went home to sleep,' Hussey says. 'He won that battle.'

Hughes won another battle the day after, scoring 120 in four-and-a-half hours to set up an exciting one-wicket victory for South Australia.

'If he was shattered by having to travel straight after the one-day international,' says Tim Ludeman, 'he didn't show it at all.'

Henderson says that this 72 hours showed the quality of all that Hughes stood for, not just as a cricketer but as a person. 'He was feeling all sorts of emotions during this game, let alone the fact he was almost asleep on his feet, but he put his head down and worked as hard as he always did; and got the result for South Australia. Pure class.'

SEVENTEEN

BALL BY BALL

As unreasonable as it had seemed, the four-day match was Hughes's only first-class fixture between the New Year's Test and the flight to Chennai in February. He ensconced himself in the Australian one-day line-up with solid scoring through a series win over the West Indies at home, but was then on the plane to India.

FOR HIS TEAM, A storm was on its way. A mishandled farewell for Mike Hussey after the Sydney Test match was one of several issues brewing within the Australian set-up. The Australian team were sent to India in dribs and drabs. Hughes did not know from one day to the next whether he would be playing a one-day international against the West Indies at home or flying to the subcontinent. 'It was confusing for him,' Greg says, 'but all he wanted was to play more one-dayers. He ended up being in the last group to go to India.'

By the time they arrived in India, some senior players were not communicating with each other and the coaching and support staff were growing weary of continuing, if minor, disciplinary infractions. The atmosphere among the large group of 17 players could be awkward, with many uncertain about their role or position from day to day.

When the on-field results began to reflect this off-field tension – Australia were pummelled in the first two Test matches in Chennai and Hyderabad – the team leadership put their collective foot down. Coach Mickey Arthur gave the 15 players several days to tell him, in writing, in person or by phone, three things the team could do better and three ways that individuals could help. When the team prepared in Mohali for the third Test match, Watson, Johnson, Khawaja and James Pattinson's responses were yet to be received. All four were suspended for the match, and Watson flew home to Australia for the birth of his son.

Amid all this, Phillip Hughes was a keen, tireless worker and an adherent to team rules, keeping his head down and staying out of the fray. When Arthur proposed what would later be mocked as the 'homework' assignment, Hughes was eager to help.

He said to Arthur, 'I'm not comfortable writing things down. Can we just have a coffee?'

And so he played his part with a minimum of fuss. When the punishments were issued, Hughes fully supported Arthur, manager Gavin Dovey, and Clarke.

'If I can do it, anyone ought to be able to do it,' he said to Cowan. 'We're playing cricket for Australia. Why can't someone do this to get better?'

Hughes and Cowan, after several years of knowing each other, grew close on that tour. Both left-handers were working at the same dilemma – how to survive and score runs against probing Indian bowlers on low, dusty wickets in intense heat amid the din of confident crowds and a claustrophobic ring of fielders. By the time of the Mohali match, Hughes had enough on his plate, having scored 25 runs in four Test innings. Had Khawaja not been demoted from the Mohali match, he might have found himself dropped yet again.

'The guys who inherently wanted the team to be winning were sticking together,' Cowan says. 'From the outside it looked as though people were treated harshly, but it needed to happen or else the team would implode. Hughesy was flabbergasted; he couldn't understand why people didn't do it. He didn't shirk. He knew it was important.'

Hughes and Cowan spent hours throwing balls to each other in the nets and talking about batting.

'Although it was a tough tour, he was relishing the job of trying to find a way to make runs,' Cowan says. 'We talked a lot about different situations, the tough conditions which were much tougher than previous tours. For instance, the nets didn't turn! You'd think you were playing spin pretty well from your work in the nets, and then in the Test it turned square, and you weren't handling it so well!'

Their friendship had endured over time but always had a competitive edge, as it must between two players often competing for the same position.

'I'd always liked him, but by the time we were in India, I saw that he was much better than me.' Cowan says. 'My Test career was going to be short and his was going to be long, and I poured a lot into helping him become a better cricketer. I was a bit older and more relaxed by then, and I could see he was going to become one of Australia's greatest players. I wanted to contribute to that.'

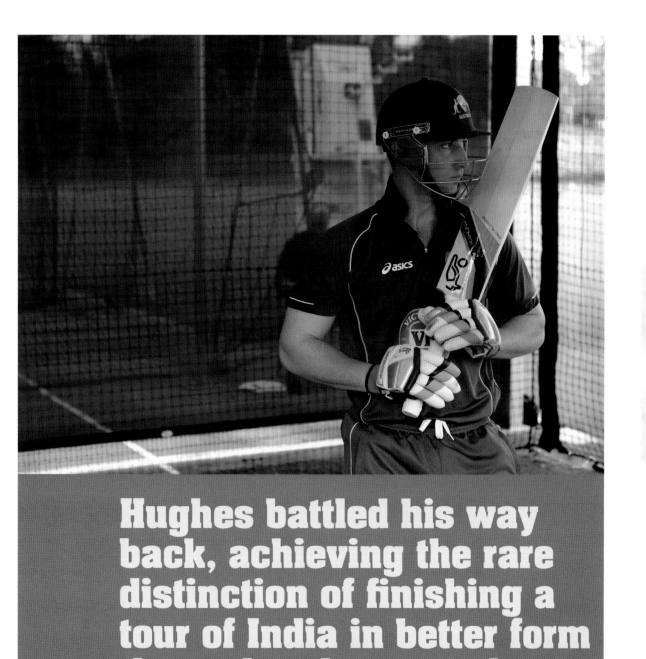

Hughes battled his way back, achieving the rare distinction of finishing a tour of India in better form than when he started

Reprieved in Mohali, Hughes battled his way back, achieving the rare distinction of finishing a tour of India in better form than when he started. His fighting second-innings of 69 in Mohali, as five partners perished at the other end, was a turning point. Even then, it could have been a greater watershed in Hughes's career if not for a perplexing lbw decision from umpire Aleem Dar that brought the innings to an end. 'I suppose they all wash out in the end,' says Greg, who as usual spoke with his son that night. 'He was disappointed, but was already looking forward to contributing in the next Test.'

Then, in the fourth Test match at the Feroz Shah Kotla Stadium in Delhi, on what Cowan calls 'the worst wicket you could imagine', Hughes's 45 provided more encouragement that he had decoded the secret of batting in Indian conditions.

'By the end,' Cowan says, 'he'd unlocked it. It took Ricky Ponting three tours; it took Hughesy two Tests. He was so malleable with his skills and found a way that suited his game. That's a one-in-a-million skill. By the end, he was saying, "Next time we come here, we're going to nail these guys".'

The Australians were condemned for their 4–0 defeat and Arthur's management of the

After seven consecutive Test matches, he was finally grasping that elusive sense of belonging

Mohali dispute would contribute to his sacking two months later, but young players such as Hughes were always able to brighten the atmosphere.

'We had such a great time on that tour,' says Wade, whose form slide would see him omitted from the Australian team. 'I just remember Hughesy going to the buffet all the time. We would go to the Asian restaurant in a hotel, and he would ask a waiter to go to a different hotel to get him a chocolate brownie. He had these little relationships with everyone, and they were so happy to do favours for him. Some of the greatest times on that tour were in the team room at the hotel, fooling around. He would have these wrestling matches with Davey Warner that went on and on.'

Cowan remembers Hughes eating a cheese pizza every night, and drinking container-loads of coffee.

'He was a very, very social guy. He hated sitting in his room. He'd rather be in the lobby drinking coffee and watching everything going on. He must have been highly caffeinated after all the coffees he had with people.'

Khawaja, who says much of the tour was 'a blur', still has one clear and recurrent memory.

'He'd just catch your eye and say, "Latte?" He was always up for it. I don't know how much coffee he drank, but it was a lot.'

Hughes was as close as ever with his old Macksville friends such as Mitch Lonergan. What had bothered him about going to India *and* not playing a game was that he would miss Lonergan's wedding. 'He was going to be best man,' Lonergan says. 'He was so excited, but then he found he was going to have to go to India.'

But even in India, his mate wasn't far from Phillip's thoughts. When Lonergan and his wife were performing their bridal waltz during the wedding, Lonergan felt his phone buzz

Hughes and Steve Smith having a laugh with the media after an Australian training session.

in his pocket. He knew he shouldn't answer, but he had a sense of who it might be. It was an overseas number. During the waltz, both Lonergan and his bride chatted to an emotional Phillip in India.

●

Far from demoralised, Hughes emerged from the Indian tour feeling optimistic. England, where he had spent three summers profitably, promised more familiar conditions. He was highly motivated to improve on his 2009 tour, and felt, at the start, that he was a part of Australia's plans. There might have been turmoil in the leadership, but after seven consecutive Test matches, he was finally grasping that elusive sense of belonging.

There was one place he had no doubt he belonged. On the eve of the tour, while he rested up in Macksville, his sister Megan was about to turn eighteen. She had not had a party before, and was worried that Greg might not approve. She and Virginia planned a party at home.

'We were going to tell him later on so he couldn't say no, because we had bought everything by then,' Megan says.

Phillip cottoned on and kept asking, 'Am I going to be here?'

Megan told him the party would be the night before he had to leave for England. He was so excited that when Megan sat down with Greg to break the news, Phillip rushed in and said, 'She's having it, she's having it!'

The party, Megan says, 'was the absolutely best time'. Phillip would tell her that his flight to England the next day was not his most enjoyable, but the hangover had been worth the pain.

One of many Australian batsmen to under-perform in the Champions Trophy one-day series at the start of the Ashes tour, Hughes was sent to Bristol to play in a three-day match for Australia A against Gloucestershire in the week Arthur was dismissed as coach and selector. In his replacement Darren Lehmann, Hughes had reason to hope he would be treated fairly at selection meetings. As coach of the Brisbane Heat T20 franchise, Lehmann had shown interest in signing Hughes, expressing a high opinion of him.

One concern was that Clarke, who might be expected to speak supportively at the selection table, was stepping down from that role. The key selectors on the tour were Lehmann and Rod Marsh, who, though not the chairman of selectors yet (the role was still occupied by John Inverarity), was travelling with the team as selector on duty.

A natural opener, Hughes had adapted to his new position at number three. In India he had been toggled up and down between three and four, but, as ever, was trying to make the best of whatever position he was given. Lehmann, however, threw a curveball when he announced that he supported Shane Watson's personal preference to open the batting with the recalled veteran left-hander Chris Rogers.

In Taunton for Australia's first game of the tour proper, Cowan and Hughes sat down for coffee and discussed the implications for themselves.

'Hughesy, a bit like me, felt unnecessarily under pressure with the change in coach,'

Darren Lehmann's appointment was a curveball for Hughes. A new coach with new ideas had him questioning his position in the order and his permanency in the side.

Cowan says. 'He said, "We're under pressure here. I might find myself down the middle order". He was a bit confused. He'd been number three in the last Test in India and there was an expectation that that would hold. Suddenly there was talk that I would be at three and he'd be at six.

'We bonded in that odd two weeks [before the first Ashes Test], which became a bit of a battle for everyone. Tour games should be about finding your rhythm and enjoying the country, but all of a sudden it's, "If you don't make runs, you're not in the Test".'

Characteristically, Hughes was able to find, and give, relief from the pressure in team social occasions. In Taunton, the team doctor Peter Brukner organised a trivia quiz night. Hughes was paired with Clarke, who says, 'I was always saying, "Doc, I don't want Hughesy!" We always came last, we were so bad. Hughesy was the worst at trivia ever. He was always cheating, too: copying from people, checking Google under the table. But the Doc kept putting him with me. I was blowing up – and then we ended up winning.'

Whenever Hughes and Clarke got a correct answer, they would receive a standing ovation. In the end, Hughes took their victory as a vindication for 'street smarts'.

Clarke says, 'He was that excited, he even acted like he'd put one over me, because I didn't want to be paired with him!'

But on the cricket field, things remained serious. Against Somerset and Worcestershire, batting at number five, then number three, then number six, then number three again, Hughes made the runs asked of him: 76 not out, 50, 19 not out and 86. In that last, carefree innings against his old county, he threw his wicket away to give a chance to Steve Smith, who had been called up at the last moment from the Australia A team into the Ashes squad. Both were chosen for the first Test match at Trent Bridge, in an unusual batting order that read Watson, Rogers, Cowan, Clarke, Smith, Hughes. Greg says it was 'a real shock to him that he was batting number six. But with a new coach and selectors, it felt like a new system.' Most surprising of all was the late inclusion of Ashton Agar, a 19-year-old West Australian spin-bowling all-rounder, at number eleven.

Hughes had always played cricket with older teammates, and sometimes the same age. Only now, at 24, was he beginning to play at a high level with his juniors. Agar had always looked up to him; at 15, he'd had a poster of Hughes on his bedroom wall

Hughes had made the required runs but, like Cowan, would be batting in an unfamiliar position. On the first day of the series, Australia bowled England out for 215, but by stumps had lost both openers, plus Cowan and Clarke for ducks. Smith and Hughes were the overnight batsmen, with Australia trailing by 140.

A wide-eyed Agar had enjoyed his first day, bowling seven overs and coming to grips with being a Test cricketer. The teammate who did most to make him feel welcome was Hughes.

'I'd first met him in India,' Agar says. 'He took his time to size you up, but then once he'd decided, he was very supportive, always checking up on me because I was new, just a question here and there, "You all right?" In India and England, at meal times he would check up on me. "How are you, youngster?" I knew someone had my back.'

The relationship was an interesting role reversal. Throughout his life, because he was such a prodigy, Hughes had always played cricket with older teammates, and sometimes the same age. Only now, at 24, was he beginning to play at a high level with his juniors. Agar had always looked up to him; at 15, he'd had a poster of Hughes on his bedroom wall. His younger brother, Wes, hero-worshipped Hughes.

On tour, far from striking him with awe, Hughes was impressing him with how down-to-earth and genuine he was.

'He was definitely someone I felt comfortable around,' Agar says. 'He got really nice bats from Kookaburra, and he gave me one. I was shocked, I was so happy . . . He was so generous, everyone said that. He was never up and down, he was the same person – the hallmark of a genuine person, always ready to give you his time.'

Having made his debut at a similar age, Hughes wanted to give Agar the benefit of his experience.

'He had played a lot of cricket, a huge amount, first-class and Test, for his age,' Agar says. 'That experience, even if he was still quite young, and had gone through a similar thing to me, was something he reassured me about.'

When Agar received his baggy green cap from Glenn McGrath on the first morning at Trent Bridge, all of his teammates congratulated him, but he particularly remembers Hughes.

'He always looked you in the eye. When I got my cap presented, he shook my hand and grabbed me on the back of my head. "Well done, youngster." Then he pulled back and he had this really serious look in his eye. I'll never forget the feeling of his hand on the back of my head.'

On the second morning of the Test match, with another healthy crowd filling the historic Trent Bridge ground, Hughes and Smith made a positive start against James Anderson and Steven Finn. The NSW pair, teammates since the under-15s, added another 33 runs before Smith nicked Anderson and was out for 53. Hughes was 17.

'I swear that each and every ball of that partnership he came up the pitch and said, "Next ball". He had such control, he was so strong mentally'
– ASHTON AGAR

When the ninth Australian wicket fell, Hughes was 21. In just 31 deliveries of reverse swing and off-spin, Anderson and Graeme Swann had wrecked the Australian innings and potentially tilted the series on its axis. Agar walked out in bright sunshine to find Hughes in the middle, unfazed by the collapse. The crowd was singing and chanting, but Hughes seemed unaware.

He looked Agar in the eye and said, 'Concentrate on each ball, next ball, forget the last one.'

Agar faced two balls from Swann, taking a single off the second. At the end of the over, Hughes, knowing that he and the young West Australian had a mentor in common in Justin Langer, said, 'Just think about Lang'.

His Langer-like intensity had a calming effect on Agar, who suddenly realised he was not feeling nervous.

For a time, Hughes farmed the strike to protect Agar, but once he saw the teenager was handling the bowling confidently, the pair batted as if they were five for 400 in a Shield match. In the thirteen overs until the scheduled lunch break, they pushed the score on by 69. Agar, on 47, had become the dominant partner, unfurling some loose-limbed drives and pulls, striking seven boundaries and a six. Hughes played the quiet man, allowing himself to be overtaken by the youngster.

'I swear,' Agar says, 'that each and every ball of that partnership he came up the pitch and said, "Next ball". He had such control, he was so strong mentally. His emotion never changed during that stand. The most he would say, when I played a good shot, was "Good boy, good boy", and then, "Next ball". He stayed so even. The more I think about it, the more it amazes me.'

The umpires extended the morning session, as Australia were still nine wickets down. The extension is meant to give the bowling team a chance to finish things off, but it was England who were silently pleading for a break. During the extra eight overs, right-armer Stuart Broad, who had been nursing a sore foot, came on for the first time in the morning. Hughes flayed three of Broad's first six deliveries to the off-side boundary.

By the time lunch was taken, Agar was 69, Hughes 63, Australia nine for 229, and England in arrears and deep shock.

In the Australian changing room, teammates gathered to backslap Agar and Hughes. Agar was all smiles, but Hughes quietly went to a corner and unpadded.

All he said to Agar was, 'You've done really well. When we start again, nothing changes, nothing changes.'

It was another side of Hughes: the intense, almost stern mentor. Agar believes the partnership was '75 per cent him getting me through, 25 per cent me getting him through. He made me feel so relaxed. Even with a look from him I knew what he meant. He didn't have to say anything.'

Agar joined the team in the dining area over chicken in white sauce followed by rice pudding. Hughes, he recalls, spent most of the break in silence.

Anderson was the danger on a wicket where he had been more successful than anywhere else in the world. From his first over after lunch, Hughes and Agar took nine runs. Agar slashed another nine off Broad's first over, and then six more off Anderson. Hughes tiptoed down the wicket to Broad and drove him sweetly past a diving Kevin Pietersen at mid-off.

'He played this amazing shot, he shuffled up the wicket and absolutely nailed it, and then he gave me a little wry smile,' Agar says. 'I will never forget it. I was in awe of that shot. Having watched him hit the ball like he was playing in the backyard, it was awesome.'

As Agar entered the nineties and Hughes the eighties, Broad tried to slow the game down and play on the teenager's nerves. He retied his bootlaces and called for sundry adjustments. Agar 'wasn't aware. Phil was helping me zone out and watch the ball. I just felt really happy, free and confident with him. I got a little bit nervous, but a hundred wasn't the goal. The partnership and getting in front of England was the goal.'

Finally, with the partnership now a world-record 163 for the tenth wicket, Broad dropped short and Agar pulled the ball to Swann, who took a good catch at deep mid-wicket. It was over.

'He patted me on the back,' Agar says. 'I was maybe a little disappointed, but the sincerity of his handshake is what I remember. It was a special bond, the greatest moment I have had and it was shared with him. It feels extra-special now.'

Agar became the instant hero, but almost in the shadows Hughes, the one-time teen sensation, had played the innings of his life, an unbeaten 81 as a calm, mature number six. Cowan, who was fighting a stomach virus and had left the ground, saw the footage later.

'He never played better. I thought, "Brilliant! The talk is about our batting being brittle, but we've found the guy for number six, he'll be the one".'

Perhaps even more incredible than the innings was how quickly it would be forgotten by the selectors. A Brad Haddin–James Pattinson partnership on the last morning would see Australia to within 15 runs of victory at Trent Bridge, but they fell short and were then thrashed on a strangely dry Lord's wicket. Hughes followed his Trent Bridge innings with three failures, but was still the highest Australian run-scorer on the tour. He had every reason to believe he would be selected for the third Test match at Old Trafford. The team travelled to Brighton for a three-day match against Sussex, and Hughes, opening with Cowan, contended with a fast opening spell from future England bowler Chris Jordan, rebounding from being hit on the helmet to score 84 before again throwing his wicket away to give a chance to Smith, who scored a century.

In Brighton, Hughes had a coffee with Khawaja, who had replaced Cowan at number three in the second Test and scored a second-innings 50.

'I'm not playing the next game,' Hughes said.

Khawaja wouldn't believe him. 'Nah, you just made 80 not out.'

'You watch,' Hughes said. 'They'll drop me.'

And they did: Hughes was dropped. So was Agar.

David Warner, who had been 'exiled' to an Australia A team in Zimbabwe after being suspended for taking a swipe at England's Joe Root in a bar during the Champions Trophy, was recalled and selected at number six for Old Trafford.

Phillip Hughes had played his last Test match.

When the team was announced, Cowan says, 'Everyone couldn't believe when he was dropped. There was genuine shock. His defence had become tight, he'd learnt how to play spin, he was all set. And then they dropped him.'

Khawaja sat down with Hughes and said, 'I feel bad for you, you shouldn't have been dropped.'

'Nah, it's all right,' Hughes said. 'I knew they'd drop me.'

'He was never the type to say the wrong thing,' Khawaja says. 'He was always a good bloke.'

'Everyone couldn't believe when he was dropped. There was genuine shock. His defence had become tight, he'd learnt how to play spin, he was all set. And then they dropped him' – ED COWAN

'We were honest with
each other, which
can be rare in cricket'
– MATTHEW WADE

But behind the scenes, Hughes was more bitterly disappointed than ever. He was *still* Australia's top run-scorer for the tour; he was *still* the player who, put in a position in the order where he had not batted since the under-19s, had made a score at Trent Bridge that only Agar, on the same day, had bettered. Behind Hughes's 81 not out, the next-highest Australian score in the series was Haddin's 71. He had failed at Lord's, but only Khawaja and Clarke had managed to pass 50 in either innings.

Greg recalls his mood during phone calls as, 'Here we go again – but I'm not finished.' Says Greg: 'It was always the same, real disappointment, but he wouldn't let it last and he didn't drop his bundle.'

He poured out his soul in Clarke's hotel room, sitting on his captain's bed and saying, 'You're not a selector anymore' before letting it all out. 'I can still see it so clearly, Hughesy sitting in my room and showing how much it hurt him,' Clarke says. 'He felt ready. He just needed a long run in the team. He was saying, "I will show that I can do it". He respected that he needed to perform, he just needed a decent run. I wasn't a selector, but as captain, I had to act like I had made the decision. I couldn't disagree with him, but in my position I wasn't able to say I agreed with him either. It was tough for the selectors too, because he wanted to play for Australia so much.'

Hughes remained 'the ultimate team man', Clarke says, 'running Gatorade, running gloves, never letting it show even if he was burning inside'. With young Agar, for instance, Hughes was unfailingly cheery and helpful.

'In the rest of the tour, we spent a lot of time running together!' Agar says. 'When we were sitting on the boundary talking, he was always keen to show me how to do things and make me feel comfortable.'

It became a difficult tour, however, as Hughes tightened his ring of those he could trust. To the team in general he showed his sunny side, but to his confidants he was, as Clarke says, burning.

'It made me consistently angry on his behalf,' Cowan says. 'He was livid after that Lord's Test when he was dropped. He was furious. He might have only let it slip to one or two people, but he was furious. They were talking about how there was no batting coming through, but we had a guy who could be the best batsman in the world and they kept doing him over.'

Back in Australia the next summer, Cowan wanted to confront Lehmann on Hughes's behalf, but Hughes stepped in, peacemaker in his own cause, telling Cowan, 'I'll do what I have to do, I'll get back there'.

For solace on the Ashes tour, Hughes spent much of his off-field time with Matthew Wade and Wade's wife Julia.

'He didn't hide away in his hotel room,' Wade says. 'He called himself "third wheel" because he was always coming out for dinner with us. Before long they'd be talking about shoes and bags. For a bloke from the country, he knew more about women's accessories than I could believe. It shocked me! Some wives get grumpy if a teammate comes to dinner with you. But for us, the first thing was making sure Hughesy was coming.'

When Wade had learnt he was not going to be Test wicketkeeper in England, the first to console him were Hughes and Clarke.

'Hughesy and I were both pulling each other along,' Wade says. 'We were honest with each other, which can be rare in cricket.'

Through the rest of the tour, as Australia lost the Test series 3–0, Hughes only played one more first-class match, against England Lions at Northampton. Before the game, Lehmann had told him he only needed to do one thing to get back into the team: score runs.

At dinner with the Wades that night, he said, 'If I bat again on this tour, I'm not getting out.'

Against the Lions, he did get out, but not before blocking resolutely for two hours.

'He was,' Wade says, 'a stubborn little fella.'

EIGHTEEN

63 NOT OUT

Stubborn, determined, still sublimely gifted, but now, in what would turn out to be the last chapter of his career, Phillip Hughes had a hard shell. His rejection in England still did not make sense to him, and over the next summer he was forced to be a spectator as Australia reclaimed the Ashes with a spectacular 5–0 whitewash, led by Mitchell Johnson in his comeback, supposedly a confirmation of the benefits of tough love from the selectors.

FOR HUGHES, THERE WAS no way back, only forward. He toured India with the Australian one-day team in the spring, making consistent starts but only one half-century. His 199 runs at 33.16 were a fair return, but he could also feel his World Cup dream slipping.

He was inseparable from his opening partner Aaron Finch. 'The boys took the piss out of us,' Finch says, 'because if we weren't both on the field, that was the only time we weren't together. He'd knock on my door at 9 am and say, "Let's go for coffee." If I wasn't ready, he'd sit in the corner waiting. Then when I was ready, he'd say, "Nah, I'm going to call Greg." He spoke to his mum and dad four, five times a day, even from India.'

During the series, Hughes renewed his bantering friendship with his one-time underage opponent, Virat Kohli. In Jaipur, where India were chasing 360 to win, Hughes walked up to Kohli, who came in at one for 176 in the 27th over, and said, 'Are you finding the target too tough? Lot of pressure!'

In his second Sheffield Shield season for South Australia, Hughes made three 100s and averaged 54.27 in another summer of machine-like run-making

Kohli replied, 'I've been in these situations many times.'

Hughes had a laugh, but Kohli laughed last, steering India to an incredible win in the 44th over after scoring 100 not out off 52 balls. In the change rooms, Hughes found Kohli and said, 'I really like your stick! I like the way it sounds. Can I have one?'

In another game, Kohli laughs, Hughes pointed out that they were wearing the same brand of sunglasses.

'You're following me!' Hughes said to the superstar. 'I'm setting the trend!'

Kohli, who had a fractious relationship with some of the Australians, found that he liked Hughes greatly. 'He would have a pleasant chat during the game, he would come and talk about anything and always had that nice smile. He was pretty excited to be where he was, playing for Australia, you could see that. He was happy to be on the pitch and to be interacting with people that he liked. I never found him as someone who was hostile. He was calm and quiet and friendly. He seemed happy to be doing what he was doing.'

●

IN HIS SECOND SHEFFIELD Shield season for South Australia, Hughes made three 100s and averaged 54.27 in another summer of machine-like run-making. He knew he had a staunch supporter in coach Darren Berry, who had publicly criticised the Australian selectors for not selecting Hughes as a top-three batsman in England.

When Hughes returned to Adelaide, he simply said, 'I can't work it out.'

'That's all he said to me about being dropped,' Berry says. 'Then he went and hit a truckload of balls in practice. He said, "I've got to get better". His attitude when he came back to us was just to pump out runs. I have never seen him not on.'

A double-century, against Western Australia at the Adelaide Oval, was the punchline to an ongoing contest with his flatmate, Tom Cooper.

Ever since Hughes had fallen twice in the 190s on the Adelaide Oval, Cooper had been teasing him for not, like himself, having a first-class double-hundred.

'My first hundred was 203 not out,' Cooper says. 'He would talk about two-hundreds and I would give him shit all the time, "They aren't that hard, mate. You've scored 23 or 24 hundreds and you can't get one two-hundred. I did it in my first go". He used to hate it. He would say, "I have more hundreds now than you will get in your whole career, blah blah blah."'

That day, says Nathan Coulter-Nile, who was bowling for the Warriors, 'He was just too good. He always seemed to make runs when I was bowling. I did run him out, though. As he went off, I said, "What are you doing?" He said, "I've just had enough".'

When Hughes came into the changing room, run out for 204, Berry was blowing up about the dismissal. Hughes simply grinned at Cooper and said, 'Gotcha, bruz.'

Hughes had scored his hundredth and two-hundredth runs off Ashton Agar, who was also battling with his time in the so-called wilderness.

'In the dressing room later, I sat with him and we chatted,' Agar says. 'I'd been searching for more consistency as a bowler. He said it was getting better that day. "You didn't bowl many bad balls at me, you've got really consistent". He was a mentor to me, strange to say, because he was often the young guy.'

At the MCG in the next Shield game, Hughes scored another century, 103 in the first innings against Victoria. It was his 25th birthday; Henderson and his DSEG offsider Richard King gave a special birthday cheer from the MCG Members. After a dubious lbw decision, Hughes joined Henderson and King for a chat. Soon a large family contingent came down. It turned out that a young cricket fan was celebrating his 10th birthday on the same day, and had asked for a day at the MCG to celebrate. 'Hughesy spent a good 15 minutes talking to the birthday boy and his family,' Henderson remembers. 'This is the best birthday present I could ever have hoped for,' the little boy said as Hughes signed his cricket bat before heading back to his South Australian teammates.

Another fortnight later, Hughes returned to the SCG as a South Australian for the first time, and reeled off another hundred. Some of his former teammates dreaded playing against him, not just because he was sure to punish them with his bat. The night before the match, he ran into Nic Maddinson and promised him, 'I'm going to make a hundred.'

And that was what he did.

'You could tell from the first ball, that's what he was going to do,' Maddinson says.

His 118 set up an outright win for South Australia, putting them on top of the Shield table.

'It was a shithouse, cracked wicket,' Darren Berry says. 'I kept saying to the younger players, "Watch Hughesy". It was a tough, scrapping hundred.'

Berry says it was a case of mixed feelings for Hughes, who 'loved his old teammates'.

'Playing against him was terrible,' says Ben Rohrer, one of the NSW team in that match. 'Our plan was to rough him up early. Why did we bother? Everyone targeted him, but he knew how to get out of the way and then when we went wide he'd crunch them. We actually bowled quite well, but he was too good.'

As far as verbal byplay was concerned, Rohrer says, 'It was actually quite fun because you could have a little joke with him. But we could deal without the hundred he scored every time. He was never bitter towards the NSW players. I think he loved us, and we definitely all loved him.'

Hughes was able to bring his sense of perspective and lightness to his South Australian teammates, too. Playing NSW, tail-ender Gary Putland came to the wicket, very nervous.

Hughes said, 'What's the matter, mate?'

'I'm a bit worried,' Putland said.

'How's your mum?'

'All right.'

'How's your dad?'

'All right.'

'How's your animals?'

'All right.'

'What's to worry about, then?'

Visits to Sydney also brought Hughes into contact with his old friends. He might only have an hour free, but he would be on the phone to one of his mates to meet him for a coffee.

'He had a way of making people come and spend time with him,' Matt Day says. Lloyd Andrews was often inveigled into lunch or coffee, while Daniel Smith was sometimes playing against him anyway, as a member of the Sydney Sixers Twenty20 outfit.

'Playing against him was definitely different,' Smith says. 'It was hard. I wanted him to come out and score 100 off 40 balls. I shouldn't say it, but I always wanted him to do well.'

When the Sixers played in Adelaide in January 2014, Smith checked into his hotel and found Hughes in his room.

'How did you get in?'

'I just told them I was part of the cricket team,' smiled Hughes, who had been in Smith's room for an hour and a half.

There was a wider consensus that Hughes was benefiting from his move to Adelaide, and was using the change in lifestyle to build a launchpad for a new tilt at the Australian team in all three formats. Ponting says it was 'no surprise to me that he really settled down in Adelaide

'Going to Adelaide was a really good move. It got him out of an environment he was used to. He worked hard, he was well liked, and he led' – GREG CHAPPELL

and Worcester, two cities that probably had a better pace of life for Hughesy so he could concentrate on becoming an even better cricketer'.

Greg Chappell agrees. 'Going to Adelaide was a really good move. It got him out of an environment he was used to. He worked hard, he was well liked, and he led.'

David O'Neil, from the Wests club, who stayed in contact with Hughes, says, 'Phil was a lot happier once he had left the things that were bothering him in NSW, and his leadership qualities were developing.'

Manager Henderson says, 'This was the best decision we could have made for Phillip's career aspirations.'

As Hughes had hoped, his leadership was appreciated at every level in the South Australian team, from young players like leg-spinner Adam Zampa, who had also moved from NSW, and left-hand batsman Travis Head, to more seasoned contemporaries such as Tom Cooper and Tim Ludeman.

'We'd have coffees and he helped me by talking about our outside lives,' Ludeman says. 'I was very cricket focused, and Phil made me remember how important family is.'

Berry, who maintained his brotherly relationship with Hughes, was offering two pathways. One was a team set-up where he could bat the way he wanted and get back into the Australian side, or, Berry says, 'if that didn't go to plan, we were looking for someone to take over from Johan Botha as captain. People were definitely drawn to Phil as a leader.'

South Australia gave him a rest in the second half of a busy season, allowing him to go home to his safety net, his Four 0 Eight Angus cattle stud outside Macksville that he had bought before leaving NSW.

'When I retire,' he told Lloyd Andrews, 'I'm getting right away from cricket.'

Cooper says, 'He got put in his contract that if he ever got homesick and there was no cricket, he could go home . . . so he could see his cows. Then I'd get a stream of pictures

on my phone of him with cows and tractors and bloody fence posts and all this stuff.'

Being a cattleman was no pie in the sky for Hughes. In 2010, at the Sydney Royal Easter Show, he had met Corey Ireland, owner of Irelands Angus, a breeding operation at Wagga Wagga.

'I had a heifer he wanted to buy, and I wasn't a cricket follower so I didn't know who he was,' Ireland recalls. 'Greg was very reserved, but Hughesy was excited and passionate and asking a lot of questions. There was a big crowd of people standing around. I thought it was for my animals!'

At that stage, Greg was helping Phillip run a handful of cattle on a small property outside Macksville. Ireland told them they were welcome to come and visit his farm, and they went down within weeks. A friendship and a mentorship quickly developed, and Ireland saw that Phillip had not just the enthusiasm but the eye.

'You meet a lot of people who come into the business but really, it's a thing you've either got or you haven't. Hughesy had it. He could walk into a paddock and pick out his top two cows, and he would be spot-on.'

In the intervening years, the Hugheses bought a larger property outside Macksville which they called the Angus Four 0 Eight Stud. By 2014, it was up to some 50 head of cattle, but the ambition was to have a herd of 500 to 600.

'Through the years, as he matured as a person, he decided he wasn't into fancy cars, he just wanted to do this so badly,' Ireland says. 'He did things carefully, not just coming in with a big wad of cash and going bang-bang-bang. Everything he did was well-planned and patient, built from the ground up.'

By 2014, Ireland was having almost daily telephone conversations with Hughes and receiving him for visits. 'He was a huge part of our family. He wanted to pick up the kids from the school bus and spend an hour with them playing cricket or riding around. It was pretty special, and he loved it. He could be himself and relax. Then we'd sit up all night talking about cows. He knew exactly what he wanted to do in his life after cricket, and he was using it to motivate himself in cricket. He'd say, "If I make a hundred here, I'm going to buy a cow".'

The Hugheses bought a larger property outside Macksville which they called the Angus Four O Eight Stud. By 2014, it was up to some 50 head of cattle, but the ambition was to have a herd of 500 to 600

Within the cricket world, teammates looked on Hughes's passion for cattle not as an amusing hobby anymore, but something to be envied. Shane Watson says that he and his wife, Lee, 'saw up close how infatuated he was with his cattle. I knew he loved it, but it wasn't until he started talking to me and all the detail and the passion he had for every animal he owned, for the business, for all that stuff. When I listened to him I would think, "This guy is set and he knows everything about it, he has a passion."... It was almost an equal passion [with cricket]. That is totally rare – I don't think I have seen anyone in his generation who had their options sorted out like that. The rest of us put all our energy into cricket and that's all we have had.'

●

HUGHES'S IMMEDIATE PRIORITY REMAINED a push for Australian selection. But the 2013–14 summer ended with a setback, when the Australian selectors chose Shaun Marsh and Tasmania's Alex Doolan ahead of him for the three-Test tour of South Africa to vie for the batting vacancy created by the axing of George Bailey after the Ashes.

Jamie Cox says Hughes was 'really upset' at not being chosen, particularly because he had 'received information prior to the announcement that he was going'.

Hughes was eventually taken on the tour as a reserve batsman, but did not play a game. Rather than dwell on his disappointment, he took it as another challenge. Rod Marsh was impressed.

'He said to me, which I thought was amazing, when he had the option of coming home and playing the last Shield game, that he'd rather be around the boys,' Marsh says. 'He wanted to do whatever he could to help them win the series. He could have gone home and made runs and staked his claim higher, but he preferred to stay in South Africa with the lads. I thought that was tremendous.'

'His eyes would demand you had to tell him what he had to do to get back in the side. There was never an acceptance that he wouldn't be back' – ROD MARSH

Marsh says that in conversations over why he had been omitted or overlooked, Hughes was clear-eyed and determined. 'He would always listen, he would always understand, he would always try and improve. If you had to drop him, he would look at you and his eyes would demand you had to tell him what he had to do to get back in the side. There was never an acceptance that he wouldn't be back.'

During the winter of 2014, Cricket Australia staged a six-week tournament of one- and four-day games involving A teams from Australia, India and South Africa, as well as a side made up of emerging Australian players, in Brisbane, Darwin and Townsville.

The series brought Hughes together with some of his closest friends in cricket, including Tom Cooper, Matthew Wade and Peter Forrest. He needed their support. His grandfather Sidney, Greg's father, passed away that month, and he would not be chosen for the upcoming Australian one-day tour of Zimbabwe, which indicated that he was not at the front of the selectors' World Cup plans.

'It was the worst I'd seen him, selection-wise,' Wade says. 'I had never seen him so angry.'

The pair had dinner regularly during the series. Some nights, Hughes was upbeat, 'fully kitted up, the clothes and the shoes and the hair', Wade says, but other nights he was flat, almost depressed, 'wearing the worst track pants and slippers. He just wanted to get back to his room with his iPad Mini to look at pictures of his cows'.

Wade, also on the outer with the Australian selectors, 'could have the conversations with him that he couldn't have with other people. It was a nice thing to be there for him when he was like that. He hadn't done much wrong, which was the hardest thing. We had hours and hours of talking about getting dropped. I just said, "We've all been there, you're going to get another opportunity".'

Right: Down but not out, Hughes's astonishing 202 blitzkreig from 151 balls against South Africa A in Darwin was a fiery statement to national selectors.

Hughes also built a strong friendship with Doolan, with whom he had first roomed during an Australia A match in Sydney in late 2012. He roomed with Doolan again during the A series. 'We clicked from the start,' Doolan says. 'He described us both as "chillers". We were similar in that we liked to chill out and not get caught up in the hype. Our only difference was that he hated movies, and I loved them, but if we had the TV on it had to be sport.' Doolan also says Hughes was 'on the phone more than anyone I've known. He'd be talking to his family or his farmer mate Corey [Ireland]. I learned a lot more about cows than I ever wanted to.'

Doolan had sometimes been picked ahead of Hughes – for the South African tour in 2013–14, and on standby for the previous summer's Sydney Test match – but while he himself thought, 'If I've been picked, it means Phil Hughes has been stiffed,' he says that Hughes was always supportive, never jealous. 'Whenever I said to him that he should be in instead of me, he said, "Don't be stupid." If one of his mates was in the team, he was happy. I learned so much from him about how to deal with disappointment. Every time he got knocked down, he got up again.'

After a moderate start to the series in Brisbane, Hughes clicked in the second innings of a four-day match against India A.

'They were quality international bowlers,' Forrest recalls. 'Watching Hughesy in the nets, he wasn't dominant. It was no surprise when he missed out at first. Then he flicked the switch, two cover-drives in one over off [Umesh] Yadav. They set a field for bowling wide outside

off-stump. He walked across and hit Yadav over mid-wicket. During the break, I said, "What are you doing?" He just said, "I'm on, bruz".'

He was on. After an unbeaten century in that game, he took out his frustrations on the visitors when the series moved to Marrara Cricket Ground in Darwin for one-day matches. He scored two half-centuries against India A, and the night before a game against South Africa A he rang Matt Day.

'I'm going to make a statement and show everyone,' he said.

'He really wanted to make the World Cup squad,' Day says. 'He had that uncanny knack of letting you know when he was going to do well. I don't think he was more determined – he was always determined. But he just had a feeling for when he was going to do it.'

What followed was an astonishing batting blitz, 202 not out off 151 balls. It was the first double-century by an Australian in one-day cricket, passing Warner's mark of 197.

'His currency was runs,' Forrest says, 'and when he got into form, he never wasted it. In the mood he was in, hundreds weren't big enough for him.'

Hughes dedicated the innings to his pa. 'I wanted to make it a special day,' he said, 'and it was a special day.'

For its last stop, the northern tour would take in two four-day matches between Australia A and South Africa A at Tony Ireland Stadium in Townsville. Hughes did not convert starts in the first game, but in the second, he was in a grinding, ruthless frame of mind. He was named captain of Australia A for that final game.

'Phillip saw this as a major milestone in his career,' Henderson says. 'He always had leadership aspirations and captaining Australia A gave him the chance to show what he had to offer but, more importantly, it was a recognition from the selectors that they were watching him very closely and his future was on the up.'

His tactical leadership was exceptional, says teammate O'Keefe.

'I got two wickets, but Hughesy got both for me. I had a bloke at square leg and he put his arm on my shoulder and said, "What do you reckon we just bring him up here, eh? Let [Temba Bavuma, the batsman] have a hit if he wants to have a hit". Next over, he brought him even further in and sure enough [Bavuma] tried to pull one because there was no one there. He just popped it up and was gone. At the end of the day, Hughesy played with fields, he put Matty Wade into bat-pad and had a leg slip on an absolute belter. One popped up and Wadey took a hanger.'

After the second day was lost to rain, the South Africans batted well into the third, ruining any chance of a result in the game.

Hughes's men asked, 'What are we going to do, Hughesy?'

'Stuff 'em, we're going to bat for two days. I'm just going to keep batting, eh?'

After the brutality of his double-century in Darwin, he produced a ten-hour marathon, wearing the South Africans away. He accumulated partnerships with Forrest, South Australian teammates Cooper and Callum Ferguson, and Wade.

'He was dominant, ruthless, just better than them,' Forrest says.

After the brutality of his double-century in Darwin, he produced a ten-hour marathon, wearing the South Africans away

Matthew Mott, who was in Townsville in a coaching role, agrees. 'He was too good for that level. He was so mature. South Africa had an off-spinner [Simon Harmer], and he didn't try to take him on, he just played to get up the other end. He was saying to the selectors, "You've got to pick me".'

Sending the national selectors a message was, says Cooper, 'One hundred per cent why he got that double-hundred, it was a "I'll show them" mentality. "If they are not going to pick me I am just going to go out and score two hundred." It was like nothing else would matter, he had that knack where he could put everything else out of his mind and bat for 350 balls to get 100 or do it in 100 balls; it was unbelievable.'

Marsh, the chairman of selectors, took notice. 'You hope they go out there and shove it right up you, and that's what he did.'

Hughes had passed his 100 when Wade joined him at three for 333.

'I was trying to get him through,' Wade says. 'I wanted him to get 200 and then 300. Just more and more and not stopping.'

Wade now has a tattoo of Hughes on his forearm, with the SCG clock set permanently at 4.08. 'I didn't want to forget. Julia sees his face and says, "Hugh-dog, stop looking at me!" They're probably having conversations about stilettos.'

Hughes was 243 when he declared. The match was over, but he was ready to restart. News had come through that Shane Watson had injured his ankle, and Hughes would be on the plane to Zimbabwe.

●

DESPITE BEING A LATE replacement, Hughes's World Cup dream remained a real possibility with two half-centuries in the triangular series with South Africa and Zimbabwe.

Cooper was out on a date when he got a call from Hughes. 'Mate, I've been picked for the Pakistan tour but I've lost my passport and my cap's in Sydney. I need help.'

Hughes had been picked for Australia's tour of the United Arab Emirates for one-day and Test series against Pakistan. Cooper spent the next day driving him around Adelaide getting a passport and other details organised, while Megan flew from Sydney with his baggy green. 'I flew to Sydney and went to Breakfast Point to get the cap out of his safe,' Megan laughs. 'Then I had to wait in Sydney for four or five hours because we didn't know if he'd be in Adelaide or in Melbourne. At the last minute, he told me to get on a flight to Melbourne. I was so scared, carrying the cap around! Finally we met for ten minutes, I gave him his baggy green and a kiss and said good luck. He went off on his flight, and I flew back to Sydney. Most of our time at home was just chilling out, we were always relaxed at home, but this time I was freaking out!'

In the UAE, he had less success in the one-day matches when moved down the order, and he did not play in the Test matches. Nevertheless, his personality continued to brighten what turned into a difficult tour, with Australia soundly beaten by a Pakistan team enjoying the hot conditions. When his old NSW teammate Steve O'Keefe was selected for his Test debut, Hughes 'was the first one to send me a message, the first one to shake my hand when I got the cap, and he was always the one who was there when things were happening, he'd be the one sitting next to you . . . When the shit hit the fan in the second Test and we had lost 2–0, he came up to me and said, "You reckon this is bad, eh? In India we lost 4–0. That's twice as bad, eh!"'

Clarke's troublesome hamstring was likely to rule him out of the first Test. Hughes was widely tipped as the replacement

Hughes spent much of his off-field time with Alex Doolan and Doolan's wife, Laura. 'We were eating together every day before she arrived,' Doolan says. 'He found a sushi train place that he kept wanting to go back to. I was feeling guilty that she was coming. But when she got there, her first question before dinner was, "What's Hughesy doing?" I think she liked going out for dinner with him more than going with me. He'd talk away with her about anything, whether he knew what he was talking about or not. By the time we finished, I'd have a cramp in my cheeks from laughing and smiling so much.'

On the way back to Australia, Hughes had the chance to spend time with Rod Marsh, the only other Australian flying direct from Dubai to Adelaide. On their way to the airport, Marsh was trying to get an upgrade from business to first-class.

'I've never flown first-class,' Hughes said.

'You never know,' Marsh said, 'sometimes you get one.'

When they checked in their bags at the airport, the attendant told Marsh he had been upgraded.

'Has Mr Hughes been upgraded too?' Marsh said.

'Yes, as a matter of fact he has.'

Marsh says the look on Hughes's face was 'just excitement. We then went into the first-class lounge, had a sit-down meal, which was unbelievable, and then we got on the plane

and we were on opposite sides of the aisle. You get a little cabin in first-class so you can close the door. I got myself organised and stood up and looked over to see where he was, and he had pulled himself up over the divider with that cheeky smile of his. He gave me the two thumbs up and I will never, ever forget that – his smile.'

Back at home, Hughes was straight into the Sheffield Shield, playing against NSW at the Adelaide Oval in the competition's first-ever day–night match. He was out in both innings to a rampant Mitchell Starc, but his second-innings 69, when the next-highest score was 30, showed that he had adapted to the unfamiliar conditions more quickly than most. He missed out in the Redbacks' next match against Victoria, but when the team travelled to Sydney he set himself for a big score.

Michael Clarke's troublesome hamstring was likely to rule him out of the first Test match against India a week and a half later, and Hughes was widely tipped as the replacement. Virginia and Megan travelled down from Macksville for the game at the SCG starting on 25 November.

His mate Lloyd Andrews also felt it. 'There was something in the air about that year that said, "Once he gets in the Test team this time, this will be it".'

In the days before the match, Hughes was suffering from a virus. 'He wasn't well,' Greg says, 'but he was so determined to score runs. He'd thought he'd batted himself out of the Test team when he didn't make runs in the previous match, but now it was clear that Clarkey was struggling with his hamstring, Phillip knew how important this match was, and he saw that bigger picture.'

After a hot Monday, the Tuesday dawned mild with high cloud: a perfect day for batting on a dry-looking SCG wicket. Johan Botha won the toss for South Australia and had no hesitation batting first. Hughes and Mark Cosgrove went out into the usual furnace of first-hour aggression, with Starc and especially Doug Bollinger peppering their bodies with accurate fast bowling. The NSW slips cordon, stacked with Australian Test representatives – Brad Haddin, Shane Watson, David Warner, Nathan Lyon – let the South Australians know they were in a match. Off-spinner Lyon and the fast-medium right-armer Sean Abbott came on to bowl, but Hughes and Cosgrove made it to the first drinks break.

Fielding in a helmet at bat-pad was Nic Maddinson, who recognised the same determination as the previous year, when Hughes had made a hundred against his old team. 'A few guys had spoken to him before, and he'd pinpointed that game. All the big guns were playing for the Blues and he said he was going to score a hundred. We were never going to get him out.'

David Warner, fielding on the off-side, has no doubt a big score was coming. 'You could see in his last innings the determination of the kid. He was making a statement. He was going to go big. He was sick the night before, he was sick that morning, but he had to play because there was a Test match around the corner.'

During the session, Darren Berry wandered up to the press box at the top of the new Bradman–Noble Stand, where he chatted with Test selector Mark Waugh.

'How's Hughesy going?' Waugh said. 'He's not looking that good against the short ball.'

Berry replied, 'He never does, but I'll put my house on him making a century today.'

Waugh indicated, without saying it directly, that Hughes was a good chance to be picked for the Brisbane Test if Clarke became unavailable.

'Just stick with him for a few Tests,' Berry said.

Rod Marsh, who had become chairman of the national selection panel, says, 'It became obvious to all and sundry that he would replace Rogers as Warner's opening partner [in the

Hughes in vintage form against NSW
on 25 November 2014, his final innings.

future]. That was the master plan going forward. I think that was the way it was going to be. We were very confident he would have a long and successful Test match career . . . It's hard to say, "Yes, he would definitely have been chosen" [for the first Test]. However, he was always going to put his name up in front of the selectors but in the final analysis whether or not he would have got chosen . . . how many runs would he have got in that innings, who knows? He was just as likely to peel off 200 and make his case irresistible.'

The hour leading into lunch was, Berry recalls, 'a torrid affair' with the NSW players 'giving it to him'. O'Keefe says it was normal for state players to try to get under Hughes's skin. This day was no different.

'He would never say a word, he'd just flick up his collar and look you in the eye and never lose your gaze,' O'Keefe says. 'Then he would bully you around.'

When O'Keefe came on to bowl, Hughes took nine runs off his first over. 'He slog-swept me for four, and then whipped one violently from off-stump out through mid-wicket, and

307

With a glint of steel, he said, 'They're not getting me out today'

then hit the single. When he got down my end he said, "You spin the ball in, eh?" I looked at him as if to say, "At least give me an over to settle".'

During the lunch break, Hughes looked haggard as he took off his gear and sat at the long table in the change room to graze on some food.

Berry put his arm around him and said, 'You're on today. Make sure you go big.'

'Tough work out there, coach,' Hughes said. 'But I like it that way.' With a glint of steel, he said, 'They're not getting me out today.'

He put his pads and gloves on and walked back out to bat. Cosgrove and Ferguson fell, but he had his mate Tom Cooper with him. NSW continued to bowl short. 'The boys from NSW hated playing him because he always churned out runs against them,' Cooper says. 'He told the coach there's no way I am getting out to that and that is why they started bouncing him. He didn't look like getting out any other way and that's why they went to that short plan. We were joking about that, saying, "What is this? How am I meant to score runs if they are going to bowl there?" They did it for quite a while and that was why he started trying a few pull shots . . . They were just trying to stop him scoring.'

Virginia and Megan sat in the Ladies Stand, at an elevated side-on vantage point. Ash Squire, his old mate from Wests, came over from the indoor nets, saw Hughes pass 50, and walked back towards the nets, thinking he would come back down later when Hughes was close to his hundred. Some of the South Australian players watched on the viewing balcony, while some were by the physio's table inside, watching on television. All around the country, Hughes's friends were either playing cricket or, if not, following him on their computers.

Berry went up the stairs from the change room, to watch from the upper deck of the Members' Stand. The conversation at lunch had given him a good feeling. He could still hear Hughes's words: 'They're not getting me out today.'

•

WHEN HE REACHED 40 at the SCG that day, Phillip Hughes scored his 9000th run in first-class cricket. On top of the 70-odd hundreds he had scored before leaving Macksville, he had made a handful more in grade cricket, 26 in first-class cricket, three of those for Australia in Test matches, and another ten in domestic and international one-day cricket. A week before his 26th birthday, he had scored more first-class centuries than any Australian at the same age with the exception of Ricky Ponting. More than Bradman, more than the Chappells, more than his hero Clarke or his contemporaries Smith and Warner. Those baskets in his bedroom in East Street had long since overflowed.

As the wind at the SCG changed direction, swinging from the west to a fresher sou'-easter, he set sail for another hundred. In the 47th over, Hughes said a few words to Nic Maddinson at bat-pad. Maddinson had tried to engage him in some friendly banter all morning, but Hughes would give him nothing. All he said now was, 'You're not getting me out.'

He was 63 not out and batting at the Randwick end when Sean Abbott dropped the third ball of the 49th over, the 161st of Hughes's innings, short of a length. Phillip thought, no doubt, 'Here's four more,' and attempted to pull Abbott's bouncer. He was through his shot a fraction early, and the ball hit him on the back of his neck. He bent, hands on his knees. He rose again and then fell forward onto the pitch.

The seriousness of the injury was apparent almost immediately to the players and umpires on the field and to the doctor who attended to him in front of the Members Stand. David Warner sprinted for the change room to request an emergency phone call, and sprinted back. Virginia and Megan watched on in shock and disbelief. The NSW players walked from the field in a daze. When an ambulance arrived, it had been 23 minutes since the first call, almost half an hour since Hughes had been struck.

Around the cricket country, the news spread. Sheffield Shield players in Brisbane and Melbourne were informed through the day. Phillip's network of mates in Sydney, up the coast, in Adelaide, and all around Australia were on their phones. Soon they were converging on St Vincent's Hospital in Darlinghurst, where their innate optimism – this is cricket, you can get hurt but you cannot die – was, over the next two days, taken from them.

Farewells were said, at St Vincent's and elsewhere, before his life support was switched off on Thursday 27 November. Clarke, Henderson and Cricket Australia doctor Peter Brukner helped to manage the press of friends and cricketers who came to the hospital. There was a discovery, for many, of how many close friends Phillip Hughes had inside and outside the cricket world. They each felt a special kinship with him.

Perhaps friendship, even more than cricket and cattle, was his greatest talent.

Opposite: Hughes had the old twinkle back in his eye as he strode out after the lunch break.

AFTERWORD

CRICKET GOES ON, AND it looks much as it had, but for the community that knew Phillip Hughes, it would not and could not be the same. Many tears were shed in the dozens of interviews that went into the making of this book. One cricketer confesses that he can no longer go past St Vincent's Hospital. Others say the game, their life's passion, lost its savour on the November day Phillip Hughes fell. Some would be implacably angry at Cricket Australia for cancelling only two weeks of first-class cricket in the early summer of 2014–15. Others accept that there was no manual to guide the handling of this situation, and that everybody managed the best they could. Some cricketers found, when they resumed, that they could not play the game the same way. All would find that they were emotionally spent by the end of the season.

From 27 November, the tributes ranged from the local to global. Paul Taylor, a 48-year-old father and former Mosman grade cricketer from Sydney's northern suburbs, put a cricket bat outside his front door at 4.08 pm that day. By the time of the funeral in Macksville on 3 December, tributes had come from around the world. Premier League football teams in England paid their respects, public figures from all walks of life recognised Phillip, and when Test cricket resumed, with New Zealand playing Pakistan in the United Arab Emirates, where Phillip had last represented his country, the sombreness of the moment drained the match of all feeling. The summer's cricket in Australia, once it resumed, was played in shadow.

Virat Kohli, who had taken over the captaincy of the touring Indian team in M.S. Dhoni's absence, reflects: 'We had to go [to his funeral] because at the end of the day we play one

The Four O Eight farm. Away from cricket, Phillip was happiest here.

sport . . . The one thing that we have in common is the sport of cricket and that bonds us in a way; we do have rivalries and fights and arguments but the one thing that we have is cricket. We felt that we needed to be there not to show anyone that we are concerned, but because we want to be there as fellow sportsmen. It is important for the world to know that we are united as one sport.'

For interpretations of why Phillip Hughes's death affected so many, there can be general statements about the place of sport in people's lives and the loss of innocence to which only the hardest hearts could be immune. There was a recognition, in public grief, of the ties that bind. Hughes's death was a unifying moment for cricket and for communities cross-cutting the borders of sport and nations. Life is fragile for everyone, regardless of their connection with Hughes or the sport of cricket.

But if anything has been clarified by those who have contributed to this book, it is to explain why such a reaction attended the death of this one cricketer, why so many were asking, in their grief, like Mike Hussey was, 'Why him?'

That clarification is not in Phillip Hughes's death, but in his life. The love that radiated from the sporting world in late 2014 was no fluke; it was an appreciation not only of all the general things that hold sports and peoples together, but of the unique and irreplaceable qualities of this young man. There would simply not have been the same mourning for just any cricketer. Phillip Hughes was a prodigy, a fallen idol who kept rising again, and his loss was not only of those 100 Test matches that so many believed he would play, not only a common loss of a future, but the loss of a beloved human being. For those who knew him, the loss was not having him in their lives anymore.

At the time of his passing, it seemed that millions knew Phillip Hughes. As time goes on, the circle of grief narrows back to the circle of those who really did know him. The grief remains palpable. In its presence, no words are possible. But over time, words and images and the great collection of talismen, the signed bats and shirts and the caps and the trophies, will encode memories, which are no substitute for the real thing, but will be the best we can do.

Phillip Hughes PLAYER STATISTICS

INTERNATIONAL

Debut	South Africa v Australia in Johannesburg, 26 Feb–2 Mar 2009
Matches	52
Innings	74
Runs	2367
Average	33.33
High score	160
100s	5
50s	11
Man of the Match	3
Man of the Series	0

	Test	ODI	T20I
Debut	South Africa v Australia in Johannesburg, 26 Feb–2 Mar 2009	Sri Lanka v Australia in Melbourne, 11 Jan 2013	Pakistan v Australia in Dubai, 5 Oct 2014
Matches	26	25	1
Innings	49	24	1
NO	2	1	0
Runs	1535	826	6
Strike rate	53.56	75.09	75
Average	32.65	35.91	6
Balls faced	2,866	1,100	8
High score	160	138	6
100s	3	2	0
50s	7	4	0
MOM	1	2	0
MOS	0	0	0
4s	199	91	1
6s	11	5	0

NATIONAL

	NSW			South Australia		
Debut	NSW v QLD in Brisbane, 26 Dec 2008			Adelaide Strikers v Perth Scorchers in Perth, 9 Dec 2012		
	First Class	List A	Twenty20	First Class	List A	Twenty20
Matches	38	30	17	15	6	8
Innings	69	30	17	28	6	8
Runs	3360	994	527	1440	358	175
Average	52.50	38.23	37.64	53.33	71.6	25
High score	198	96	83	204	114	74
100s	10	0	0	5	1	0
50s	20	9	4	6	2	2
Catches Taken	29	9	10	13	4	5
Not Out	5	4	3	1	1	1

	FIRST CLASS	LIST A
Debut	NSW v Tas in Sydney, 20 Nov–23 Nov 2007	Vic v NSW in Melbourne, 28 Nov 2007
Matches	111	90
Innings	203	88
NO	14	12
Runs	8645	3,607
Strike rate	57.09	77.94
Average	45.74	47.46
Balls faced	15143	4628
High score	204	202
100s	25	8
50s	45	23
4s	1183	359
6s	45	34

WORCESTERSHIRE	
Debut	Worcestershire v Gloucestershire in New Road, 17 June 2012
Matches	8
Innings	8
Runs	402
Strike rate	126.81
Average	100.5
High score	87
100s	0
50s	4
MOM	3
MOS	0
4s	37
6s	7

Author acknowledgements

The authors would like to express their greatest appreciation to the Hughes family for their warmth, hospitality, energy, patience and kindness.

The authors would also like to thank the following, who generously gave their time to be interviewed for this book: Ashton Agar, Lloyd Andrews, George Bailey, Terry Baldwin, Sharnie Barabas, Darren Berry, Daniel Burns, Beau Casson, Steve Cazzulino, Greg Chappell, Michael Clarke, Kay Clews, Tom Cooper, Trent Copeland, David Cotton, Nathan Coulter-Nile, Ed Cowan, Jamie Cox, Brendan Cunningham, Joel Dallas, Matthew Day, Neil D'Costa, Ian Dinham, Alex Doolan, Jason Ellsmore, Aaron Finch, Peter Forrest, Brett Forsyth, David Freedman, Brett Geeves, Stan Gilchrist, Darren Goodger, Mitchell Harvey, James Henderson, Michael Hill, Gregory Hughes, Helen Hughes, Ian Hughes, Jason Hughes, Megan Hughes, Virginia Hughes, David Hussey, Mike Hussey, Corey Ireland, Shariful Islam, Phil Jaques, Alan Jones, Brady Jones, Simon Katich, Simon Keen, Usman Khawaja, Virat Kohli, Justin Langer, Josh Lawrence, Warwick Lawrence, Barry Lockyer, Tim Ludeman, Mitch Lonergan, Morrie Lonergan, Nic Maddinson, Andrew Maggs, Tom Mann, Rod Marsh, Bryce McGain, Ken McNamara, Matthew Mott, Tim Nielsen, Steve O'Keefe, David O'Neil, Ricky Ponting, Nino Ramunno, Angela Ramunno, Steve Rhodes, Sam Robson, Ben Rohrer, Daniel Smith, Nathan Smith, Warren Smith, Ash Squire, Steve Tomlinson, Damian Toohey, Michael Townsend, Matthew Wade, David Warner, Shane Watson.

Thanks also for their assistance: Jason Bakker, Malcolm Conn, Tony Connelly, Matt Costello, Angus Fontaine, Jodie Hawkins, Phil Hillyard, Jim Kelly, Richard King, Foong Ling Kong, Jim Robson, Jonathan Rose, Danielle Walker, and especially James Henderson. Thank you to Michael Clarke for his foreword.

Picture credits

Daniel Boud: page i, iv–v, x–1, 4, 8, 11, 15, 18–19, 20–21, 23, 24b, 24c, 25a, 29, 30, 34, 39, 40, 42–43, 47b, 48, 53, 54, 57b, 58, 60, 63, 65, 66, 69a, 86, 92, 94, 96–97, 102, 103, 104, 124, 138, 148, 149, 173, 192–193, 199, 200–201, 236, 297, 314e, 316–317, 318–319, 320.

Hughes family: page vi, 3, 7, 12–13, 14, 16, 24a, 24d, 25b, 26, 27, 31, 33, 37, 41, 42, 43, 45, 47a, 50–51, 55, 56, 57a, 69b, 70, 73, 75, 76, 79, 80, 83, 84–85, 90, 91, 95, 98, 100, 107, 109, 113, 114, 115, 118–119, 120–121, 125, 126, 131, 133, 139, 150–151, 152–153, 154, 163, 176, 208–209, 214–215, 253a, 269, 279a, 288, 294, 296.

AAP Image/Dale Cumming: page 255.

AAP Image/Dan Peled: page 275.

AAP Image/Joe Castro: page 272, 321.

AAP Image/Lukas Coch: page 315e.

AAP Image / Nikki Short: page 314d.

AAP Image/Tracey Nearmy: page 127, 166.

AFP PHOTO/GIANLUIGI GUERCIA: page 180–181.

AFP PHOTO/William WEST: page 252.

ANDREW YATES/AFP/Getty Images: page 196, 280–281.

Anthony Johnson/Fairfax Syndication: page 251.

AP Photo/Andrew Brownbill: page 276.

AP Photo/Themba Hadebe: page 179.

AP via AAP/Shakil Adil: page 315h.

Bradley Kanaris/Getty Images: page 137.

Cameron Spencer/Getty Images: page vi–vii, 127, 218, 315b, 326.

Chris Hyde/Getty Images: page 314a.

Christopher Lee/Getty Images: page 228.

Clive Rose/Getty Images: page 194–195, 198.

Craig Golding/Getty Images: page 213.

Daniel Kalisz - CA/Getty Images: page 315d.

Darren Pateman/Fairfax Syndication: page 165, 204.

DAVID GRAY/REUTERS/PICTURE MEDIA: page 271.

EPA/DAVID JONES: page 283.

Evan Morgan/Newspix: page 298.

Ezra Shaw/Getty Images: page 147, 149.

Gallo Images/Getty Images: page 182.

Gregg Porteous/Newspix: page 164.

Hamish Blair - GCV/Getty Images: page 210.

Hamish Blair/Getty Images: page vii, 106–107, 170, 174, 180, 181, 184, 185, 187, 197, 201, 226, 229.

Homebush Boys High School: page 116.

Ian Hitchcock/Getty Images: page 291, 299.

Joosep Martinson/Getty Images: page 314g, 315g.

LAKRUWAN WANNIARACHCHI/AFP/Getty Images: page 245.

Laurence Griffiths/Getty Images: page 284.

Lucas Dawson/Getty Images: page 167.

Mark Evans/Newspix: page 89.

Mark Kolbe/Getty Images: page 161, 235.

Mark Metcalfe/Getty Images: page 310.

Mark Nolan/Getty Images: page 157.

Matt King/Getty Images: page 142–143, 241, 268.

Michael Dodge/Getty Images: page 315f.

Morne De Klerk - CA/Cricket Australia/Getty Images: page 263.

Morne De Klerk/Getty Images: page 264, 313.

Paul Kane/Getty Images: page 314c.

PA/Tony Marshall: page 196.

PA via AAP/Chris Ison: page 242.

Phil Hillyard/Newspix: page 111, 122, 129, 134, 144, 158–159, 183, 188, 221, 278, 292, 306–307, 308, 314b, 323.

Quinn Rooney/Getty Images: page 257.

Renee Nowytarger/Newspix: page 132–133.

Robert Cianflone/Getty Images: page 169, 230, 270, 277.

Robert Prezioso/Getty Images: page 222-3.

Ryan Pierse - CA/Getty Images: page 309, 311.

Ryan Pierse/Getty Images: page ii, 191, 201, 216–217, 225, 239, 258, 267, 279b, 287, 304, 314f.

SAEED KHAN/AFP/Getty Images: page viii, 315a.

Scott Barbour/Getty Images: page 300–301, 315c.

Sebastian Costanzo/Fairfax Syndication: page 233.

Simon Alekna/Fairfax Syndication: page 110, 117.

Steven Siewert/Fairfax Syndication: page 295.

Stu Forster - GCV/Getty Images: page 207.

Stu Forster/Getty Images: page 261.

Sunday Night/Channel Seven: page 248.

Photo courtesy of The Land/Shan Goodwin: page 253b.

Tim Clayton/Fairfax Syndication: page 140–141.

Tom Shaw/Getty Images: page 202.

WILLIAM WEST/AFP/Getty Images: page 247.